SEND IN THE CLOWNS!

SEND IN THE CLOWNS!

Popular Politics after Neoliberalism

Seán Kennedy and James McNaughton

OR Books
New York · London

© 2025 Seán Kennedy and James McNaughton

Published by OR Books, New York and London

Visit our website at www.orbooks.com

All rights information: rights@orbooks.com

First printing 2025

Cataloging-in-Publication data is available from the Library of Congress.
A catalog record for this book is available from the British Library.

Typeset by Lapiz Digital Services. Printed by Bookmobile, USA, and CPI, UK.

paperback ISBN 978-1-68219-514-7 • ebook 978-1-68219-515-4

This book is dedicated to Sheldon S. Wolin

Contents

Introduction

How to Read a Blockbuster

We all know what a blockbuster is. Posters, fanfare, and a splashy trailer herald its arrival. And in its aftermath follow plastic figures and Lego sets, franchise and spinoff. "Blockbuster" was originally coined by the US military during World War II to describe a bomb of such stunning violence it could destroy a whole block of buildings. But by the 1950s, the word shrinks to what's now familiar: a metaphor for the cutting-edge technology and commercial impact of the big movie. In the theater, the blockbuster cranks alive the motorized seats, jerks the popcorn bucket in a spray of sound. Special effects aim to thrill. And once the blockbuster ends, we reemerge to the parking lot, ears stunned by quiet humid air, eyes never so surprised that humans merely stroll, that cars stop at red lights on the empty drive home.

Todd Phillips's *Joker* (2019) is a bona fide blockbuster. Big stars, big budget, and, with a wise nod to the Batman franchise, it grossed over a billion dollars in cinemas worldwide.[1] But *Joker* is a different kind of blockbuster, because it asks us to rethink blockbusting itself. Early in the movie, when Arthur Fleck cracks, he strikes his own head against the wall and window. He literally busts his own block, blaming himself for the stress of mental illness, for gig-work precarity, for welfare cuts, for his struggles to look after his mother, and for a media machine that mocks

---

1   "Joker (2019)," the-numbers.com, nd, np.

him as a loser. Things are so bad, he fears he will die homeless. By the movie's end, however, from the back of a police car, Fleck watches fellow clowns, inspired by his own TV performance, bust up an entire Gotham block. "This isn't funny," a policeman scolds him (1:47:30). But Arthur laughs because blockbusting has undergone a witty reversal: no longer a symptom of self-blame and humiliation, blockbusting has been exteriorized, transformed into a collective venting, a frenzy of riot against a city whose policies humiliate. The catharsis is so profound that Fleck leaves Arthur behind altogether. Moments later, he mounts the hood of the smashed police car, paints a bloody smile on his face, and exults in the adulation of the crowd. He embraces his new identity as the prince of mayhem—the Joker—and confirms his status as a blockbuster.

That transformation is the central triumph of *Joker*, the most exciting, and the most tragic. It is exciting because the rage aimed at Gotham expresses the indignity of being told by the mouthpiece of an elite corporate class, Thomas Wayne, that success and failure reflect only your character: whether or not you are a clown. Wayne doesn't ask whether an economic system is rigged, why the state cuts healthcare, why the media goes in for blame rather than structural diagnosis. Rage against Gotham is the inarticulate anger against this state of affairs. It reclaims for blockbusting its aerial bomb violence—not against fascist cities as in World War II, but against the inequalities unleashed by modern neoliberalism emerging in 1981, when the movie is set.

But this transformation is also tragic. We lose the sensitive, beleaguered Arthur Fleck. Instead, we get a mentally ill man who murders his mother, stabs his former friend in the eye with a pair of scissors, shoots his TV idol, and possibly rapes and kills his Black neighbor. With that loss, we also lose "Clown for Mayor!"—the political movement that had emerged to confront Wayne's bankrupt ideology through collective organization. We witness instead the birth of a blockbuster villain

2

whose final act is to kill an overworked government social worker—a class of occupation that oligarchs like Wayne would be happy to see disappear anyway.

What makes this tragedy so effective is that Todd Phillips gives Joker a sympathetic background and origin story in Arthur Fleck, performed masterfully by Joaquin Phoenix. Joker's main antagonist, Batman, was given an origin story from his inception. When he first appears in *Detective Comics* #27, in 1939, we learn that Batman is the alias of the feckless socialite billionaire Bruce Wayne. The next year, in *Batman* #1, we discover his backstory. Young Bruce Wayne witnesses his parents gunned down in a botched robbery of his mother's pearl necklace. Bruce devotes his life to bodybuilding, scientific study, and "warring on all criminals."[2] By contrast, Joker has typically lacked a backstory. He is the face of irrational evil, a maniac spiffed up in a sharp purple suit. In one sense, he embodies the fear of 1940s fascism, helping kids cope. Like a miniature Hitler or Mussolini, this Joker gains authority by using the radio to make predictions that he flawlessly executes: "The Joker has spoken!"[3] Even when the police gather to protect the predicted victim, each one nevertheless dies smiling at the exact specified hour.

In another way, Joker is there simply to validate Bruce Wayne's neurotic idealizations formed by the childhood trauma of the theft and murder of his parents. Like his parents' killer, Joker also likes to steal ladies' necklaces and murders for no apparent reason. (Catgirl also has a thing for stealing wealthy women's necklaces, which sets up love as another way to resolve Bruce's childhood damage.) But with the introduction of a backstory in Arthur Fleck, Phillips's *Joker* mounts a challenge to how

---

2   Bob Kane and Bill Finger, *Batman #1* (New York: Marvel, 1940).

3   Erika Rothberg, ed. *The Joker: 80 Years of the Clown Prince of Crime!* (Burbank: DC Comics, 2020), 9.

Batman—and the entire Batman franchise—imagines crime, goodness, violence, and even economics.

Send in the Clowns! takes its cue from the magic of backstory. Without backstory, *crime* is merely the irrational evil of individuals; it is never the systematic theft of an economic system, legally coded to steer assets to the rich while outsourcing costs to the poor and nature. Without backstory, *evil* is merely a devious mastermind capable of predicting the future, while systems supposedly grounded in spontaneity, such as capitalism, are exonerated. Without backstory, *mental illness* is an individual affliction, not a political symptom. Without, not simply backstory, but an understanding of narrative itself, we might accept the satisfactions of Batman melodrama without question, accept that our saviors should work beyond the bounds of the law, backed by murky corporate accounting, untouchable family wealth, and police who are willing to kill rather than arrest. Without backstory, we cannot recognize why the invisible hand of the marketplace wears an iron glove, why a modern free trade regime is accompanied by an explosive expansion of prisons.

Without backstory, what's more, we misrecognize psychic outcomes in late capitalism—where mothercare inverts to smotherhood, where broculture slips to incel. Without backstory, conspiracy theorizing and violent protest appear merely irrational rather than as performative strategies to be judged based on the aim of disrupting melodramas the state employs to justify its own violence, or by how well they reinvigorate failing democratic processes. *Joker* gives us a backstory in Arthur Fleck; we take the cue and, reading the visual language of the movie, elaborate chapter by chapter these other backstories that are central to getting a grip on our present condition.

Maybe a popular movie is an unusual place to grasp these paradoxes. Movies, after all, move us through currents of feeling, not analytic frameworks. We become attached to characters through sympathetic lighting that darkens their fears or celebrates their triumphs, through music that deepens our connection to their emotional transformation. The cello saws over the pivotal scene when Fleck moves his torso and arms slowly before the mirror after he has killed three stockbrokers. We watch—and feel—Fleck center himself, self-satisfied in his body, perhaps for the first time in his life: the music plumbs the melancholy of achieving needed dignity through violence, even as flickering green light cautions us that something is seriously off with restoring self-worth this way. In the theater, we sweep along these counter currents, moved through sensory flows.

But if we slow down a movie—if we grip a scene carefully—we can distill from the visual language, common to everyone, analytical frameworks that are useful for unfolding the backgrounds of the most difficult modern problems. When, near the movie's beginning, for instance, Fleck spins an <u>EVERYTHING</u> MUST <u>GO!!</u> sign under a marquee for the porno *Strip Search*, we ask: why is a notorious form of police abuse in New York City, strip searching, the name for an erotic fantasy of whiteness in Gotham? Why, in the 1980s, does the modern United States accept police humiliation and lust after carceral punishment? (Here we might remember another meaning of blockbusting: the tactic used in the real estate industry to consolidate white property and privilege in American suburbs after the war.)[4] Or, later in this scene, when Fleck gives chase to a group of kids who steal his sign, we ask: what are the effects on workers who are asked to chase their employer's sign as if it were their own, bearing the risks of loss but sharing in none of the rewards? Slow-reading film, what we call *grip-reading*, allows *Clowns!* to split apart, chapter by chapter, the conundrums of late capitalism. Broadly put, *Clowns!* explores how, under neoliberal regimes, equality can reverse into hierarchy,

---

4   Thomas J. Sugrue, *The Origins of the Urban Crisis: Race and Inequality in Postwar Detroit* (Princeton: Princeton University Press, 2014), 46, 194–197.

economic liberty suppresses political liberty, and populations denied political power attempt to restore their dignity through conspiracy and violence, exposing them to anti-democratic authoritarianism. In a final chapter, we also provide ways forward.

By backstory, then, we do not mean that this book will lay out the various past histories of Batman and Joker. Plenty of expert books already document them well.[5] And many readers will know that Fleck's backstory is not the first past given to Joker. When Bob Kane—with Bill Finger and Jerry Robinson—created the stylish mass murderer who kills for the joy of villainy, the absence of backstory darkened Joker's evil. By 1951, however, the comic explains Joker's smile: the Red Mask escaped a robbery of the Monarch Playing Card Company by diving into a vat of chemical waste, and the subsequent reaction marred him with a permanent smile, creating a Joker with a bad dose of toxic masculinity. Alan Moore's *The Killing Joke* (1988) later torqued this plot by revealing that mobsters coaxed a hapless man into the heist, forcing the red mask on him. He first considered the larceny out of shame at failing to support his pregnant wife as a stand-up comic, then agreed to participate because his wife was killed the morning he had to decide.

Even in Moore's comic, when backstory makes him sympathetic, Joker's resulting sociopathology is so spectacular and outrageous that it eclipses our ability to consider background trauma as mitigating condemnation. He kidnaps Gotham's police commissioner James Gordon, strips him naked, binds him to a rollercoaster, and sends him through a funride that features oversized images of the commissioner's own daughter shot and raped. In Paul Dini and Bruce Timm's *Batman: The*

---

5   Daniel Wallace, *The Joker: A Visual History of the Clown Prince of Crime* (New York: Universe, 2011). Travis Langley, *Batman and Psychology: A Dark and Stormy Knight* (New York: Wiley, 2012). Robert Moses Peaslee and Robert G. Weiner, eds. *The Joker: A Serious Study of the Prince of Crime* (Jackson: University of Mississippi Press, 2015).

Animated Series (1992–1995), Joker reveals his background as an abused child to the intern therapist at Arkham Asylum, Dr. Harley Quinn. But these accounts, Batman explains, are fabrications to manipulate her sympathy. No, mostly, Joker's backstory is absent, misdirection, or fraud, so that Joker's violence appears the more psychotic, whether in *Batman: Cacophony* (2009), when he destroys a schoolful of children, or in *A Death in the Family* (1989) when, as Iran's diplomatic representative to the UN, he attempts to murder everyone in that august body in an act of state-sponsored terrorism.

Todd Phillips draws Fleck from some of these well-known details: the failed stand-up career, the desire to care for a family, a tortured childhood, a stint at Arkham Asylum, and a therapist who grapples with his toxic behavior. But Arthur's damage is revealed differently than these earlier Jokers. His wounds are also inflicted by a wider society that fails ordinary people. If we want to discover Fleck's background, in fact, we'd best look not to DC comics, but to an older source for Joker's character in *The Man Who Laughs*, the 1928 Paul Leni movie set in seventeenth-century England.[6] In this melodrama, based on a novel by Victor Hugo, King James II has a surgeon carve a perpetual grin into the face of Gwynplaine, the son of a rebel leader. That way, the rebel's own orphaned child will always laugh at what a fool his father has been for challenging a king. Now an adult, played by Conrad Veidt, the rebel's child works as a strolling player with other clowns. Psychically wounded by a lifetime of people laughing at him, he feels unworthy of the love of a blind woman devoted to him: "Hear how they laugh at me—nothing but a clown!" (24:03). At the movie's end, Gwynplaine is dragged before the court of Queen Anne to be ridiculed by the most powerful and wealthy. Except, in this case, he stands up to the mockery, declaring that a King made him a clown, but God made him a man. Then he escapes with the help of the city mob, a hero.

---

6   *The Man Who Laughs*, directed by Paul Leni (Universal Studios, 1928).

Joker works this melodrama in ways that matter to *Clowns!* Like the man who laughs, Fleck makes money by making others laugh, yet doing so also means taking abuse on the job. Fleck suffers a psychic crisis because even outside of work people expect him to be always "Happy"—Fleck's mother's nickname for him. But Fleck is often insecure and sad. What's more, Fleck's clown name is Carnival. Carnival was traditionally a time when fools and jesters confronted and mocked the rich and powerful, to remind them that their privileged station comes from divine chance, that the servant could have been the master, the laborer the landed. The rich should have more humility. In this tradition, Fleck confronts Wayne and challenges his own TV idol, Murray Franklin. He also asserts himself a man. But in late capitalism, carnival mockery will not humble a wealthy class, especially when convinced they have earned their station—never mind about inherited wealth or the legal fortifications protecting capital from the damage it creates. *Joker* asks whether carnival laughter, in these conditions, requires an accompanying dose of violence. *Clowns!* asks how violence functions in traditions of democratic renewal, and we examine the alternatives.

Like *The Man Who Laughs, Joker* is a melodrama—an emotion-driven genre in which the fate of a person moralizes, often in oversimplified ways, the structural injustices faced by a people. The mob helps our smiling hero escape as well. But *Joker* knows that the original democratic energies of melodrama have been co-opted by *Batman* and other superhero movies. Superhero melodrama has us believe that evil can be isolated into individual lunatics and terrorists, that critique of inequality is secretly a catastrophist desire to destroy Gotham itself. Superhero melodrama extols wealthy saviors who work beyond the law, like Batman, and who deploy corporate wealth in everyone's interest. These generic structures make for good movies. But *Joker* says, in the era of yawning inequality, there really is something naive in finding the basis of heroism in canny corporate accounting, trust babies, and tech bros.

INTRODUCTION

Clowns! elaborates *Joker*'s confrontation with superhero melodrama to reveal the meaning in these forms, but also because we think everyone should recognize how melodrama functions. It's not just that we need to identify what's going on when Elon Musk posts selfies of himself as Dr. Strange, a superhero sorcerer who protects Earth from fantastical peril.[7] It is that today, even sober political and economic theory employs melodrama. Friedrich A. Hayek's neoliberal political economy, to give one influential example, frames his work with melodrama's moral binaries: he counterposes good, self-reliant individuals who uphold unfettered capitalism to those who, in pursuing social justice, inevitably produce totalitarian evil.[8] Melodrama also dominates entertainment news. It prepares us to accept mass incarceration. It is used to justify war. Elisabeth Anker says modern propaganda relies on an "orgy of feeling," so that melodrama can replace a civic life based on reasoned deliberation with what *feels* true.[9] Melodrama substitutes politics with what feels like politics. Melodrama allows demagogues to describe themselves as saviors and to decry political opponents as criminals, undermining the foundations of democracy itself. Neoliberalism takes the form of a genre. *Send in the Clowns!* shows the cost.

It's likely that few people trust the blockbuster, certainly not as a place to find a deep critique. A blockbuster might confirm the widely felt disillusionment that our democratic birthright has been severed, that fewer people than should share in the formation of political power. But even if a movie were to accomplish a countercultural critique, awaken an

---

7   Patrick Cavanaugh, "Elon Musk Claims to Be Doctor Strange, but Marvel Director Lets Him Know Otherwise," comicbook.com, June 29, 2018, np.

8   Friedrich A. Hayek, "'Social' or Distributive Justice," in *Law, Legislation and Liberty: A New Statement of the Liberal Principles of Justice and Political Economy* (London: Routledge, [1973] 2013), 226–266.

9   Elisabeth R. Anker, *Orgies of Feeling: Melodrama and the Politics of Freedom* (Durham: Duke University Press, 2014).

audience to the radical sense that the world really ought to be different, others would point out that capitalism easily co-opts critique, that critique sells movie seats, that counterculture is its own commodity. What's more, everyone knows that the system is broken. The real problem is that we have to *act* as if we do not know this. We might leave a movie exhilarated by its radical critique and the possibility of defying convention, but we still follow the law when we drive quietly home. Mark Fisher called this critical melancholy "capitalist realism," the widespread cynicism that results when we realize there are no "political alternatives to capitalism."[10] For Fisher this melancholy is also the fault of culture: the young are unable to be surprised anymore because there is nothing formally new in culture, everything sold out in advance.

Clowns! takes a different approach to popular culture, to critique, and to capitalism. We engage *Joker* not because it is a movie of stunning formal innovation. Rather, we grip this movie because we believe that, in order to imagine political change, we must first ground analysis in a language we share in common. We might need to change, not the movies we watch, but *how* we watch them. What's more, when Fisher represents capitalism as a political system, he risks creating a new melancholy, a new impotence, by divesting in advance the political power available to us. Capitalism and liberal democracy overlap, it's true: they share a theoretical basis in individuals who exercise rights, whether making economic contracts or exercising free speech. But economic liberalism and political democracy also contest one another. Advocates for capitalism often prioritize economic rights over civic equality. They seek to limit political participation, not simply to forestall regulation and taxation, but also to hinder voting and legislative power. The power available to populations to change the laws—whether that be to tax the rich, to remove

10   Mark Fisher, *Capitalist Realism: Is There No Alternative?* (London: Zero Books, 2014), 7.

legal protections for capital, or to protect nature—can only be recognized, and then harnessed, if we articulate the background that explains our present-day pathologies.

A main contention of this book, and one that defines how we read this movie, is that *Joker* is an *allegory*: a tale that unfolds on two levels. On one level, the mundane, we see the story of a broken family, the Flecks. On another, the figurative, we see the disintegration of the social contract under neoliberalism, terms we will come to understand clearly in the pages ahead. Allegories condense their themes into the names of their characters: Arthur, a famous name for the King of the Round Table, is still a quest hero. But by now, he is a fleck, a piece of dirt, a stain on the social fabric. His clown name is Carnival, a name that remembers how carnival once had comic performers who confronted the injustices and abuses of the powerful. His mother, meanwhile, is Penny. But she hasn't got a penny to her name. Their nemesis, Wayne, rules the world, though his world may be waning too. *Joker* tells their story, using it to reflect on broader questions of economic and social justice in America. But *Joker* also knows that to turn a person into an allegory, to make them a blockbuster, is to ask hapless individuals to embody impossibly complex social and structural problems. They are made to bear the brunt of, to live out, the contradictions of the systems within which they exist. That won't end well.

Clowns! makes the case that we all need help understanding complex social problems and the contradictions they present for the individual. How is it, we ask, that modern societies, founded on individual freedom, fashion so many individuals who feel unfree? How is it that modern societies based on the pursuit of individual happiness have produced the unhappy and insecure? How is it that political and economic theories which protect individual liberty by limiting the power of the state, create so many who are drawn to authoritarian power?

Chapter One

Trash

On Neoliberalism

A group of clowns put on their faces in a clown shop on Thursday morning. Gotham City Radio news talks over the opening shot, which closes up on Arthur Fleck before the dressing mirror: "It's day eighteen of the garbage strike. With ten thousand tons of garbage piling up every day, even the nicest sections of the city are looking like slums." Face whitened, eyes set in blue diamonds, the clown applies red lips with a paint brush. "Health commissioner Edward O'Rourke is declaring a city-wide state of emergency for the first time in decades. 'There's no need to wait until somebody dies or comes down with typhoid fever. It's already a serious situation.' It's something that affects almost everyone in the city no matter who they are or where they live." On Arthur's profiled face, a tear catches the light just above his cheek bone. A catalog of Gotham residents complain: "'You can't go down no one avenue without seeing nothin' but garbage and rats' . . . 'It's starting to affect my business when customers can't get in here because of the garbage situation.'" Listening, Fleck frowns— then he tries to smile. "To look at it, it's terrible." "The very bad smell." His fingers, inserted into his mouth edges, tug up the lips, straining into a happy face. They pull down a frown. "The idea of the National Guard moving in and cleaning up is a good idea." They release in anger. The tear, full in blue makeup, wobbles on his cheek, then courses down. (00:22–01:18)

Joker opens with a clown crying on account of a trash strike. Why such an emotional reaction to garbage? What's it to a clown that trash is mounting and people have gone on strike? By answering these questions we reveal the sophistication of *Joker* and lay out the aims of this book. The answer starts by acknowledging that to become a clown, at least in the oldest tradition of clowning, one must do more than make up the face and don the outfit. The clown must also absorb the perspectives of regular people and ready a challenge to the powerful with jest. So on voice over, Gotham's citizens react to the loss of a basic city service, which leads to rats and trash piles. And on the screen, a clown performs these reactions. He forcibly works to keep a brave smile on his face, already painted there, by finger-pulling his lips. But as the citizen's complaints compound, with businesses suffering and the awful smell, and as they become unsure who to blame, his face falls and tears mar the makeup. One way to understand this scene, then, is to simply notice that, whatever the strike means, our clown feels this disintegration in the social order personally and has internalized its emotional impact.

Whether or not the clown knows it, a trash strike marks this disintegration for a good reason. Gotham's trash strike borrows from the Great Garbage Strike of New York in 1968, an infamous standoff in which Mayor John Lindsay hoped to "break these public-service unions."[1] *Joker* recalls some of the details: Mayor Lindsay threatened to call in the National Guard, but Governor Rockefeller rebuffed him, then used the threat of a health emergency to take state control of the Sanitation Department and negotiate a settlement. The goal of breaking the unions, however, was not put aside. In fact, just a few years later, those powerful New York unions would be hobbled by neoliberal economic policies that aimed to destroy them, and with them, the entire "postwar consensus." That consensus, which existed from roughly 1940 to 1970, was an accepted agreement that, as the economy made strides in productivity and income, workers would also profit through gains in wages and benefits. Dismantling that consensus, in brief,

---

1   Quoted in Janos Martin, "Today in New York History: The Great Garbage Strike of 1968," untappedcities.com (February 11, 2015).

prevented workers from sharing in economic gains over the next forty years, enabling the yawning wealth inequality we witness today.

Joker opens with that postwar consensus in trouble. We hear it outwardly in the confused radio voices, and we see it in Arthur's face, as he is unable to integrate their views. In this chapter, we'll show that what fractures and eventually replaces consensus are neoliberal policies. Like many classical liberal thinkers before them, neoliberal thinkers advocate that liberty be found in a "minimal state," a state in which the government should limit itself to preserving public order and refrain from meddling in the economic sphere. Rather than consider social wellbeing, neoliberalism advocates that we dismantle the welfare state and insists each individual become responsible for themselves, even in a downturn. But when Arthur Fleck registers the citizens' reactions to the economic and political crisis in Gotham, *Joker* wants us to recognize the mistake of such an approach. It's crazy to expect individuals to take on themselves what is, in reality, society-wide economic and political dysfunction. This is true for the clown who absorbs the people's discontent, for Fleck who internalizes as a personal failing the effects of economic cuts, and for Joker who solves what are political challenges through personal vendetta. Arthur will crack up under this impossible burden.

One thing Arthur lacks is economic and political context, something Gotham media fails to provide. What is this trash strike about? Why does it backdrop a movie that stages a confrontation with Gotham wealth? Why does the radio fail to give the worker's perspective? This chapter begins here. We take the cue from *Joker* to explain why a garbage strike matters. Then, we push deeper into the objectives and paradoxes of neoliberalism itself. Neoliberalism prioritizes economic liberty over political engagement. In doing so, it cultivates strategies to suppress democratic politics. To achieve self-regulating markets, economic liberals paradoxically employ state intervention and force, and they suppress workers' freedom to strike.[2] Gotham City Radio hints at this prospect when the commissioner invokes the specter of typhoid, peddling fear of a health crisis to justify a "state of emergency." A "state of emergency" literally means to suspend democratic laws and norms, just as calling up the National Guard implies breaking the strike with the threat of state violence. Here we begin to answer a major question that unfolds across this book: why does an outlook that advocates for liberty and mistrust of government paradoxically call for increased state violence and a disregard for democracy?

We end this chapter by showing that one way *Joker* responds to this question is by making trash a central visual metaphor. Trash appears in nearly every scene. Trash obviously makes visible the hidden labor of garbage workers that Gothamites generally take for granted. *Joker* also suggests that by dismantling the postwar consensus and by shifting social costs onto individuals, neoliberalism generates a trash problem. We all know the trash problem as pollution: without political checks on economic activity, nature is trashed, species disappear, the planet cooks. But trash is also figurative, the social costs of economic policy that pass through to people. And trash is also the language used to shift these social costs, whether in the guise of "government waste" that justifies shrinking the state, or as the label for individuals who pay most dearly when social democracy is dismantled: those branded "wasters," and "trash," and "clowns."

It's starting to affect my business

When Arthur looks in the mirror, and finds it difficult to maintain a smile, he does so both as Arthur Fleck and as Gotham's clown. For Fleck,

---

2   Karl Polanyi, *The Great Transformation: The Political and Economic Origins of Our Time* (Boston: Beacon Press, [1944] 2001), 155.

sustaining a smile is to comply with his unhappy mother's expectations: to be "Happy," as she nicknames him. But for the clown who absorbs the Gothamites' views, smiling while crying also allegorizes the conflict portended on the radio: that the unionized sanitation strikers, and by extension most all working-class laborers in the US, will be brought to heel. They will be forced to smile, even as they see their power and their aims of sharing in national wealth gains dismantled.

New York Gotham is the right place to situate these concerns because, according to David Harvey, New York was the laboratory for neoliberalism in the United States. New York was the first front in a larger war that would establish new class relations, new philosophies of state, new definitions of freedom, new methods of distributing gains in national productivity, and new strategies for inducing the working class to accept their defeat. In one sense, New York's story is familiar and describes other US cities entering the 1970s. The city had deindustrialized, with corporations moving jobs overseas. And, in the wake of civil rights demands and urban unrest, it had suburbanized—eroding the economic base of the city and leaving swaths of the metropolitan center impoverished.

But if those problems afflicted many cities, what made New York singular was its solution. True, in the short term, the sanitation strikers won concessions. But the fiasco of trash on streets eroded public support for workers and emboldened those forces bent on defeating the unions in order to undo the entire postwar consensus. President Richard Nixon took up this charge. He first claimed, unbelievably, that urban unrest in US cities was over, which allowed him to yank traditional federal support for urban development, public employment, and public services. Next, major banks refused to refinance New York city debt, which pushed the city into "technical bankruptcy." Then came the bailout.

Here we see neoliberalism in action. Financiers structured the bail-out so that bondholders would be paid first, and essential services only afterward:

> The effect was to curb the aspirations of the city's powerful municipal unions, to implement wage freezes and cutbacks in public employment and social provision (education, public health, transport services), and to impose user fees (tuition was introduced into the CUNY university system for the first time). The final indignity was the requirement that municipal unions should invest their pension funds in city bonds. Unions then either moderated their demands or faced the prospect of losing their pension funds through city bankruptcy.[3]

Harvey calls this "a coup by the financial institutions against the democratically elected government of New York City." Unions are forced to invest in the very bailout bonds that strip their power. Financial engineering secures cutbacks in city services, what's called austerity. It does so by moving social and policy debate beyond democratic governance. Life becomes grueling and civic culture turns mean.[4] In the radio voices, we hear the new political subject this system produces: frustrated, confused, stripped of their politicalness—that is, stripped of political consciousness and agency. This is the crisis with which *Joker* begins. Streets are grubby and restless, social services gutted, and democratic resistance to austerity—either through unions or voting—hobbled by the deals of a financial elite arrogantly convinced that they alone can fix the problem.

Though Harvey and *Joker* center this story in New York, crushing the postwar consensus occurred precisely when, both nationally and

---

3   David Harvey, *A Brief History of Neoliberalism* (Oxford: Oxford University Press, 2005), 45.

4   Joshua B. Freeman, quoted in Harvey, *Neoliberalism*, 46.

internationally, advocates for racial justice—those fighting for the political liberation of minority and postcolonial populations—advanced from seeking equal political rights to advocating fair participation in economic growth.[5] Martin Luther King, Jr., for example, was assassinated the day after he gave his final speech to another group of striking sanitation workers in Memphis Tennessee. The Memphis Sanitation Strike began two days after the Great Garbage Strike in New York ended. The conditions and pay for all workers were appalling. They were especially bad for Black workers who did the dirty work of trash loading, yet were denied equal pay and basic decencies, such as showers at work. King was seeking ways to expand his political movement into common cause with poor workers everywhere: the Poor People's Campaign. He supported the sanitation workers' demands to form a union and improve their conditions, and he called for a general strike.[6] King understood that unions would strengthen democratic processes and open political pathways to reduce economic inequality and workplace indignity—precisely what neoliberal theories most feared and railed against.

Neoliberalism does not directly advocate for racial inequality or racist suppression, but it stridently rejects social justice, which allies it with new forms of racism. Neoliberalism, which consolidated into a theory after World War II, promotes radical economic individualism as the best bulwark against communist and fascist totalitarianism. But in positioning itself against totalitarianism, neoliberalism melodramatically reads *all* state intervention, *all* modes of collective action, including pursuit of social justice, as kinds of tyranny. The classic neoliberal text, Friedrich Hayek's *The Road to Serfdom*, appeared in 1944 and was targeted against

---

5   Arun Kundnani, "The Neoliberal Idea," in *What Is Antiracism? And Why It Means Anticapitalism* (London: Verso, 2023), 155–182.

6   Martin Luther King, Jr., *"All Labor Has Dignity"*, edited and introduced by Michael K. Honey (Boston: Beacon Press, 2011), 167–195.

"the socialists of all parties." Hayek argues that the marketplace can regulate itself without government intervention—the principle of laissez faire—and that social justice is not something that governments can, or ought, to pursue. Hayek venerates the pillars of Western civilization as he sees them: "liberalism and democracy, capitalism and individualism, free trade and any form of internationalism and love of peace."[7] But the version of democracy that Hayek extolls is a minimalist one: he extends people the right to vote for representatives, but denies those representatives much say over the economy. This leaves economic decisions to owners of capital, making those decisions autocratic. In other words, while Hayek endorses electoral democracy, he rejects social democracy, which allows voters to participate in economic policymaking. And he vehemently rejects "any increased equality in the distribution of economic power, with the result" as Noberto Bobbio notes, "that the right to vote often amounts to nothing more than a mirage."[8] MLK's fate reflects these limits: political participation is one thing. Mobilizing democracy to address racialized economic inequality is quite another.

Because it aims to limit democratic power over the economic sphere, in the 1940s neoliberalism remained both theoretical and fringe. The United States avoided fascism and socialism by fashioning instead a social democracy that actively redistributed economic power. The United States entered the 1950s, for example, with hard-won redistributive tax rates; guarantees of Social Security for disability, work accident, and old age; regulations to protect labor; expanded free college education; and federal healthcare systems that patch up private markets. This postwar consensus has also been called the New Deal Consensus or "embedded

---

7   Friedrich A. Hayek, *The Road to Serfdom*, fiftieth anniversary edition (Chicago: Chicago University Press, [1944] 1994), 41, 26.

8   Norberto Bobbio, *Liberalism and Democracy*, translated by Martin Ryle and Kate Soper (London: Verso, [1988] 2005), 77.

liberalism."[9] Hayek might argue social democracy was the same as totalitarian socialism, but Americans liked their Medicare and Social Security, still do, and know otherwise.

Yet, as we see, by the 1970s in New York—and more expansively in the 1980s with Reaganism in the United States, Thatcherism in the United Kingdom, and globally through what is called the Washington Consensus—neoliberalism begins to steer governing policy decisions. It takes root in the United States and internationally, partly to address the economic crisis of stagflation, as we will see in the next chapter, but also to prevent minority populations from seeking social justice through advocacy for economic reparations and to stymie former colonies from nationalizing Western industry in their countries.[10] As neoliberalism steers policy decisions, it produces a democratic deficit: it resists democratic power that seeks to make society more equitable. It manufactures social consent, creating a sense that there is no alternative, in part through financial engineering put beyond the recourse of participatory politics. It fosters neo-racist discourse when it claims postcolonial peoples who seek social justice through economic regulation "prove" they are incapable of Western values and merely culturally inferior.[11] And when political resistance appears, the gospel of reduced government will turn to governmental force, violating neoliberalism's own commitment to non-interference.

The trash strike that opens the movie signals the sputtering resistance to this coming development. The radio commentary explains how blame will be allocated and consensus produced. According to the media and the politicians, organized labor behind the strike is the nuisance. But

---

9   Mark Blyth, *Great Transformations: Economic Ideas and Institutional Change in the Twentieth Century* (Cambridge: Cambridge University Press, 2002), 49–95.

10   Kundnani, "Neoliberal Idea," 179–180.

11   Kundnani, "Neoliberal Idea," 181.

the public doesn't know what to think. They want the standoff to end, that the parties negotiate and settle, no matter "how long it takes" (01:14). No striker is interviewed to provide context. And the specter of a state of emergency is in the offing. Frustrated citizens, seeing no alternative, turn against labor as they call for "the National Guard" (01:16).

Smile and put on a happy face

Notice, then, that the clown's tortured smile also captures a building conflict between democracy and liberalism. Though neoliberals like Hayek argue that one can be for both democracy and liberal capitalism, when push comes to shove, democracy gets restricted. Everyone is offered liberal rights—the right to vote, to trial by jury, to privacy, and to non-interference—but denied what democracy also offers: the political dignity of sharing in the formation of power, especially over matters of social justice and economic equity. Social democrats are forced into compliance. They must act as if smiling, even when humiliated. *Joker* presents this tortured predicament as the movie's premise: in a neoliberal world that treats him like trash, can A. Fleck be Happy? The movie also gives a straightforward answer. If people like Fleck are severed from political agency, they will resort to conspiracy thinking and personal revenge. One cost of cutting people from the dignity of democratic power is that you can end up with neither Arthur Fleck nor Happy. You can end up with Joker.

Smiling is the visual language of this crisis in *Joker* because the cherished liberal value of happiness itself is in trouble. By "liberal" we don't mean the Democratic Party or progressive politics, as the phrase is now commonly used. By liberalism we mean the philosophical foundations of economic and political modernity which rest on theories of the free individual. In economic philosophy, this liberal individual is imagined as free by being able to go to the market and negotiate contracts—for wages, or to sell goods. The eighteenth-century Scottish philosopher Adam

Smith championed liberal economic theory as he called for negotiation of contracts in an "open and free market."[12] Another term for this is laissez faire—when government leaves the market to its own devices. In political philosophy, the liberal individual is described as having inalienable rights and can participate in the project of self-government. No longer subjected to the king, liberal citizens imagine themselves political subjects in their own right.

As a matter of historical fact, liberal freedoms were slowly won, wrested from monarchs only gradually: in the case of England, from the Magna Carta of 1215 to the beheading of Charles I some four centuries later, and more suddenly as well as thoroughly in the case of Revolutionary France. But in liberal political and economic philosophy this rational, self-interested individual, who trades and votes, was theorized as universal, as if men have always had natural rights that precede society, as if all societies are made up of individuals who think in terms of trade, barter, and individual self-interest. History shows this myth is inaccurate. But as Karl Polanyi wrote of Adam Smith: "no misreading of the past ever proved more prophetic of the future."[13]

These ideas of an economically and a politically free individual might appear similar, but the concept of the individual is riven by deep conflict. Liberal philosophy often tries to smooth the conflict by combining these hypothesized individuals into one, conflating politics and economics through the concept of a contract. The *social contract* is generally understood as an implicit agreement among members of a society to cooperate for social benefits. Liberal social contract theory argues that political states are fashioned when people come together, forgoing some of their natural rights, in order to gain security enough to pursue their

---

12   Adam Smith, *The Wealth of Nations*, introduction by Alan B. Krueger (New York: Bantam, [1776] 2003), 828.

13   Polanyi, *Great Transformation*, 45–56, 45.

own happiness.[14] But liberalism conflicts internally when seeking to limit universal rights, and liberalism produces conflicts between economic rights and political rights. Finally, liberalism also conflicts with the aims of universal participatory democracy.

For the first, the contradictions are stark: Thomas Jefferson declared that all men are entitled to "Life, Liberty, and the pursuit of Happiness," while he himself owned slaves. That is, from its inception liberalism grounds its claim to truth in universal applicability—*all men*—while violating that truth claim in practice: *not Black people.* Liberalism justified such contradictions by limiting who was included inside what John Stuart Mill calls the "civilized community," so that those deemed outside that community, those deemed currently outside of adulthood, or forever unable to achieve personhood, could claim neither the political agency nor the individual autonomy to fashion their own contracts.[15] This line of thinking goes back to John Locke, the seventeenth-century English politician and philosopher.[16] Outside were placed minors, women (though the nineteenth-century Mill wanted women to be included), as well as the vast sweep of colonized peoples—"barbarians" Mill names them—all variously denied the protection of political participation. Here, we should join Nancy Fraser in recognizing the difference between liberal exploitation and expropriation. Liberal contracts might *exploit* someone—sometimes circumstances compel people who are endowed with equal rights before the law to accept bad economic contracts: low pay, say. But racism allows liberalism to fashion boundaries beyond which liberal political rights

14   Jean-Jacques Rousseau, *On the Social Contract*, translated by G.D.H. Cole (Mineola: Dover Thrift Editions, [1762] 2003), 8–9.

15   John Stuart Mill, *On Liberty*, in *On Liberty, Utilitarianism and Other Essays*. Edited and introduced by Mark Philp and Frederick Rosen (Oxford: Oxford University Press, [1859] 2015), 13.

16   John Locke, *Two Treatises of Government*, edited by Peter Laslett (Cambridge: Cambridge University Press, [1689] 1988), 308.

are denied altogether—"barbarians" deserve only despotism—and for them liberal economic rights are irrelevant. Beyond these boundaries we find *expropriation*: theft, slavery, rape.[17] Perhaps more important than deciding whether expropriation and racist dehumanizing are necessary contradictions within liberalism is to recognize that, without constant vigilance, liberalism's economic logics produce these ghastly recidivist tendencies, whose consequences are then ambered in legal and financial structures that benefit wealth preservation, long after racist expropriation has ended.

Even *within* the liberal community, the sheer fact of economic exploitation also causes a rift between political and economic liberalism, a rift that appears in liberal ideas of happiness. Jefferson adopted the idea of pursuing happiness from John Locke. For Locke, individual pursuit of happiness is the foundation of liberty, provided we recognize that true happiness is not necessarily one's immediate pleasure, but rather a reasoned view of how what you do now relates to the good of your future happiness as well.[18] This view of liberty—that basically you know what is best for your happiness and others shouldn't interfere unless it harms them—is a foundational liberal idea. It leads liberal thought to advocate for a minimal state and to insist that citizens keep an antagonistic eye on the government. Democracy, for its own part, overcomes that suspicion by allowing universal participation and encouraging pursuit of common agreement within that framework.[19]

But, already by Jefferson's writing, and especially in the nineteenth century, this moral foundation for liberty insists we consider the happiness

17   Nancy Fraser, *Cannibal Capitalism: How Our System Is Devouring Democracy, Care, and the Planet—and What We Can Do About It* (London: Verso, 2022), 41.

18   John Locke, *An Essay Concerning Human Understanding*, edited by Roger Woolhouse (Harmondsworth: Penguin, [1689] 1997), 249–250.

19   Bobbio, *Liberalism and Democracy*, 43.

of other people too. Jeremy Bentham famously adopted the idea of "utility" as the benchmark for determining good legislation: that lawmakers should try to maximize the happiness of the greatest number of people. Yet Bentham's utilitarianism stopped short of regulating the economy to improve people's happiness. Instead, he advocated precarity as the way to motivate workers and accepted general misery. Even "in the highest state of social prosperity," he wrote, "the great mass of the citizens will most probably possess few other resources than their daily labor, and consequently will always be near to indigence."[20] True, he grudgingly recommended "a regular contribution" to mitigate poverty, but "not to exceed simple necessities," else it would "punish industry."[21] Government should keep people hungry so they'll be motivated to work.[22] Central to theories of general happiness is a work ethic grounded in precarity.

Mill, after Bentham, eventually came to recognize the conflict between the goal of general happiness and the astonishing misery of the masses under unregulated industrial capitalism. He identified the moral basis of liberty not in *individual* utility, but in *social* utility; that is, not in "the agent's own happiness" but in the happiness of "all concerned."[23] Though Mill is one of the recognized laureates of liberalism, he was also anti-democratic in key ways, as our discussion of his idea of "civilized communities" above shows. And he never developed a theory of power that explains how capitalism produces new hierarchies of concentrated

---

20 Jeremy Bentham, *Principles of the Civil Code*, in *The Works of Jeremy Bentham, vol. 1*, edited by John Bowring (Illinois: Liberty Fund, [1802] 2011), 562.

21 Bentham, *Civil Code*, 572.

22 Polanyi, *Great Transformation*, 123.

23 John Stuart Mill, *Utilitarianism*, in *On Liberty, Utilitarianism and Other Essays*, edited and introduced by Mark Philp and Frederick Rosen (Oxford: Oxford University Press, 2015), 130.

wealth that suppress political equality, as would Karl Marx.[24] Mill fails to explore fully how liberal economic rights conflict with the political rights of the many.[25] Nevertheless, with an eye to the happiness for "all concerned," even Mill eventually admits and advocates that the state must regulate wealth and property; must root out capitalism's tendency to reward fraud. He suggested experimenting with communal modes of ownership advocated by many socialists. What's more, he rebuffed familiar liberal attempts to blame misery and precarity on individuals themselves. Instead, he saw poverty as resulting from the arrangement of society, and as presenting a political obligation:

> So in the economy of society; if there be any who suffer physical privation or moral degradation . . . this . . . is *pro tanto* a failure of the social arrangements. And to assert as a mitigation of the evil that those who thus suffer are the weaker members of the community, morally or physically, is to add insult to misfortune.[26]

The liberal economy treats a lot of people like trash. To blame that evil on the people themselves only adds to the insult.

Fleck's weeping smile performs a crisis in happiness that occurs when the lessons Mill learns about general happiness are undone. On the radio, Fleck hears the rumblings of a new liberalism, a neoliberalism that aims to unwind the clock to a time before the postwar consensus, a time before theories of liberty concerned themselves with general happiness. Mill wants us to look at "social arrangements," but the coming breed of neoliberal leaders will instead baldly insist, as does British

---

24 Matt McManus, "Was John Stuart Mill a Socialist?" jacobin.com, May 30, 2021, np.

25 Christoph Menke, *Critique of Rights*, translated by Christopher Turner (Cambridge: Polity Press, 2020), 1–5.

26 John Stuart Mill, *Socialism* (Chicago: Belford, Clarke, and Co., 1879), 28–29.

prime minister Margaret Thatcher, that "there is no such thing as socie-ty."[27] Hayek, approaching the matter with more sophistication, will claim that we cannot legislate rules for general happiness. We can only create "opportunities" and encourage people to "accumulate a stock of tools . . . in short to accumulate 'capital' in the widest sense of the term" to pre-pare them for an unknown future.[28] But it amounts to the same thing: individuals should be fully responsible for their own happiness. Political attempts to regulate an economy that produces inequality and misery will be increasingly resisted. Because *Joker* is set in 1981, we know all too well what Hayek's unknown future holds. Neoliberalism will unleash *neo*inequality, *neo*restrictions on political participation, *neo*privations, and *neo*degradations. It will produce new people it will see as trash, peo-ple such as Arthur Fleck, who, according to Hayek's approach, have only themselves to blame. Of course, a clown would weep at this new turn: clowns are professionally invested in making everyone happy. Of course, Arthur Fleck would weep at this new turn as well: he must work as if to make everyone happy, when he is precisely the kind of individual whose happiness will matter little in the new dispensation.

What do you get if you cross a mentally ill loner with a society that abandons him and treats him like trash?

In every scene, Gotham spawns black trash bags. They pile up on the edge of sidewalks and accumulate against alley walls. Huddled among them disappear the homeless. When the title of the movie, *JOKER* in enor-mous yellow capitals, covers the screen, the camera rolls at street-trash

27 Iain Dale, ed. *Margaret Thatcher: In Her Own Words* (Hull: Biteback, 2010), 260.

28 Friedrich A. Hayek, *Law, Legislation and Liberty: A New Statement of the Liberal Principles of Justice and Political Economy* (London: Routledge, [1973] 2013), 190.

level. Trash bags are the movie's visual language, there to remind us from scene to scene that something in this new dispensation is metastasizing into a crisis. Literally, trash bags are produced by the unresolved conflict between city authorities and sanitation workers. Allegorically, mounting trash represents a reality about this new economy: that it will treat growing numbers of working people as disposable. Arthur makes the connection too. When he's invited on *Live! With Murray Franklin,* near the end of the movie, he rhetorically asks what you get when you "treat [people] like trash." As Joker, he answers with revenge.

Clowns! is not a book about trash, nor for that matter is it a book about revenge violence. But just as *Clowns!* insists we take seriously Arthur's question to Murray, even as our book urges starkly different answers, so the visual metaphor of trash allows us to sketch the pages ahead. Broadly put, by rolling back the postwar consensus, neoliberalism imagines that an economy based on individual contracts produces a largely self-regulating and spontaneous system. In truth, such an economy not only requires force to be enacted and sustained, but also produces leftovers and trash. In one sense, leftovers are the literal problem of refuse—the underpriced, and so hidden, shadow of capitalism's extraordinary productivity. According to the Plastic Pollution Coalition, for instance, the United States exported 1.07 million tons of plastic waste in 2018, about one third of its recycling, 78 percent of which went to countries with poor waste management.[29] Neoliberalism sometimes acknowledges these consequences euphemistically as unintended externalities. Milton Friedman calls them "neighborhood effects,"[30] his benign term for free market inefficiency. Some suffer from economic growth and do not

29 Brendan Lui, "US Waste Exporting Explained," rePurpose.global, April 16, 2019, np.
30 Milton Friedman, *Capitalism and Freedom,* fortieth anniversary edition (Chicago: University of Chicago Press, [1962] 2002), 14.

get recompensed, just as some benefit from good outcomes they have not paid for. But this trashing of nature owes more to deeper contradictions within liberalism's philosophical approach. Liberalism is encoded to see the natural wild as a wasted opportunity. As far back as Locke, we find him marveling that America offered so much "waste in common,"[31] readying both colonial appropriation and the view that Native Americans were wasters for neglecting to exploit their bounty. That we all now find ourselves living through the sixth great species extinction in the history of the planet, uncertain whether climate change has already spiraled irreversibly out of control, owes something to this same liberal insistence that wasted nature is not a predictable side effect of exploitation, but the tragedy of leaving nature unexploited. Climate denialism is the refusal to countenance a trash problem.

When Arthur talks of being abandoned and treated like trash, however, he means something else. Arthur is a victim of insecure, disposable labor, the subject of our next chapter. There, we describe the sociology of labor insecurity, and how a work ethic—valuing hard work as a moral good and labor as a political force—fails to make sense under such conditions. The Flecks are also abandoned by welfare systems—left dangling from a rope of sand, to use Tom Waits's words. Changes to welfare, as Chapter Three shows, were ushered in by President Ronald Reagan, who repeatedly invokes the language of "waste" to fire government workers, privatize public works, and deregulate capital. He channeled public unease about the sanitation workers' strikes of New York and Memphis to advance his project of disciplining unions: "Our citizens feel they have lost control of even the most basic decisions made about the essential services of government, such as schools, welfare, roads, and even

---

31   Locke, *Two Treatises*, 294.

garbage collection."[32] Yet, despite this advocacy for smaller government, as Chapter Four shows, the newly precarious will also be targeted by the police, and fed into the maw of a steadily engorging prison system. Loïc Wacquant puts it this way: "the prison operates as a judicial garbage disposal into which the human refuse of the market society are thrown."[33] As we'll see in Chapter Five, this project of incarceration is made possible by a melodramatic media, willing to use the metaphorical language of trash to allocate blame to the poor, who will be branded "wasters," "trash," and "clowns." Together, these moves depoliticize the democratic population, compel them into compliance, and eventually, as later chapters show, bring about a backlash.

Further reading

Norberto Bobbio, *Liberalism and Democracy*, translated by Martin Ryle and Kate Soper (London: Verso, [1988] 2005).

Charles W. Mills, *The Racial Contract*, twenty-fifth anniversary edition (Ithaca: Cornell University Press, [1997] 2022).

Chantal Mouffe, *The Democratic Paradox* (New York: Verso, 2000).

Wendy Brown, *In the Ruins of Neoliberalism: The Rise of Antidemocratic Politics in the West* (New York: Columbia University Press, 2019).

Christoph Menke, *Critique of Rights*, translated by Christopher Turner (Cambridge: Polity Press, 2020).

32 Ronald Reagan, "State of the Union Address," Joint Session of Congress, January 26, 1982, reaganlibrary.gov, np.

33 Loïc Wacquant, *Punishing the Poor: The Neoliberal Government of Social Insecurity* (Durham: Duke University Press, 2009), xxii.

Chapter Two

Making Cents
On Flexible Labor

Arthur Fleck is on the job: a gig clown for Ha-Ha's clowning agency. Trash bags edge the sidewalk, and drably dressed Gothamites mill by. In the midst, a clown whirls a yellow sign: <u>EVERYTHING</u> MUST <u>GO!!</u> He sports a luminous green wig and a tiny hat, a mustard vest and a bright red nose. He's advertising Kenny's Music Shop, which is going out of business. Next to Kenny's is a typewriter repair store. A pianist, impeccable in a lavender suit, churns out a carnivalesque "Temptation Rag." Fleck beams from ear to ear. Oops! He's holding the sign upside down! Out of sight, down the street, a group of youths approach. They are bored and they see business: a clown and his sign. Snatching it, they scatter laughing. Fleck reacts instinctively to protect what's his. It is a quintessential chase scene—in size twenty loafers. The camera switches to the boys' point of view: it's a trap. Whacked by his own sign, Fleck goes down. The boys move in: "Beat his ass up," "This guy's weak," "He can't do nothin'," "Harder!", "Take his stuff." They kick and punch, then disperse, leaving Fleck in a groaning heap on the ground. His sign is in bits. (01:31–03:33)

What makes this scene so gripping is that little about it makes sense. Nonsense is everywhere. A bankrupt business in a dull, depressed city is advertised by a jolly, colorful clown. Arthur smiles broadly, though we know he is unhappy. Kids rob him, but the cardboard sign they steal has little value. Arthur gives chase, but in comically oversized shoes. From the literal perspective of his job, it is true, Arthur's behavior makes sense. He has been hired to draw attention to Kenny's wares and, like others who work in services, he must smile. His boots are big and his palette outrageous, but that's what makes clowns funny and attracts eyeballs. Arthur chases the sign because he needs it to advertise the store. Yet all of the elements are so grotesquely exaggerated—the smile, the boots, the danger in devotion to an employer's sign—that we recognize the presence of allegory: in the coming economy, it seems to say, the joke is on the flexible worker.

The movie's tropes guide us. Arthur chases after the "sign" of his temp employer as if the employer's interests were his own. He does so as if he's happy with this state of affairs: he has a cheerful smile painted on his face. Yet, he's frantic, and the risks he takes are clearly excessive. He pursues happiness wearing shoes that are too big for him: taking on societal risks and responsibilities too large for any one person to handle alone. We might put it this way: Arthur has absorbed the ideology of a work ethic. But does such loyalty to work make sense for someone in Arthur's position? Arthur might be flexible at work: he dances and spins and bends over backward. But he's about to learn that in an era of growing labor insecurity, flexibility for the likes of Fleck means being humiliated on the job, then fired once things go south. Arthur runs headfirst into a new era of flexible exploitation, and it whacks him to the ground.

In this chapter, we begin with this stinging reality check: neoliberalism, celebrating a self-regulating economy with minimal state intervention, increases insecure labor under the ideology of increased flexibility. But in these conditions, does it still make sense to chase an employer's sign? Is the joke on those who maintain a work ethic? True, a work ethic may still make sense for highly skilled workers sought out by companies for stable, even lifetime employment and perks. But for the growing class that sustains this professional elite—the subcontracted factory workers who make the products and clean the office, the underemployed who mow their lawns, the temps who dash and deliveroo their food, the personal assistants who organize their lives—for them, has the work ethic become a relic? *Joker* hammers Arthur with this question twice: after being whacked at work, Arthur's boss Hoyt accuses Arthur of himself thieving the sign and Hoyt deducts the cost from Arthur's paycheck. He treats Arthur as a clown to avoid paying him for clowning.

As Arthur confronts the widespread reality of wage insecurity, we come to grips with the broader costs. As one class of elite workers find their work ethic channeled into corporate allegiance, millions of others are expected to remain motivated by personal poverty, workplace surveillance, and character shaming. For both groups, the political meaning of work—its collective dignity—disappears, and worker solidarity fractures. Insecure work, as we will see, has many sources. But the costs to the worker are magnified when labor is imagined as merely a commodity in a self-regulating market, rather than an integral part of a healthy society. To explain what we mean by this, we return again to the raw dramas of early industrial capitalism, when liberal theorists first advocated that wage workers become fully mobile and flexible. Workers were asked to run in oversized boots, absorbing staggering societal costs. In response, workers staged a long political backlash as they organized together to protect society. But in *Joker*, when Arthur realizes he's being exploited, he zones out. We cut to him stomping trash in an alleyway. Without a political outlet, the movie asks, what happens to the rage of the humiliated?

We got the sign!

On the surface, casting Arthur as the representative of a changing work ethic doesn't make a whole lot of sense. When scholars consider the decline of the working-class work ethic, they rarely mention the clowns. They focus on "productive" workers. In 1776, Adam Smith urged that we draw a line between productive laborers and unproductive laborers.

Productive laborers, he said, are those in manufacturing—and, later we can add, in heavy industry—whose labor adds tangible value that endures after the work is finished: something that can be sold or used to make money. Unproductive laborers, for Smith, do jobs whose value ends when they stop working. Think servants such as Penny Fleck at Wayne Manor or, in our modern economy, those who serve others: the grocery and rideshare drivers, the waiters and masseurs. Unproductive labor, in Smith's formula, includes esteemed servants of democracy, such as judges and lawyers. It includes pastors. It includes the artists, the "players, buffoons, musicians, opera-singers, opera-dancers": it includes the clowns.[1]

The modern crisis in the work ethic, which André Gorz dates to 1965, is a story told in terms of productive workers, because they experience a tangible erosion in the meaning of their work that has political ramifications. The loss owes partly to rationalization: manufacturing jobs are steadily standardized into rote tasks so workers can be switched out. Industrial jobs rely less and less on a specific individual's talents. Workers find fewer occasions to take pride in how their unique skills help solve tricky material problems: in shipbuilding, mining, railroads, and construction, for example. The loss also owes to technology and hyper-specialization: modern industry requires so much expertise, it can be hard to see oneself personally reflected in the final product.[2] Finally, the work ethic implodes when neoliberal regimes break and discredit unions, robbing workers of their dignity as a political force that can shape the direction of a nation's economy. In Britain, Thatcher goes to war with the coal miners' unions. In the US, Reagan crushes the air-traffic controllers. He excludes unions from participating in

---

1   Adam Smith, *The Wealth of Nations,* introduction by Alan B. Krueger (New York: Bantam, [1776] 2003), 423.

2   André Gorz, *Critique of Economic Reason,* translated by Gillian Handyside and Chris Turner (London: Verso, 1989), 18–22.

government councils and guts regulations that protect workers within the National Labor Relations Board.[3] The result is that popular faith in labor as a transformative political force collapses, an outcome exacerbated because so much industrial labor is simultaneously off-shored, subcontracted, and automated.

Even though he's not in these classes of workers, a clown spinning a sign outside of Kenny's music shop also depicts the crisis. True, Fleck finds himself near the bottom of the capitalist work hierarchy to begin with: he puts in shifts at a clowning agency and his current job helps to hustle a music shop out of business. His loyalty to a temp agency—"I love this job," he tells Hoyt as he's getting fired—looks naive or desperate (28:45). It is true that, as a small-time entertainer, Arthur's work connects him personally to those he makes laugh, a source of immediate fulfillment. He clowns at a children's cancer ward, brightening their hospital stays: meaningful work. But Arthur's gig job also alienates him (alienation is Marx's term for what happens when you no longer see yourself reflected in your work).[4] Outside Kenny's, Arthur is hired as a living billboard, his talents reduced to flogging discount instruments. Even the kids who prank him intuit how lame this is: "If you're going to be a clown, at least you could be a good one, you know that, right?" (02:08). Clowning itself as a profession is likely going the way of the typewriter repair shop behind him. Feeling it himself, Fleck dreams of making the switch to a career in stand-up comedy: an entertainment job where personality and individuality are still professionally valued. Now there's a career he could devote himself to fully, and own his sign: but what are the prospects for permanent work?

---

3   David Harvey, *A Brief History of Neoliberalism* (Oxford: Oxford University Press, 2005), 52.

4   Karl Marx, *Economic and Philosophical Manuscripts of 1844* (Buffalo: Prometheus, [1844] 1988), 69–84.

Arthur makes a good representative of these changes because, spinning and twirling, Fleck literally embodies the fate of a flexible worker. His gig-labor forecasts the coming expansion of freelance, seasonal, and "temp" employees, whose presence grows exponentially during the neoliberal reversion. These changes radically transform the work ethic, and, for millions of workers, increasingly source motivation not in an ethic at all, but in precarity. Already by the late 1980s, automation, subcontracting, and just-in-time corporate supply strategies split US working populations into two types of flexible workers. At one end we find the "privileged stratum of permanent workers" attached to enterprises: this stable core of employees, about 25 percent of the workforce, "must be functionally flexible,"[5] skilled, and adaptable. For them, the work ethic is reinvented as corporate loyalty, demanding long hours but offering benefits, dry cleaning at work, maybe even daycare. At the other end, we find the "reserve army" of laborers on the workforce periphery. Some have permanent jobs. And within the 36 percent of US workers now in the US gig economy, some have well-paid contingent jobs: the IT consultants or accountants who secure healthcare insurance from spouses' jobs, allowing them flexibility and autonomy.[6] But for the vast millions of contingent laborers, on-call workers, temporary workers, and even many independent contractors, flexibility means to be "numerically flexible," to be let go when demand dries up.[7] For this peripheral workforce, flexibility is corporate-speak for lower pay, no promotion structure, and stripped out sick-benefits, retirement, and vacation pay. Most of these workers would prefer secure and permanent work.[8]

---

5   Gorz, *Critique*, 65–67.

6   Shane McFeely and Ryan Pendell, "What Workplace Leaders Can Learn from the Real Gig Economy," gallup.com, August 16, 2018, np.

7   Gorz, *Critique*, 67.

8   US Bureau of Labor Statistics, "Contingent and Alternative Employment Arrangement Summary," bls.gov, June 7, 2018, np.

The immense effects on workers overall are told in the numbers. In the US, in 1956, there were 20,000 in employment services (which includes temp jobs); in the early 1970s, there were 200,000. By the 1990s, such jobs ballooned to 1.1 million, only to more than double by 2008, to 2.3 million. These workers are the first to be laid off in a downturn. In the recession of 2001–2003, temp workers accounted for more than 25 percent of job losses, despite making up only 2 percent of employment.[9] By 2017, there are another 2.6 million "on-call" workers and another 5.9 million workers who don't expect their job to last the year. Contingent positions, such as these, earn only 77 percent of what a permanent worker makes. In more recent years, exploitative gig models have vastly proliferated. Large data app services—not only Uber and Doordash, but also Instawork and Gigpro—classify gig workers as independent contractors, a larger labor category that includes 10.6 million workers.[10] Doing so allows these app-based services to skirt federal minimum wage laws as well as obligations to workers' Social Security and Medicare, even worker compensation. If attacked on the street, as Arthur is, or injured or killed on the job, these employers offer no insurance. The race to the bottom between different national economies means that such worker insecurity is global. Today, it is estimated that fully half the world's workforce is "vulnerable" or employed "informally."[11]

Growing labor insecurity appears in the data as a divergence between gains in labor productivity and wages. From 1948 until 1979, when productivity rose, workers shared in the gains through commensurately

---

9   Tian Luo, Amar Mann, and Richard J. Holden, "The Expanding Role of Temporary Help Services from 1990 to 2008," *Monthly Labor Review* (August 2010): 3–16.

10 US Bureau of Labor Statistics, "Contingent and Alternative Employment," np.

11 Mike Davis, *Old Gods, New Enigmas: Marx's Lost Theory* (London: Verso, 2018), 4.

higher pay. From 1979 to 2022, however, as overall productivity rose by 72 percent, wages only went up by 17 percent.[12] The minimum wage of 1979, adjusted to productivity and inflation, should be $19.43 by 2022, instead of $7.25.[13] When this divergence begins, in the late 1970s, corporate tax rates are slashed and personal income tax rates for the upper class collapse from 70 percent to 28 percent.[14] Productivity gains are funneled to shareholders, even as the wealthy are asked to pay far less to support society's functioning. Inequality widens, deficits balloon, and the upper class solidifies its political power. "Flexibility" is the rhetoric deployed to sell these changes: flexible labor is held to extend individual liberties with freedom of choice. The reality for so many, however, is precarious working conditions and generalized insecurity. The reality is that labor shrinks as a political force. These are the signature modes of economic existence under neoliberalism. Call it Fleck's exploitation. Call it "flexploitation."[15]

Why does anybody do anything?

What flexibility adds to profits, it subtracts from meaning at work. Remember the unpleasant scene in Hoyt's office, when Arthur is asked what happened to Kenny's sign. Central to this scene is the acknowledgment that things don't make sense. Hoyt initiates the motif: "I like you Arthur . . . I don't even know why I like you" (17:53). He then accuses Arthur of stealing Kenny's sign, and that doesn't make sense either:

12   Economic Policy Institute, "The Productivity-Pay Gap," epi.org, updated October 2022, np.

13   Calculated from productivity and inflation data on bls.gov.

14   Harvey, *Neoliberalism*, 26.

15   Pierre Bourdieu, "Job Insecurity Is Everywhere Now," in *Acts of Resistance: Against the Tyranny of the Market*, translated by Richard Nice (New York: The New Press, [1997] 1998), 85.

ARTHUR
Because I got jumped. Didn't you hear?

HOYT
For a sign? That's bullshit. It doesn't even make
sense. Just get him his sign back.
He's going out of business for
God's sake Arthur—

ARTHUR
Why would I keep his sign?

HOYT
(snaps)
How the fuck do I know. Why does
anybody do anything? If you
don't return the sign, I gotta take
it outta your paycheck. Are we clear?
(18:04–18:29)

Little is, in fact, clear. Arthur cannot see why Hoyt would accuse him of stealing a near-worthless sign. Hoyt cannot see why Fleck would expect him to believe the bullshit cover story. The scene stages a crisis of signs and signification: of how "work" works and what motivates workers and employers.

Yet so far from being nonsense, this drama captures perfectly the conflict between employees and employers implied by contract wage labor. This conflict is old and exacerbated again in the modern gigging era. Running a contract talent agency, Hoyt neither expects a corporate work ethic from Fleck, nor provides one in turn. He asks Arthur about his other career plans in stand-up, after all. He dismisses the work ethic outright: "why does anybody do anything?" And when Arthur goes for a chair, Hoyt keeps it transactional: "no don't sit. This will be quick" (17:45). There's no worker's compensation for getting beat up on the job. The joke's on Arthur for having treated the employer's sign as his own, only to get hammered trying to protect it. The sign belongs to Kenny. Arthur's just the clown who's left to hold it. Whether Hoyt really believes Arthur's story hardly matters. The economic logic overriding wage labor dictates that before the worker gets paid, other things must be paid first: rent, the cost of tools, the margin for profit. His boss identifies with Arthur in a limited way—may even want good things for him. But economic rationality governs, and—unwilling to absorb workplace risk for a disposable gig worker—Hoyt resorts to attacking Arthur's character to justify the painful deduction. He humiliates Arthur by implying he's a thief, he isolates Arthur by telling him the other workers "think you're a freak," and he steers Arthur's sympathies to fellow entrepreneur, Kenny: "he's going out of business, for God's sake" (17:49–17:51). Why would Arthur stay motivated to work there? Hoyt's tone reveals he doubts Arthur could find another job, certainly not in stand-up. Workers absorb the risks and can be disciplined by character attacks and by poverty.

Told this way, the scene even mirrors the exploitation basic to an emerging industrial capitalist economy. When he describes wage labor in the eighteenth century, for instance, Adam Smith, like Hoyt, doesn't bother invoking a work ethic either. "A man must always live by his work," Smith simply states, and "his wages must at least be sufficient to maintain him."[16] Like Hoyt, Smith identifies with the misfortunate. He wrote the *Theory of Moral Sentiments* (1759), after all, which argues that "how selfish soever man may be supposed," he is interested in other people's happiness, even just "the pleasure of seeing it."[17] But when it comes to wage work, Smith knows that the cost of the sign will be deducted from the paycheck. From a workers' wages, Smith writes, "rent [to the landowner]

---

16   Smith, *Wealth of Nations*, 67.

17   Adam Smith, *The Theory of Moral Sentiments* (New Delhi: Gyan Books, [1759] 2017), 7.

makes the first deduction"; then the tools and materials, plus a margin for profit "makes a second deduction." It wasn't always so. There was a time before "the appropriation of land" into private property and before "the accumulation of stock" by the landlord and merchant classes, when "the labourer enjoyed the whole produce of his own labour."[18] Working for themselves, workers could then produce surplus they could trade. But "it would be to no purpose to trace further what might have been" if workers were able to reap the full rewards of their growing productivity under new manufacturing.[19] Smith's melancholic pragmatism about the exploitation embedded in wage labor stops the conversation short. The idea that no alternative exists takes root.

It's valuable to stay with the early history of industrial capitalism a little longer, because although Smith recognizes that wage workers are exploited when they lose productivity gains to the owners of capital, and accepts this as necessary, he would have been horrified to witness the full costs industrial capitalism extracted from workers in the coming years. Smith anticipated what economists now know happened, that the early Industrial Revolution would produce astonishing inequality, especially from 1770 to 1840 when workers' wages failed to match blistering produc-tivity gains and profit rates doubled. But economic data fails to account for the staggering *cultural* catastrophe that ensued. Settled villagers of the English countryside, within a few decades, transformed into "shiftless migrants" and the "political and social conditions of their existence [were] destroyed."[20] When Smith was writing, poor relief remained in effect. And, until 1834, the Speenhamland system guaranteed workers the "right

---

18 Smith, *Wealth of Nations*, 67.

19 Smith, *Wealth of Nations*, 67.

20 Karl Polanyi, *The Great Transformation: The Political and Economic Origins of Our Time* (Boston: Beacon Press, [1944] 2001), 164–165.

to live": no matter a worker's pay, the parish to which they were attached ensured they received a minimum wage, based on the price of bread.

To unleash an industrial market economy, however—for labor to become commodified—these laws were abolished. Labor became mobile and flexible, and the social fabric was torn to shreds. Wage floors were dismantled. Set loose from parishes and their community supports, workers crammed into shoddy slums near factories. A new theory of discipline emerged. Workers would be motivated not by the promise of higher wages but with the threat of hunger. "Hunger will tame the fiercest animals," liberal theorist Joseph Townsend enthusiastically reasoned. "It will teach decency and civility, obedience and subjection."[21] No need to compel workers through legislation; the force of the physical sanction would be "sufficient," Jeremy Bentham put it.[22] Later, Thomas Malthus supported this application of the self-regulating market to the biology of human life. In *An Essay on the Principle of Population* (1798), he claimed starvation was simply nature's way of killing off the superfluous.

When a modern economist, such as Robert C. Allen, writes of this period that "cities were built on the cheap, and the purchasing power of wages stagnated,"[23] what his economic metrics fail to capture is the staggering human and social cost of such developments. Male life expectancy in Liverpool plummeted to fifteen years old.[24] Infant mortality soared. Childhood education evaporated. Religious participation collapsed. And

---

21 Joseph Townsend, *A Dissertation on the Poor Laws* (London: Poultry, 1786), 20.

22 Jeremy Bentham, *Principles of the Civil Code*, in *The Works of Jeremy Bentham, vol. 1*, edited by John Bowring (Illinois: Liberty Fund, [1802] 2011), 547.

23 Robert C. Allen, "Engels' Pause: Technical Change, Capital Accumulation, and Inequality in the British Industrial Revolution," *Explorations in Economic History* 46.4 (2009): 430.

24 John Rule, *The Laboring Classes in Early Industrial England, 1750–1850* (London: Longman, 1986), 89.

people's ability to raise a family—to reproduce society—faced annihilation. Capital was being made hand over fist. But workers suffered degradation and starvation wages. Their whole way of life was destroyed by a market mechanism with no way to value—*no way to make sense of*—those things it could not profit from: the stability of family, the endurance of workers, a neighborhood of friends, pride in a craft, music and the arts, secure housing, enjoyment of a clean natural environment—in short, a healthy society. Grappling to communicate the scale of the destruction, Polanyi compares how imperialism ravages the lifeworld of indigenous peoples.[25] Market capitalism demands that land and people be transformed into commodities. But, as Polanyi points out, labor and land—humans and nature—can only ever be "fictitious commodities."[26] When we fully desocialize labor into wage work, when we rip it from the world in which it is embedded, we inadvertently debase other necessary modes of human labor: childcare, political participation, clowning around. Similarly, when we treat nature as a commodity we can exhaust it, destroying its organic basis for renewal, and eventually our own.

The social destruction in England produced a spontaneous and pragmatic backlash and catalyzed agitation for regulation to protect society. These regulations were also pursued by paternalist aristocrats and a few liberals, but it was the working class who mounted the political defense of society, coordinated around a work ethic.[27] True, early regulations mostly went unheeded: in 1833, children under nine were banned from working in textile factories, and by 1842 no boys under ten were allowed in underground mines.[28] True, the socialist worker utopias of Robert Owen

---

25 Polanyi, *Great Transformation*, 164–165.

26 Polanyi, *Great Transformation*, 71–80.

27 Polanyi, *Great Transformation*, 105.

28 Encyclopaedia Britannica, "Factory Act, United Kingdom [1833]," britannica.com, nd, np.

in both the United Kingdom and the United States eventually failed: these were the cotton mills where workers found shorter working hours and safe housing, where they bought goods at wholesale and shared care for children. But Owen's advocacy charted the way for worker co-ops, laid the groundwork for unions, and championed all manner of legislative reforms, including the eight-hour workday, child labor laws, worker's compensation, universal education, and so on. The forefathers of the twentieth-century's neoliberals, A. V. Dicey and Ludwig von Mises, labeled this double movement—the pendulum swinging from the liberalizing prerogatives of capital (free markets and flexible commitments) to the self-defense of society achieved by workers (unions, holidays, benefits, safety)—a "collectivist" socialist conspiracy.[29] But as Polanyi points out, the reforms were piecemeal, practical, and pragmatic, hardly the result of coordinated planning. The working class insisted that the market economy had to make more than money: it also had to make sense.

The postwar consensus fashioned between corporate capital and workers in the United States is a late stage in this same double movement. By the late nineteenth century some US mining unions had won eight-hour workdays, and before the 1930s some large corporations instituted pensions, such as those federal workers had earned. But it took the Great Depression and the massive expansion of unions in the 1930s to set up the postwar force of collective bargaining and to push through Roosevelt's New Deal which federalized minimum wages; instituted near-eight-hour workdays; and launched Social Security, the housing authority, and food stamps. These programs had gaps that disadvantaged women and minorities. When Penny writes to Wayne that she "has no insurance or opportunities for any future" (48:43), *Joker* reminds us that even before neoliberal attempts to roll back New Deal welfare benefits, domestic workers—largely female and Black populations—had no Social Security,

---

29   Polanyi, *Great Transformation*, 147.

because their employers were exempted from paying in. For the bulk of so-called productive workers, however, loyalty was routed through a union, which could rationally valorize a work ethic and a reason to smile when holding your employer's sign, because worker protections were won and defended.

By the late twentieth century, such utopianism has evaporated. We know it even through the movies. When Arthur has his sign stolen, *Joker* sets up a near parody of films from another era. In Sergei Eisenstein's masterpiece *Strike* (1925), for instance, when a boss unfairly accuses a factory worker of stealing tools, the worker's indignation leads him to hang himself from a factory pipe.[30] The suicide catalyzes the entire factory to mobilize into strike, a titanic struggle that pits the workers' community against the capitalist class, who employ infiltrators, then the police, to water cannon and eventually massacre the unarmed strikers. In *Strike*, a work ethic means not just pride in one's individual skill at a specific job— because few others could do it as well. It also means coming to recognize the transformative political power inherent in industrial labor, visualized in camera shots where thousands of workers and their families mill across the screen. Harnessed in solidarity with others, Eisenstein's early Soviet melodrama says, industrial labor can shape the direction of a nation.

US unions pursued social democratic goals, not socialist revolution. They threw their lot in with Democrats rather than supporting progressive or socialist candidates. Yet by Arthur's time, even these compromise strategies have collapsed, and neoliberal policies swing the pendulum of the double movement back again. More people slide into precarity. Now, a gig-worker accused of theft is reduced to venting his spleen in a back-alley and lamenting in his journal: "I just hope my death makes more ~~sen~~ cents than my life" (06:25). For the modern flexible worker, indignity is

---

30   *Strike*, directed by Sergei Eisenstein (1st Goskino Factory, 1925).

felt alone, and the most redeeming outcome imagined from death is not workplace solidarity or job security, not collective bargaining or political power, not recognition or respect, but merely making more cents. Even in fantasy, the work ethic is reduced to the banal, if understandable, dream of making a little bit more money.

Don't bother sitting down

When Hoyt reveals the foolishness of Arthur's work ethic—that the sign will be deducted from his paycheck—Arthur glazes over with a deadpan smile. The camera tightens on his face, and the sound of kicking and grunting drowns out Hoyt's waxing tirade about how "the other guys, they don't feel comfortable around you, Arthur" (18:39). We cut to Fleck in a narrow alleyway lined with trash bags, kicking, then furiously stomping something behind a dumpster. The violence and setting mirror Arthur's own alley beating, which makes us briefly wonder if Arthur might be kicking an unseen person. But, defeated by his exertion, Arthur slips, then finally sits down in the middle of the filth. He has merely been venting his rage on trash. The trash stands in for another version of himself: kicking himself, as the expression goes, out of humiliation and regret. But kicking trash, taking it out on something deemed worthless, is also the logic of Arthur's initial beating: boys growing up on the street with few chances happen upon a clown on whom to vent their protest. Here, we return to our initial question about making sense of humiliation: if the new economy enrages, because it humiliates, who will be the target of this fury? The first alley scene ends in a vision of male degradation and impotence: Arthur clutching his genitals and his clown's flower dribbling its squirt of water. In the second scene, Arthur sits in a fetal position and the joke of humiliation has become visually generalized: in the distance, a giant Ferris wheel looms, motionless.

Further reading

Karl Polanyi, *The Great Transformation: The Political and Economic Origins of Our Time* (Boston: Beacon Press, [1944] 2001).

André Gorz, *Critique of Economic Reason*, translated by Gillian Handyside and Chris Turner (London: Verso, 1989).

David Harvey, *A Brief History of Neoliberalism* (Oxford: Oxford University Press, 2005).

Chapter Three

Tough Times

On Welfare

Fleck's laughing face fills the entire, darkly lit frame. The laughs are confused, joyless, and pained. His throat chokes for breath, and his gasps and sniffles resemble crying. He's humped in a chair in a cramped office. The shelves are overburdened. So is his social worker. The dim aqua light presses the darkness around them. "Is it just me," he asks, "or is it getting crazier out there?" A deep and slow timpani drum begins, beating one . . . two, one . . . two, as if the ticking of the clock of bureaucracy spells impending doom. "It is certainly tense. People are upset. They're struggling. Looking for work. These are tough times." She asks for Arthur's therapy journal. He's agitated, but hands it over. It is also a joke diary, he explains. The social worker asks if he's thought more about why he was committed. The camera cuts to a white-tiled, overlit hospital room, where Arthur repeatedly bashes his head against the observation window. The clock on the hospital wall, identical to the one on the social worker's office, records the same time. "Who knows?" he responds. Arthur asks for increased medication dosage but is refused. (04:46–07:11)

This scene in the social worker's office sets Arthur's impending medical crisis in the heart of an economic crisis. The economic crisis began in the 1970s and was called *stagflation*: the word combines "inflation," meaning the average price level, which in the 1970s was rising, and "stagnation," because the economy was floundering with unemployment growing. This new term came about because the phenomenon was new:

inflation normally accompanies an economic boom. The social worker calls it "tough times." The economic historian Mark Blyth puts it this way: "[t]here was indeed a crisis, and the state had lost control of its diagnosis."[1] The crisis is written into Arthur's bodily predicament. He's inflating with laughter, but the laugh indicates pain rather than pleasure. And despite his treatment, his mental health is stagnating. He might prefer the hospital to a social worker's talk therapy and medication, but the clock time is the same in both places. There's no progress. These choices are presented visually as black and white, the dim lighting of the therapy office and the blazing light of the hospital. But Gotham's way out of the impasse is darker again. In the subsequent scene with the social worker, we learn social welfare services and medication will be cut altogether and Arthur will be abandoned by the state.

That crisis is already portended in this scene. We see it when the social worker turns Arthur's visit into an interrogation about individual responsibility: "and have you thought more about why you were locked up?" (07:01). The therapist's shift to isolating responsibility individually, as well as the language that criminalizes mental health ("locked up"), mirror the sleight of hand that will accompany the economic response to stagflation as well. The old solution for economic stagnation and unemployment was to increase fiscal medication: to increase government spending on those losing out in a downturn, as economist John Maynard Keynes had long recommended.[2] But in 1981, when *Joker* is set, Ronald Reagan rides to power with a new economic prescription: to gut social services and to compel the unemployed and the disabled to accept individual responsibility for their predicament. Arthur is on the front line of that coming change.

1   Mark Blyth, *Great Transformations: Economic Ideas and Institutional Change in the Twentieth Century* (Cambridge: Cambridge University Press, 2002), 138.

2   John M. Keynes, *The General Theory of Employment, Interest and Money* (New York: Harcourt, Brace and Co., 1936), 321.

The language of Reagan's counterrevolution is also cast in melodramatic terms that catalyze drastic changes. In his inaugural presidential address of 1981, Reagan describes a nation on the brink of disaster. The problem is not an external enemy, but internal policies: the New Deal. Taxes are high, yet never high enough to meet the demands of government spending. Welfare commitments are growing all the time, destroying America's work ethic and perverting the free market. Historically, America's greatness had resided in its commitment to personal freedom and industry: "the energy and individual genius of man." But dependency culture, Reagan claimed, had changed all that. Ordinary people have become lazy and are living beyond their means. Unemployment is rising, inflation too. America has lost its way.[3] In response, he proposed a new economic program.

> In the days ahead I will propose removing the roadblocks that have slowed our economy and reduced productivity. Steps will be taken aimed at restoring the balance between the various levels of government . . . It is time to reawaken this industrial giant, to get government back within its means, and to lighten our punitive tax burden. And these will be our first priorities, and on these principles, there will be no compromise.[4]

Pro-business and anti-welfare, Reagan's election signals the end of the New Deal consensus in American politics. No longer could those out of work expect a sympathetic hand from their government. Rather, they would be pushed back into the workforce or penalized for their indolence.

---

3   Ronald Reagan, "First Inaugural Address," Speech to US Capitol, January 20, 1981, reaganlibrary.gov, np.

4   Reagan, "First Inaugural Address."

Who knows?

When he's asked why he was committed to Arkham Asylum in the 1970s, Arthur responds: "Who knows?" The same shoulder shrug mirrors the confused policy response to stagflation, an economic confusion that gave neoliberalism, called in this era Reaganomics, an entryway to transform the national economy. Economic policies shift, says Blyth, when governing ideas fail to explain the behavior of the economy.[5] New Deal Keynesianism was discredited because it was unable to manage the simultaneous rise in unemployment and inflation. Typically, it was believed, these phenomena are meant to regulate each other. In tough times, the job market shrinks but prices and wages fall. In good times, prices rise, but wages rise as well and there are more jobs. But stagflation troubled the Keynesian consensus. That consensus argued that to reduce inflation one should either raise the tax rate (a fiscal policy) or increase the rates of borrowing from the central bank and tighten the money supply (monetary policy). These moves take money out of the economy to slow overheating and lower inflation in the good times, when the economy is doing well. The money raised from such measures can build a surplus for use in a future recession. But in truth, for Keynes, slowing a booming economy was never ideal. He called it "the species of remedy which cures the disease by killing the patient." Better simply to manage the economic downturn when it inevitably comes. In a downturn, Keynesianism prescribes the reverse of the policies just described: to reduce unemployment, government should increase fiscal stimulus by "redistribution of incomes or otherwise." In other words, government should fund people directly through unemployment benefits or social welfare (this is the "redistribution of incomes"), or else should create new jobs by increasing federal spending, useful in a downturn when

---

5   Blyth, *Great Transformations*, 30–34.

businesses are fearful (this is the "otherwise").[6] These policies are called "compensatory" because they increase economic demand by helping those most harmed by a downturn, keeping support for capitalism intact through crisis and targeting relief to those most likely to spend the money rather than save it.

Stagflation introduces a conflict into these policies because unemployment calls for *increased* stimulus whereas inflation calls for *decreased* stimulus, both at the same time. Stagflation also puts into conflict the two mandates of the Federal Reserve (the US central bank, often called the Fed): one is to strive for "maximum sustainable employment"; the other is to keep inflation in check ("stable prices").[7] The Fed controls the money supply and the interest rates. It can increase the interest rates for borrowing, which reduces inflation. But doing so simultaneously suffocates the economy, increasing unemployment. The reverse is also true: lowering interest rates expands the economy because everyone can borrow more cheaply, creating jobs, but risking inflation. Managing a balance between monetary and fiscal policy at the same time is tricky.

According to Blyth, stagflation in the 1970s was caused largely by massive fiscal spending on the Vietnam War, much of it hidden from economists, which generated outsized inflation. President Lyndon Johnson lacked the political will to raise taxes to check inflation. President Nixon raised taxes, and his Fed chair also raised borrowing rates by 3 percent, depressing the economy and raising unemployment. Inflation came down. But, on account of the enormous spending on the Vietnam War, it still remained high. Then, the Organization of Arab Petroleum Exporting Countries' oil embargo hit in 1973–1974, supercharging inflation by quadrupling in the oil price. Nixon introduced government price controls, but

---

6   Keynes, *General Theory*, 322–324.

7   Federal Reserve Bank of Chicago, "The Federal Reserve's Dual Mandate," chicagofed.org, updated October 20, 2020, np.

incoherently, and by the time he resigned "wholesale" price inflation was 44 percent and unemployment 7.6 percent.[8] The business community felt sorely betrayed by big-government Republicanism—tax increases, meddling price controls, and that on top of new environmental and work safety regulations that the Nixon presidency signed off on, the Environmental Protection Agency and Occupational Safety and Health Act.

For the neoliberals, the stagflation crisis spelled opportunity. Just as the Great Depression smashed the credibility of laissez-faire economics, stagflation demolished the postwar consensus in ways that allowed a reprioritization of how resources should be allocated: who should receive money to stimulate the economy, and from whom money should be taken to cool inflation. A new policy—monetarism—gained credence. Monetarists called on the Fed to prioritize cutting inflation over reducing unemployment. They argued that promoting full employment was misguided because it ignored the need for "labor mobility" in a "dynamic world." In Chapter Two, we called this the flexibility problem. Milton Friedman, the leading monetarist, contested the Keynesian consensus by arguing that an economy finds a "natural level" of unemployment: people change jobs; jobs become obsolete.[9] This is not an index that something is wrong. The market will, if left to itself, stabilize itself.[10] In any case, for Friedman, unemployment is less of a concern than misguided state intervention in the economy.

Downplaying the ills of unemployment, Friedman trained everyone's eyes, instead, on the evil of inflation, identifying three main sources: excess government spending, the "unduly ambitious" Keynesian policy of

---

8   Blyth, *Great Transformations*, 138–139.

9   Milton Friedman, "Nobel Lecture: Inflation and Unemployment," *Journal of Political Economy* 85.3 (Jun 1977): 451–472.

10 Milton and Rose Friedman, *Free to Choose: A Personal Statement* (New York: Harcourt Brace Jovanovich: 1980), 264–265.

full employment, and misguided fiscal policies at the Fed.[11] Monetarists argue that inflation should be controlled by decreasing the money supply (a supply regulated by the Fed) and by cutting fruitless federal stimulus. This antagonistic view of government was a mainstay of Friedmanism: "government is the problem."[12] Governments *produce* inflation, Friedman suggested, by placating the unemployed with stimulus that will not work in the long term.

When Friedman described his policy of cutting federal spending and tightening the money supply for *Playboy* in 1973, he admitted it would be painful: "the bad effects are felt right away. People are out of work. Interest rates go up. Money gets tight. It's unpleasant."[13] Monetarism was not a popular policy, he admitted, but that did not make it wrong. The real problem was "educating the public."[14] And this was the purpose of the neoliberal counter-revolution. The public had to learn that less money in its pockets was the solution to its problems. This would take time to inculcate. Reagan's *State of the Union* addresses were integral to the effort. And business got behind the project too, learning, as Mark Blyth puts it, to "spend as a class." They exploited loopholes in the Campaign Finance Reform Act (1971) and set about buying as much influence as they could. The business community would steer the GOP toward becoming the pre-eminent party of small government and big business.[15]

What Friedman never admits is that the "bad effects" of monetarist policy are not shared by the entire public: money isn't tight for everyone.

---

11   Milton and Rose Friedman, *Free to Choose*, 264.

12   Milton Friedman, *Why Government Is the Problem* (Stanford: Hoover Institution on War, Revolution, and Peace, 1993).

13   Milton Friedman, *"Playboy* Interview," in *There's No Such Thing as A Free Lunch: Essays on Public Policy* (La Salle: Open Court, 1975), 3.

14   Milton Friedman, "Steady as You Go Revisited," in *There's No Such Thing as a Free Lunch*, 51.

15   Blyth, *Great Transformations*, 155, 154–161.

Monetarism tries to steer Fed policy toward only one of its mandates—inflation—as it argues against helping the unemployed. To *Playboy*, Friedman claims that inflation primarily hurts "people without much political voice—the poor and retired people on fixed incomes."[16] But Blyth points out this right-wing canard is not true. "*Inflation is a class-specific tax*. Those with credit suffer while those with debt, relatively speaking, prosper."[17] For indebted middle-class and working poor people, inflation is not much of a crisis. After all, wages then tended to go up with prices, keeping things more or less even. And if you hold debt such as a mortgage, inflation reduces your debt burden over time, since your payment stays the same even as your wages rise. Social Security payments to retirees also increase to match inflation. On the other hand, if you are wealthy and lend money (are a saver or a bank, or, yes, a wealthy older person), unexpected inflation costs you because it reduces the value of future payments on bonds, for instance. Inflation hysteria conceals a class position. The same can be said for the title "monetarism" itself. It can sound like a rejection of Keynesian fiscal policy. But more precisely, Friedman's policies, especially as developed under Reagan, only oppose those fiscal policies that help the poor and unemployed. The enormous tax cuts overseen by Reagan were also fiscal stimulus after all, well within a Keynesian remit; it's just that such stimulus accrues narrowly to the wealthy and corporations, who are less likely than the poor to spend it. Reagan would argue that such largesse "trickles down" to the poor when the wealthy spend or invest. Instead, inequality widened dramatically, and has continued to widen until the present.[18] Whereas under the postwar consensus, fiscal and monetary policies tilted to benefit the broader working

---

16   Friedman, "*Playboy* Interview," 3.

17   Blyth, *Great Transformations*, 149.

18   Thomas Piketty, *Capital in the Twenty-First Century*, translated by Arthur Goldhammer (Cambridge, MA: Belknap of Harvard University Press, 2014).

and middle classes, Reagan tilted those policies upward to benefit the wealthy. Keynes called for a "redistribution of incomes," and Reagan obliged—only, he redistributed *upward*. Here, we call this *sadofiscal policy*, because it pleasures the rich while punishing the poor. That is the real Reagan revolution.

They don't give a shit about people like you

Neoliberalism preaches individual happiness, but in Gotham this means abandoning, then pursuing, Happy.

> SOCIAL WORKER
> The city's cut funding across the board.
> Social services is part of that. This is the last
> time we'll be meeting.
>
> *Arthur nods, not hating the idea.*
>
> [· ·]
>
> They don't give a shit about people like you,
> Arthur. And, they really don't really give a
> shit about people like me either.
>
> (41:26–41:46)

Here is the abandonment. When well enough to work, the state wants to make Arthur wholly responsible for his healthcare, even though he apparently has neither the mental nor financial resources to manage it himself. Yet without healthcare, the state will take away his freedom: commit him. Here is the pursuit. The social worker points out that the victims of welfare cuts include people like herself with good tax-paying jobs. Fiscal policy that aids the poor hires people directly. Ironically, *Joker* suggests that all is not lost on this count. Neoliberalism will pay for work in the criminal and prison system, where the social worker will end up treating Arthur at the movie's end. (We'll examine the penal turn in Chapter Four.)

To bring about this change in economic policy, the Reagan revolution had to convince people to change their attitudes, both to the state and to their fellow citizens. Responsibility for economic downturns now belonged to the individual. Some people would need to be treated like shit.

To popularize sadofiscalism, to make it worth voting for, required popular intellectual support. On the eve of Reagan's election, Milton and Rose Friedman offered a classic statement of the conservative case against social welfare in *Free to Choose*. Published in 1980, the book was a popular restatement of aspects of Friedman's *Capitalism and Freedom* (1962). It carried the imprimatur of the Nobel Foundation, which had awarded Friedman its prize for economics in 1976, and was part of the neoliberal drive to change the conversation about what being American meant. It was accompanied by a ten-part TV series, privately funded by conservative lobbyists, but aired on the Public Broadcasting Service (PBS).[19] This made Friedman a household name. Reviving the age-old distinction between the working poor and the welfare poor (the worthy and the unworthy), the Friedmans framed welfare as *the* issue dividing America, ideologically and economically. Welfare is "a tax on work": "What nine out of ten working people are now doing is paying taxes to finance payments to persons who are not working."[20] In the welfare state, Adam Smith's invisible hand was being repurposed as a pickpocket. The victims were ordinary, hard-working Americans, and Friedman excelled at speaking to them: "If you pay people not to work, and tax them when they do, don't be surprised if you get unemployment."[21] Friedmanism assumed the self-sufficient individual as the proper basis of liberal society, and the morally incompetent individual as the likely recipient of welfare. This

---

19   Blyth, *Great Transformations*, 159.

20   Friedman and Friedman, *Free to Choose*, 104.

21   "Top 300 Milton Friedman Quotes," quotefancy.com, June 23, 2024, np.

condensed two founding assumptions of the neoliberal counterrevolution: taxes are punitive; welfare ought to be.

Joker communicates in stark lighting the false choices of a mental health crisis, whose solution to revoke care completely will instead make things worse. This cinematic strategy, of presenting polarized choices, chimes with the rhetorical strategy in Friedman's analysis. The strategy derives from Friedman's beloved source, the urtext of neoliberalism, Hayek's *The Road to Serfdom* (1944). Written in the shadow of Hitler and the Stalinist purges, Hayek's book depicts history as a simple clash of civilizations: a war between free-market liberalism and Stalinist socialism, between Western humanism and Hitlerist atrocity. For Hayek, it is either them or us; good or evil. There can be no "middle way."[22] Morally, this was about as sophisticated as *Star Wars*. Yet, such melodramatic framing would help construct a "counterimaginary" to the New Deal.[23]

Even before Friedman became the popular voice of that counterimaginary, the reach of the New Deal in the US was limited by the polarizing rhetoric of the Cold War which targeted the Soviet Union. (To this day, socialism is considered a "terrorist" ideology by the American military.)[24] Stark ideological posturing enabled business and finance leaders to limit the US welfare state, "without abandoning the strong state." Heavy military spending replaced more expansive forms of social welfare offered by other advanced democracies, such as national healthcare. A strong state remained but, in order to limit social spending, participatory

---

22 Friedrich A. Hayek, *The Road to Serfdom*, fiftieth anniversary edition (Chicago: University of Chicago Press, [1944] 1994), 47.

23 Sheldon S. Wolin, *Democracy Incorporated: Managed Democracy and the Specter of Inverted Totalitarianism* (Princeton: Princeton University Press, 2008), 22.

24 Ken Klippenstein, "US Military Training Document Says Socialists Represent 'Terrorist' Ideology," theintercept.com, June 22, 2021, np.

democracy would have to be limited.[25] Under this regime, even some proponents of the New Deal became spooked by the prospect of too much government.[26] Overall, the new liberal cared less about socioeconomic reform, was lukewarm or indifferent toward social democracy, and was increasingly unreceptive to egalitarian ideals.[27] Friedman overlaps here. He advocates for freedom instead of equality or welfare.

Under Hayek's influence, Friedman—in *Capitalism and Freedom*—could conflate, without irony, communism, socialism, and the welfare state.[28] Government planning, especially social planning, tended to "dictatorship."[29] Social justice programs are unjust, because they impose distribution outcomes on free people in a free society. That is, taxes force some people to pay for the well-being of others. Hayek, in his classic statement of the neoliberal position, privileges "general welfare" over social welfare. General welfare subsumes social welfare, he argues, and is best achieved in a free market. Market institutions have endured because it was found that they "improve for all or most the prospects of having their needs satisfied."[30] In fact, the market is itself a source of social justice because, as Friedman puts it, if an exchange between two parties is voluntary, it will not take place unless both believe they will benefit. This was the "key insight" of Adam Smith's *Wealth of Nations*: fair exchange

---

25   Wolin, *Democracy Incorporated*, 26.

26   Theodore Rosenof, "Freedom, Planning, and Totalitarianism: The Reception of F. A. Hayek's *Road to Serfdom*," *Canadian Review of American Studies* 5.2 (1974): 161.

27   Wolin, *Democracy Incorporated*, 27.

28   Milton Friedman, *Capitalism and Freedom*, fortieth anniversary edition (Chicago: University of Chicago Press, [1962] 2002), 34.

29   Hayek, *Road to Serfdom*, 78.

30   Friedrich A. Hayek, *Law, Legislation and Liberty: A New Statement of the Liberal Principles of Justice and Political Economy* (London: Routledge, [1973] 2013), 229.

is no robbery.[31] Under this spell, Friedman compares rules that prohibit racism in hiring decisions to principles employed in "Hitler Nuremberg Laws."[32] Linking principles of social justice to Nazism made it easier for neoliberals to frame social welfare as an assault on democracy. In Europe, democratic socialism was considered an heir to the liberal tradition. To neoliberals in America, the child was the progeny of fascism.

Binary thinking is prone to simplistic oppositions that can be moralized into good and bad, regulating blame and concealing contradictions. Within Hayek's and Friedman's liberalism, *good* is "competitive capitalism" imagined as individuals entering into economic contracts voluntarily; *bad* is government when it oversteps its limited mandate to keep enemies at bay, maintain order, and to enforce such contracts. This framework ignores how social reproduction is threatened when people (labor) and earth (land or resources) are treated only as commodities without provision for their organic sustenance (food, sleep, community, child rearing, clean water, health). It also overlooks how power concentrates in capitalist societies into corporate organization that deeply influences governmental power. Instead, Friedman argues that "competitive capitalism . . . promotes political freedom because it separates economic power from political power and in this way enables the one to offset the other."[33] Yet, as Michael Best and William Connolly argue, in a prescient analysis from 1976, the neoliberal model displaces blame for the negative effects of corporate capitalism onto the welfare system designed to mitigate these harms: "Behind the symptoms of welfare state malaise lies the illness of corporate capitalism."[34] Feigning compassion for the

---

31   Friedman and Friedman, *Free to Choose*, 1.

32   Friedman, *Capitalism and Freedom*, 113.

33   Friedman, *Capitalism and Freedom*, 9.

34   Michael H. Best and William E. Connolly, *The Politicized Economy*, second edition (Lexington: D.C. Heath, 1982), 201.

poor, while making credible claims about America's "cumbrous welfare bureaucracy,"[35] the neoliberals hide corporate power from their model, while exacting the price of public accountability from the welfare system. Unregulated capitalism produces massive inequality which the welfare state is then expected to alleviate, but with ever diminishing means.

Reagan adopted the Friedman view in substance while moderating his rhetoric. He couldn't abolish the social security system of pensions or privatize the national parks as Friedman advocated,[36] but he saw other opportunities. A main strategy was to stigmatize welfare recipients as irresponsible, even to themselves. In his *State of the Union* addresses, Reagan staged America's problems in the familiar pattern that Sheldon Wolin describes as "a confrontation between parasitism and the work ethic."[37] Reagan combined tough talk on paternalist social protection with promises to lift the poor out of poverty by teaching them to be fully responsible for themselves: to "reach out a hand when they fall, heal them when they are sick, and provide opportunities to make them self-sufficient."[38] He transformed the age-old distinction between the worthy and unworthy poor into catchy phrasing: "the needy" and "the greedy."[39] He publicized the alleged demoralizing effects of welfare dependency, while granting more than $600 billion in tax breaks to business and energy interests.[40] Tax breaks were framed as the cost of putting America back to work. Somehow, Reagan justified spending cuts and tax cuts as

---

35 Milton Friedman, "Negative Income Tax II," in *There's No Such Thing as a Free Lunch*, 200.

36 Friedman, *Capitalism and Freedom*, 35–36.

37 Sheldon S. Wolin, "Democracy and the Welfare State," in *The Presence of the Past: Essays on the State and the Constitution* (Baltimore: Johns Hopkins University Press, 1989), 159.

38 Reagan, "First Inaugural Address."

39 Ronald Reagan, "State of the Union Address," Speech to Joint Session of Congress, January 26, 1982, reaganlibrary.gov, np.

40 Blyth, *Great Transformations*, 179.

dual means to the same end: "to stimulate the economy and create jobs."[41] To his detractors, in 1986, he cited Franklin Roosevelt himself, the grand architect of the New Deal, saying "welfare is a narcotic, a subtle destroyer of the human spirit."[42] The welfare system, Reagan argued, was rife with corruption: both "waste and fraud."[43] In his first year, Reagan cut over $40 billion in welfare benefits, and intended more.[44] Slashing public spending—a policy known as austerity—made it possible to discredit welfare on the basis that it doesn't work. *Joker* dramatizes the moment in Manhattan when this austerity policy begins to bite. The social worker is buried in a basement of files, and Fleck's downward spiral is made to seem quasi-inevitable as his social safety net disappears.

Is it just me?

A mentally ill character losing his healthcare, Fleck is on the fast track to complete individual responsibility. When he asks, "is it just me or is it getting crazier out there?" he avoids the obvious interconnection. The economic situation presented a crisis, which mobilized arguments to cut social welfare and, with it, Fleck's medication: one crack-up catalyzes another. Friedman celebrated the strategy in a 1982 reprint, aware that his moment had come: "Only a crisis—actual or perceived—produces real change. When that crisis occurs, the actions that are taken depend on the ideas that are lying around."[45] Crisis is a medical term, designating the moment in treatment when health is either won or lost: a life-or-death

---

41 Reagan, "State of the Union Address," 1982.
42 Ronald Reagan, "State of the Union Address," Speech to Joint Session of Congress, February 4, 1986, reaganlibrary.gov, np.
43 Reagan, "State of the Union Address," 1982.
44 Blyth, *Great Transformations*, 179.
45 Friedman, "Preface 1982," in *Capitalism and Freedom*, xiv.

scenario.[46] In this sense, too, *Joker* is a crisis narrative. Fleck's mental situation deteriorates quickly. It is a systemic meltdown. Socially, he suffers from what critics of austerity call the death of a thousand cuts.[47] He loses his job and his social support. This would put most of us under. But Fleck is also mentally ill, and this might matter most of all.

Disability advocates talk of their shock at finding out the burden of adapting to society is wholly on them.[48] They demonstrate how society disables them, time and again, by refusing to recognize their impairments. It is always they who must accommodate ableist norms and expectations, and never the other way round. Fleck knows this, writing in his therapy journal: "The worst part about having a mental illness is that people expect you to behave as if you d☺nt" (26:49). Friedman's binarisms leave little room for such subtlety. "We do not believe in freedom for madmen or children," he writes.[49] The principle is an old one that goes back to John Locke. Liberalism does not extend a freedom based on voluntary contract to those unable freely to make such contracts. In such instances, the state must be paternalistic. Though Friedman's paternalism will generally advocate cash payments instead of specific welfare programs, it also harbors a telling rhetorical bias.[50] By essentializing mental illness into an extreme and fixed category—"madmen"—Friedman discourages us from envisioning individual treatment for those such as Arthur who might just need reliable support and medication to keep on track, to continue working and caring for his mother. Friedman collapses mental illness into a type of person, a "madman," then the person into a group,

---

46   Dario Gentili, *The Age of Precarity: Endless Crisis as an Art of Government* (London: Verso, 2021), 11.

47   Alexandros Kentikelenis and Thomas Stubbs, *A Thousand Cuts: Social Protection in the Age of Austerity* (Oxford: Oxford University Press, 2023).

48   Joanne Limburg, "Am I Disabled?" aeon.co, December 10, 2020, np.

49   Friedman, *Capitalism and Freedom*, 33.

50   Friedman, *Capitalism and Freedom*, 178.

"madmen." Later in his book, the category "children and madmen" is neatly replaced by "children and other irresponsible individuals."[51] It is not simply that to be free means to forgo social welfare. It is that by taking social welfare, one must admit oneself to be irresponsible or mad.

Knowing this, we can better understand why the financial savings of cutting welfare were only part of the point in Reagan's policies. The welfare poor had to be punished at the level of character, by internalizing their classification as "irresponsible." They needed to be scrutinized, constantly: to be reminded of their responsibilities and feeling their freedom always in the balance. Reagan instigated periodic reviews of the 2.6 million people on disability, such as Arthur Fleck. These people had to prove they were being treated for their conditions and, if deemed sufficiently improved, were declined further aid. They were subject to routine medical checks and required to submit (and resubmit) evidence of their eligibility. In this way, over half a million people were removed from the rolls.[52] For the others, government exacted obedience in the form of procedural hurdles and bureaucratic uncertainty that generated insecurity. In other areas of the economy, Reagan called for deregulation: for privatizing public assets and weakening environmental regulations. But the poor would feel a significant *expansion* of state regulation. Even their designation as "needy"—their classification as objects of state benevolence—fortified state power in its paternalistic form.[53] Reagan's signature move, a hallmark of neoliberal thought, was to characterize good government of the nation as individual self-government. For this to work, however, individuals had to learn to behave like agents in the putative free market. They had to learn to self-regulate: "if no one among us is capable of governing himself, then who among us has the capacity to

51   Friedman, *Capitalism and Freedom*, 86.
52   Wolin, "Democracy and the Welfare State," 159.
53   Wolin, "Democracy and the Welfare State," 154.

govern someone else?"[54] Fleck's response is to burst out laughing—not out of free pleasure, as laughter normally signifies, but in pain.

In *Joker*, the question of Arthur's treatment is a bait-and-switch that justifies his abandonment and then his pursuit: revoking his medication and later locking him up. Rhetorically, Friedmanism made this maneuver possible, and Reagan's policies ensured it. There were always contradictions within the liberal tradition, between economic freedom and political engagement. Hayek and Friedman resolve those in one direction: the economy comes first. We must choose, they say, between the individual *or* society, liberalism *or* socialism, work *or* welfare. Neoliberals wished the contradiction away: economic freedom *produces* political equality, they claimed, but never the other way round. "A society that puts equality ahead of freedom will end up with neither," Friedman stated, whereas "a society that puts freedom before equality will end up with both greater freedom and greater equality."[55] This had been Hayek's main contention. Market freedom is the necessary precondition of its political equivalent. In this present crisis, Friedman told America, government is the problem. It had become bloated and self-defeating; had expanded, Reagan declared, "beyond the consent of the governed."[56]

As in *Joker*, this either-or rhetoric formed the pretext for advocating neoliberal economic policies, "economic program[s] . . . completely different from the artificial quick fixes of the past."[57] Despite such avowals, Reagan also retained Keynesian modes of fiscal stimulus—he just limited them to the wealthy. Reagan's Fed chair Paul Volker certainly tightened the money supply by raising interest rates to crush high inflation. Reagan certainly aimed to apply the neoliberal package of privatizing

---

54   Reagan, "First Inaugural Address."
55   Friedman and Friedman, *Free to Choose*, 148.
56   Reagan, "First Inaugural Address."
57   Reagan, "State of the Union Address," 1982.

government assets, cutting regulation, and breaking unions. But Reagan's budgets counterweighted this tightening with massive fiscal stimulus for the wealthy and the military-industrial complex, which significantly expanded national debt. Even as business elites benefited from state subsidies, the poor and unemployed were told a different story: that fiscal stimulus for *them* was bad. That unemployment was their own fault. That taking government help made them irresponsible. For them, freedom meant abandonment. And since the abandoned were imagined fully responsible, they could expect to be criminally pursued even for minor infractions. With that, we turn to the rise of the neoliberal prison state.

Further reading

Sheldon Wolin, "Democracy and the Welfare State," in *The Presence of the Past: Essays on the State and Constitution*, 151–179 (Princeton: Princeton University Press, 1989).

Joel F. Handler, *The Poverty of Welfare Reform* (New Haven: Yale University Press, 1995).

Michael B. Katz, *The Price of Citizenship: Redefining the American Welfare State*, updated edition (Philadelphia: University of Pennsylvania Press, [2001] 2008).

Frances Ryan, *Crippled: Austerity and the Demonization of Disabled People* (London: Verso, 2019).

Chapter Four

Strip Search

On the Carceral State

Take two! Hands free by their clipped handguns, two policemen walk by. A panhandler stands behind bags of trash. Close up to the piano, the bare hands of the musician confidently finger the keys. Arthur's hands sport white gloves which grip the edge of the yellow <u>EVERYTHING</u> MUST <u>GO!!</u> sign. His shoulders shim to the beat, and he snaps the sign above his head. His hands invisible, the sign whirls as if unaided. Above Arthur is the cinema marquee. It advertises bondage porn: STRIP SEARCH. Three entwined naked white women, none looking at the other, handclasp breasts, and more hands butterfly open legs. "Adult Stars" who are "Sexier than you can imagine." A boy thwaps Fleck's sign from his hands, and laughing in chase across the road, another raises his hand and gives the finger to the oncoming yellow cab. Arthur on the ground clutches his genitals in his hands. (01:31–03:36)

In *Joker*, social crisis and the desire for a solution unfold as a confusion of hands. "Hand" is an old term for someone who works manually. All hands on deck! The "manual" worker derives from Latin, "manus," which you still hear in the Spanish "mano," hand. *Joker*'s manual hands include the piano player's, the actors' in the porn, the clown's on the street. "Hand" has other meanings, too. A hand that grips suggests agency and control: get a grip, we say, he's losing his grip. The police like to know where hands are: "Hands where I can see them!" When the law is given a "free hand," it suggests latitude, maybe too much, perhaps abuse. An "invisible hand" is a term from economics, from Adam Smith.[1] Smith uses this metaphor to explain how under capitalism, if everyone operates from self-interest, not to worry, things will work better for society, as if orchestrated by an invisible hand. Giving the finger is an old gesture going back to ancient Greece to represent the phallus. Raise the middle finger and the knuckles on either side resemble testes. It says: fuck you!

We can read this allegory of the hands in Gotham as the consequence for urban populations confronting increasing contradictions in the neoliberal economy of the late 1970s. Industrial wage labor is being dismantled. Worker solidarity is fragmenting. Urban populations are becoming marginalized. With social fragmentation comes a rise in low-grade nuisance behaviors. The result will be sterner policing and imprisonment strategies: the criminalization of poverty.

Fleck is center sidewalk, working his hands to become a living advertisement. His best trick is the invisible hand where he spins the economic sign, as if by magic or a riot of spontaneity. (This is made possible by a mechanism behind the sign.) The better Fleck does his work—the sooner everything goes—the sooner Fleck loses this job. This is unsurprising: he's a gig worker, which, by definition, means repeatedly working oneself out of a job. But in urban cores from the 1970s onward, flexible wage employment steadily replaces secure industrial work. A new class of urban proletariat in this economic spin won't be rehired: a panhandler lurks behind trash bags, self-medicating through a brown bag. Fleck has to keep his grip. Pranked, he finds no solidarity. His piano playing colleague doesn't budge. In chase, Arthur cries "stop them!" (02:19). But what should a passerby do? Forcibly stop a group of children running from a roaring clown? The kids' behavior escalates from spontaneous horseplay,

---

1   Adam Smith, *The Wealth of Nations*, introduction by Alan B. Krueger (New York: Bantam, [1776] 2003), 572.

to pissing off city traffic with a vulgar, joyful salute. It turns into alley crime proper. They beat and urge each other to rob Arthur. Out of school and work, facing a future of insecure wage labor themselves, these children dramatize street delinquency that accompanies the post-industrial marginalized proletariat. That delinquency constellates into cultural hysteria: not panic about how to help marginalized male populations in a changing economy, but rather about how to neutralize and contain them.

The response that first New York, then the United States proper urges can be seen in the porno hands: *Strip Search*. Set earlier, *Joker* doesn't directly depict over-policing nor the classist and racist patterns of bias of increasingly locking people up. That carceral turn begins in the 1970s but becomes fully visible in the mid-1990s, after another recession, when Mayor Giuliani promotes hard-nosed policing tactics.[2] *Joker* occurs in historical parenthesis: in between. The urban economies are collapsing, and social services are revoked. But we're not yet arrived at the explosion of policing and imprisonment that replace them. In this limbo between welfare and prison, characters in *Joker* make provision for their own security, there is a rise in homelessness, and there swells an erotic penal fantasy of managing a newly insecure urban population.

In this chapter, we examine why the market's invisible hand comes to wear what Loïc Wacquant calls an "iron fist."[3] Why does neoliberalism, which disempowers the state in economics, re-empower the state with vastly expanded police power and prison reach? So far *Send in the Clowns!* has depicted neoliberalism mostly as it imagines itself: as the economic man who whistles praise for a self-regulating market economy, free of government interference. We've argued that the self-regulating market is a historical myth, argued too that by financializing everything

---

2   Neil Smith, "Giuliani Time: The Revanchist 1990s," *Social Text* 57 (1998): 1–20.

3   Loïc Wacquant, *Punishing the Poor: The Neoliberal Government of Social Insecurity* (Durham: Duke University Press, 2009), 6.

and by stripping social services with sadofiscal policies, neoliberalism exacerbates inequality and fosters precarity. What we see now is that neoliberalism's anti-government ideology is haunted by a mocking shape. Everywhere neoliberal man strides, he casts a strange, disfigured shadow. The shadow cast is the carceral state, the policing network and prison complex that trail wherever neoliberal policies tread. Look upmarket, neoliberalism speaks of fewer government restrictions: the editorial writer who praises the free market, the business professor who lectures from the better-appointed university halls, the IMF and World Bank representative who speaks softly at Davos. But downmarket, we find something altogether darker: the "punitive regulation of racialised poverty."[4] In this form, neoliberalism is not an anti-government economic ideology, but a political project that expands the state.

EVERYTHING MUST GO!!

The marquis plays up New York City's sex work and rollcalls the wider cast of characters emblematic of urban grit: *"STREET WALKERS and PIMPS, HUSTLERS and BONDAGE FREAKS"* (01:53). On the literal level, pornography and sex shops are simply part of urban decor, what we know of late-1970s Manhattan or other urban centers. Yet these urban outcasts, and others like them, will pique the indignation of classes above, who will insist they be cleaned from American streets to make way for urban renewal. The title of the movie—*Strip Search*—is an ironic reminder of the police abuses that will help achieve that end.

Strip Search refers literally to policing abuses that scandalized New York. In 1986, the Supreme Court made it illegal to strip search someone arrested with a misdemeanor. But that didn't stop tough-on-crime

---

4   Loïc Wacquant, "Three Steps to a Historical Anthropology of Actually Existing Neoliberalism," *Social Anthropology/Anthropologie Sociale* 20.1 (2012): 67.

Mayor Giuliani in the 1990s. Under his watch, even minor arrests in New York led to this abuse and humiliation. By the late 1990s, strip searching had become so routine that New York was hit with a class-action suit on behalf of tens of thousands of people strip searched between 1996 and 1997.[5] By then, Mayor Giuliani had built a reputation for cleaning up New York. Not, to be sure, by "indict[ing] capitalists for capital flight, landlords for abandoning buildings, or public leaders for a narrow retrenchment to class and race self-interest." No, Giuliani took revenge on the least fortunate, specifically identifying as the enemy "homeless people, panhandlers, prostitutes, squeegee cleaners, squatters, graffiti artists, [and even] 'reckless bicyclists.'"[6] As part of that strategy, Giuliani outsourced regular police booking to New York corrections officers at Central Booking, which meant that everyone arrested in Queens and Manhattan had to fully strip when processed for arrest, as if entering prison. Many had their genitals inspected, their bodies mocked, or were threatened with rape.[7] At least one case of corrections officers sodomizing a man with the stick of a toilet plunger was prosecuted.[8] Let's not think this was a one-off phase, either. In 2010, New York City paid out $33 million to people illegally strip-searched between 1999 and 2007. Though the Supreme Court, in a divided 2012 decision, made strip searching for misdemeanor arrests legal again, in 2019, the city paid out $12.5 million for illegal searches of *visitors* to jails between November 2012 and October 2019.[9]

Porn eroticizes this abuse of police power as titillation. Why? In one form, this compression merely borrows actual tough-on-crime rhetoric.

5   Ron Feemster, "Naked City?" salon.com, June 1, 1999, np.

6   Smith, "Giuliani Time," 3.

7   Feemster, "Naked City?"

8   American Civil Liberties Union (ACLU), "NYPD Officer Pleads Guilty in Torture Case," aclu.org, May 26, 1999, np.

9   Anthony Accurso, "$12.5 Million to Settle Class Action Suit Over Strip Searches of NYC Jail Visitors," *Prison Legal News*, October 2018, 54.

Lorna Goodman, a top staff lawyer for New York City, defended strip searching because, after all, some of the people arrested were sex workers anyway: "To the 90th percentile, the persons who were strip-searched had been in the system before. They had been through it all. If a striptease person is strip-searched, the injury is less than the injury to a 17-year-old parochial school girl who's never been arrested."[10] The marquis in *Joker* sardonically puns the sadism in such official rhetoric which implies that certain adults, depending on their job, do not deserve constitutional protections. In another form, the marquis is another of *Joker's* symbolic compressions. The title *Strip Search* compresses time, between the bankrupt 1970s and the response after the recession of the 1990s. It does so to collapse how neoliberalism first strips social services, then, when a recession hits, solves the ensuing disorder not by restoring services, but by unleashing police brutality and rights violations. Literally, Arthur's "<u>EVERYTHING</u> MUST <u>GO!!</u>" signals the attempt to shake the last profits out of a bankrupt business after a recession. Symbolically, it refers to the physical stripping of clothes. Allegorically, it also signals the literal outcome for lost citizen protections. Everything, including rights and dignity before the law, must go. Arthur clutching his genitals at the end of this scene forecasts the subject trying to protect himself from that outcome.

Fusing pornography and police power is more revealing still. Pornography generally works by removing sex from the context of real relationships, from causes and complexes grounded in reality, so that illicit acts become a spectacle. A strange man knocks on the door and before we know it, she's got him banging her against the kitchen counter. The boyfriend comes home and, no surprise, he is excited by this turn of events, so joins in. The positions and formulations are so patterned and routine that they can be searched by scene and category. Wacquant argues that the drive for law-and-order punishment works analogously

---

10   Quoted in Feemster, "Naked City?"

to pornography: he calls it "penal pornography" for this reason. He has in mind how tough-on-crime culture, first appearing in the United States in the 1980s, then two decades later in Europe, shares much with pornography's spectacle, routine, and evisceration of causality. Penal pornography produces predictable scenes: the bonanza drug seizures, the politician before the camera promising reductions in crime, the complaints about lenient judges, the "sacrosanct 'rights of crime victims.'" It gives us television visuals that later become the stuff of dramatic news segments and popular cop reality shows: *911, Cops, America's Most Wanted, Dog the Bounty Hunter*. Wacquant describes the cast of those targeted: "teenage scofflaws, repeat offenders, aggressive panhandlers, drifting refugees, immigrants waiting to be expelled, street prostitutes, and the assorted social detritus that litter the streets of the dualizing metropolis to the indignation of 'law-abiding' citizens."[11]

We know this kind of TV spectacle from the press conferences in *Batman* movies, where the people of Gotham are promised streets safe from criminals. District Attorney Harvey Dent (Aaron Eckhart) in *The Dark Knight* announces "that everything that can be done over the Joker killings is being done" (1:10:59) and that "one day the Batman will have to answer for the laws he's broken" (1:11:46),[12] and Police Commissioner Gordon stands before the microphones praising Dent (2:22:32). Dent and Gordon stage these scenes as a conscious performance to manipulate the public: Batman, we know, is not the real agent of mayhem. But these films don't question the spectacle itself. *Joker* does, and it responds by calling out the very *form* of penal pornography. Like porn, catching the bad guys titillates us by freeing people and crime from context—from causes—and from real relationships. For Wacquant, the causes of "punitive and pornographic penalty" are clear: "the spread of policies of economic deregulation and

---

11   Wacquant, *Punishing the Poor*, xi, xii.
12   *The Dark Knight*, directed by Christopher Nolan (Warner Bros, 2008).

welfare disciplining."[13] That is, as US factories departed city centers in the late 1960s, first for the suburbs, later for Mexico or Asia, the result gutted urban economies. At the same time, government cut social services and villainized the poor themselves.

In *Joker*, *Strip Search* knows something about the composition of the urban poor who will suffer hyper-incarceration. The film boasts a diverse cast of pimps and hustlers—"in color" (01:53). Gotham streets, similarly, are in color: Arthur in green hair and red nose dances to music played by a Black man before Hispanic youths harass him. But *Strip Search*, the images imply, is borne from a fantasy of whiteness. It is a racialized fantasy. The women getting it on in the image are all blond and white. Let's read this contrast carefully. Police abuses, it suggests, are tolerable, desired even, because they prepare the city for the fantasy of whiteness, whites getting (it) on only with whites. That condensation of sexy image and prison procedure splits those who can get excited by this kind of policing from those who will be its target.

This split, we might say, is economic man and neoliberalism's carceral shadow, which will disproportionately affect urban people of color. The statistics make it startlingly clear. From 1950 to 1970, there were a steady 100 convicts per 100,000 residents in the US; by 2000, there were 478. In 1950, 70 percent of the prison population was white; by 2010, only 30 percent. In 1980, $27 billion was spent on public housing and $6.9 billion on corrections; by 1990, the numbers had reversed. By 2003, 2.3 million people were crammed into prisons, with another 4.7 million under judicial supervision outside. "One Black American citizen in six is doing or has done hard time and one in three is destined to serve a sentence of imprisonment in the future."[14] Neoliberalism splits society into two separate domains. In

---

13   Wacquant, "Three Steps," 75.
14   Wacquant, *Punishing the Poor*, 117, 160, 37.

one, a laissez-faire society indexes freedom and fulfillment to a hands-off government. In the other, a shadow society matches this one, step by step, pace by pace, with strides in "zero tolerance" policing, boot camps for juveniles, mandatory minimum sentences, and three-strike laws. In the ensuing decades down to our own day, boys such as those who beat Arthur will be treated to school policing, juvenile prisons, and eventual incarceration.

The state does not recede as neoliberal theory argues. Rather it manages the poor by castigating and warehousing them, by expanding the corrections system, police forces, probation rolls, and prisons. Those who lose out from the "dissolution of the Fordist-Keynesian compact," those who lose well-paid jobs and social benefits that kick in during recessions, experience the *penalization of poverty*. Cities become polarized. Depending on your class, and your skin color, there are two different Americas. Here is Wacquant:

> The neoliberal Leviathan resembles neither the minimalist state of 19th-century liberalism nor the evanescent state bemoaned by economic and governmentality critics of neoliberalism alike, but a *Centaur-state that displays opposite visages at the two ends of the class structure*: it is uplifting and "liberating" at the top, where it acts to leverage the resources and expand the life options of the holders of economic and cultural capital; but it is castigatory and restrictive at the bottom, when it comes to managing the populations destabilized by the deepening of inequality and the diffusion of work security and ethnic anxiety.[15]

Life is a vanilla threesome for those at the top; but those at the bottom get frisked and strip searched by the cops.

---

15   Wacquant, "Three Steps," 67, 74.

Fucking savages

All of this is, literally, above Arthur's head. But across the movie, Fleck registers this development in two crises of feeling. The first appears in Arthur's fear of homelessness, which like *Strip Search*, symbolically condenses a coming change in American life. Homelessness appears between the loss of the welfare state and the rise of the penal state; between the decline of the protective state, which provisioned for mothers and public housing, and the rise of the carceral state, where resources are directed to policing and imprisonment. Homelessness is a transitional phase for mentally ill patients like Arthur, who are "deinstitutionalised" when hospitals close in the 1970s and who will be "reinstitutionalised" in jails and prisons.[16] In the 1980s, homeless people are neglected and vilified as the visible symptom of societal malaise, often treated to lethal violence. In the 1990s, the state takes over with policing, incarceration, and removal.

The film takes place on this trajectory, shadowing Arthur with homeless men, grounding his character in legitimate fear that people could be treated this way. In *Joker* the homeless are everywhere, visually aligned with the trash on the street. The disheveled man under the marquis has trousers the color of the trash bags beside him (02:03). When Arthur enters the pharmacy before going home to his mother, another homeless man roots in trash bags, his face huddled into them (09:18). All movie long Arthur is troubled by the dead homeless man he saw on the sidewalk, people just walking over him. These visual cues and anxieties are a reminder that Arthur himself is only a few steps from being targeted himself. He gets re-institutionalized at the end of the film for committing murder. But there's a good chance he would have been incarcerated anyway in the coming city-wide push to criminalize

---

16   Wacquant, "Three Steps," 74.

homelessness. "How does someone wind up in here?" he asks the clerk at Arkham Asylum (1:10:41). It is a fair question.

In Giuliani's period, clearing out the homeless meant the creation of police databases to track homeless individuals, police-sweeps of city encampments, and a concerted effort to demonize homeless people as "dangerously mentally ill street people." The homeless were pushed further out into the exurbs, to underpasses, scrublands, and airports. Meanwhile Giuliani also exacerbated homelessness by evicting squatters and canceling city contracts with neighborhood organizations that housed hundreds homeless people, even as landlords mobilized to cancel rent-control policies. The number of homeless people actually increased between 1994 and 1997 by 15 percent. Welfare was slashed, city jobs were axed, and the planned shrinkage of public spending in the 1970s turned into a full-blown expulsion of poor people themselves from the city, easing the way for white gentrification. It was a new revanchist politics rooted in sadism, as Neil Smith argues.[17]

The second crisis of feeling appears when Arthur refuses to villainize the boys who attacked him. Villainizing will justify the emerging carceral state, so Arthur's uneasiness is an ethical moment. When Arthur returns to work, his co-worker Randall is quick to place blame. "I heard about the beatdown you took. Fucking savages" (16:00). Arthur demurs at this chance to criminalize the Hispanic youth: "It was just a bunch of kids. I should have left it alone" (16:06). The song playing in the background agrees: "before you do anything rash, dig this: everybody plays the fool, sometime." But Randall tunes out and doesn't accept Arthur's answer. "No. They'll take everything from you if you do that. All the crazy shit out there. They're animals" (16:10). Lawyer Goodman says we shouldn't feel bad for strippers who are forced to strip before corrections officers. Randall disregards lives in a different register. He implies that street

---

17   Smith, "Giuliani Time," 5, 7, 8.

hoodlums are subhuman, animal, and outside of civilization: savage. The threat of violence is the only thing they'll understand.

Such language is integral to strategies of domination, even in a liberal tradition. As mentioned in Chapter One, John Stuart Mill, the nineteenth-century champion of liberal democracy and early advocate of women's suffrage, argues in *On Liberty* that "despotism is a legitimate mode of government in dealing with barbarians." "Provided," he adds, "the end be their improvement, and the means justified by actually effecting that end."[18] That addition is the secret logic of the carceral state: that the poor, and especially poor people of color, must be disciplined *for their own good*. Racism adopts a similar strategy. First, characterize a group as outside of civilization. Then, there's no need to uphold the usual civilized values when dealing with them. Randall hands Arthur a gun. Given the astonishing rates at which Americans are stripped of their right to vote when charged with a crime, it really does become democracy at one end of the class spectrum and growing despotism at the other. In 2020, over five million Americans were disenfranchised, at a rate 3.7 times greater for African Americans.[19] In some states—Alabama, Florida, Tennessee, Kentucky, Wyoming—fully one in seven African Americans is stripped of the right to vote, this fifty years after the civil rights movement fought to gain it. The carceral complex is the institution that preserves much of the racial bias once enforced by Jim Crow segregation.[20]

---

18   John Stuart Mill, *On Liberty*, in *On Liberty, Utilitarianism and Other Essays*, second edition, edited with an introduction and notes by Mark Philp and Frederick Rosen (Oxford: Oxford University Press, [1849] 2015), 13.

19   Christopher Uggen et al., "Locked Out 2020: Estimates of People Denied Voting Rights Due to a Felony Conviction," sentencingproject.org, updated October 30, 2020, 4.

20   Loïc Wacquant, "Race as Civic Felony," *International Social Science Journal* 57.183 (2005): 127–142.

Randall's language, then, participates in something more modern: the formation of new "social types" that arise in neoliberalism's carceral shadow. Drug use itself becomes a clear basis on which to form selective moral categories. There is no "cocaine head" in modern parlance, because crack, which is just cocaine cut with other ingredients, is a drug mostly used by poorer people. This biased moral classification also manifests in the law, which, in the 1980s, targeted crack use with flagrantly disproportionate and punishing prison sentences. The most infamous social type might be the "superpredators," a term coined in the 1990s for repeat offenders. In the UK, we find "feral youth" and "yobs." In France, "sauvageons": the same epithet, *savages*, that Randall uses.[21] The Great Replacement Theory spouted by the likes of Tucker Carlson—the theory that white populations in Western societies are being replaced systematically by non-white peoples—lurks in these categories, too. All of them are made possible by modern law and media, which imagine crime as contagious, even as the legal system, incarceration complexes, and media categories themselves produce the contagion. In the 1980s, for example, California introduced one thousand new laws expanding the use of prison sentences, sending the state on a massive building spree to lock up these newly discovered "repeat offenders," and expanding the budget outlays to prison.[22]

But Arthur resists Randall's logic. Even though he accepts the gun, the scene treats Randall's anger on Arthur's behalf and kindness toward him as at best a misguided paternalism—his honest Hobbesian interpretation of the streets without a social contract—and, at worst, a form of abuse. Joaquin Phoenix pitches Arthur's voice high and responds like a timid child, an image reinforced because Arthur's having trouble lacing up his shoes. Randall's imposing figure leaves little room visually. When

---

21   Wacquant, *Punishing the Poor*, 31.
22   Wacquant, *Punishing the Poor*, 291.

he hands Arthur the gun, he may be looking out for him, but his language is from the script of an adult trying to mislead a child by coaxing them with a gift:

RANDALL

Here.

ARTHUR

What is it?

RANDALL

Take it. It's for you.

(16:31)

Arthur laughs nervously, and talks in a stage whisper, just like a kid not wanting to get another kid in trouble: "I'm not supposed to have a gun!" "Don't sweat it, Art," says Randall, "no one has to know. And you can pay me back some other time. You know you're my boy" (16:56). That last phrase, "my boy," uses US slang for equals, a loyal friend. But in this scene, it also captures a power dynamic that mixes the transactional ("pay me back") with parental authority ("my boy") and introduces an unseemly, exploitative element.

Randall's point here is that the new street subproletariat needs to be met with new forms of hyper-masculinity. To be a man means to provide for your own security, which trumps worrying whether someone mentally unfit should be given a gun. That aggressive masculinity also means disparaging others, such as Gary—mocking downward, not up. Arthur laughs uproariously at Randall's joke about miniature golf, which derides Gary's diminutive stature. Gary shoots a look of disappointment in Arthur's laugh, indicating that Arthur doesn't normally participate in such bullying humor. So, when Arthur laughs wildly, we know it's less an authentic response to Randall's joke than a sign that Arthur feels coerced by Randall's macho worldview, a suspicion confirmed when Arthur eerily switches off the laugh immediately upon leaving the room (17:22). We can see here that this mode of masculinity causes Arthur's psyche to fissure. Such masculinity insists we interpret "a bunch of kids" "playing the fool" as "animals" or "fucking savages" that we can legitimately shoot, like so many seventeen-year-old Trayvon Martins. Stand Your Ground Laws aside, those state will overtake Randall's vigilante masculinity by herding, in the hundreds of thousands, the newly created sub-proletariat of urban males into a vastly expanded and expensive carceral system.

Have they all committed crimes?

Now we see more clearly why Wacquant argues that, under neoliberalism, the invisible hand of the market actually strikes with an iron fist. For all its anti-government pretense, neoliberalism actually expands the state in strategic ways. Punition might seem like a contradiction within neoliberal ideology; it is in fact a core principle since it stabilizes the legitimacy of neoliberal rule:

> The penal state . . . restores the authority of the governing elite by reaffirming "law and order" just when this authority is being undermined by the accelerating flows of money, capital, signs and people across national borders, and by the constricting of state action by supranational bodies and financial capital.[23]

Wacquant argues that policing distinguishes "the neoliberal Leviathan" from the "minimalist state of 19th-century liberalism." This much is certainly true: incarceration rates explode wherever the United States exports neoliberal economic policies. Wacquant admits that even the most marginal citizens "circulating in the lower regions of social and urban space enjoy an extensive array of well-established social, economic, and civil

---

23   Wacquant, "Three Steps," 76.

rights, and the minimal organizational means to see those respected to some degree. This is true even of nonresident foreigners."[24] But he also knows that the US Congress passes laws that link prison sentences for drug offenses to revoking educational funding, housing assistance, government jobs, and voting rights. Criminals who are well-off face no equivalent sanctions; they do not lose their mortgage interest deductions, those state housing benefits for the middle class and wealthy that already far outweigh those offered to the poor.[25]

Nevertheless, this contradiction—that the self-regulating market paradoxically requires more government intervention—appears early in liberalism as well, and indeed is acknowledged by Adam Smith himself. As noted above, Smith coined the phrase "invisible hand" to explain how man's self-interest benefits society inadvertently: "By pursuing his own interest he frequently promotes that of the society more effectively than when he really intends to promote it."[26] Today the phrase is taken as a religious commandment, as if Smith were not only deifying a self-regulating market economy but also arguing that economic self-interest provides principles of governance superior to politics in fashioning the most beneficial society for everyone. Smith, a humanist, meant nothing of the kind: his view of wealth in *Wealth of Nations* was deeply embedded in a political framework of the nation as a whole, embedded in views of security and safety, and within an understanding of how state policy can favor the countryside, industry, or agriculture. There is nothing in Smith's thinking that suggests economics can sub in for a moral law or political obligation.[27]

---

24 Wacquant, *Punishing the Poor,* 27.
25 Wacquant, "Race as Civic Felony," 132.
26 Smith, *Wealth of Nations,* 572.
27 Karl Polanyi, *The Great Transformation: The Political and Economic Origins of Our Time* (Boston: Beacon Press, [1944] 2001), 116, 117.

Instead, and ironically, when Smith articulates this idea of the "invisible hand," he is addressing a central anxiety people share about capitalism: that traders and manufacturers might not keep the nations' interests at heart, might prefer, for instance, foreign to domestic industry. Smith says business will always prefer domestic industry because doing so is safer; owners can see their goods and workers. Under capitalism you don't need to worry so much about capital (and jobs) moving overseas, so there's no need to regulate it. Here's the passage in full:

> By preferring the support of domestic to that of foreign industry, he intends only his own security; and by directing that industry in such a manner as its produce maybe of the greatest value, he intends only his own gain; and he is in this, as in many other cases, led by an invisible hand to promote an end which was no part of his intention. Nor is it always worse for the society that it was no part of it. By pursuing his own interest he frequently promotes that of the society more effectually than when he really intends to promote it. I have never known much good done by those who affected to trade for the public good.[28]

We all know, of course, that manufacturers do, in fact, move jobs and industry overseas, that they off-shore headquarters to avoid national taxes, that they seek lower standards for labor rights, wage rates, and environmental protections—all to maximize profits. Some domestic workers do indeed lose out. After all, this is precisely the situation for urban centers such as depressed Gotham. History has demonstrated incontrovertibly that the very reassurance Smith offers when coining his invisible hand has proved unreliable and false.

What's more, elsewhere in his work, Smith is no fool about what the invisibility of self-interest actually means. By "invisibility," Smith

---

28 Smith, *Wealth of Nations*, 572.

means—as noted—that our individual actions can have beneficial consequences for the whole structure of society even when that is unintended.
Smith also knows, however, that in ordinary conditions ("the natural state
of things"), when a dispute arises between employees and employers, the
"masters" have an enormous power advantage. The owners, "being fewer
in number, can combine more easily; and the law, besides, authorises, or
at least does not prohibit their combinations, while it prohibits those of
workmen." Though a free market should have no problem with unions,
workers are, in fact, forbidden from unionizing. Not so for bosses, who

> are always and everywhere in a sort of tacit, but constant and
> uniform combination, not to raise the wages above their actual
> rate . . . We seldom, indeed, hear of this combination, because it
> is the usual, and one may say, the natural state of things, which
> nobody ever hears of.[29]

For Smith, workers' wages "must at least be sufficient to maintain him.
They must even upon most occasions be somewhat more; otherwise it
would be impossible for him to bring up a family, and the race of such
workmen could not last beyond the first generation." But masters sometimes try in secrecy to reduce wages "even below this rate." Workers
become desperate, and "must either starve, or frighten their masters into
an immediate compliance" with their requests for higher wages. But,
Smith notes, the law has been enacted "with so much severity" against
workers unionizing, that the workers gain no advantage but the "punishment or ruin of the ring-leaders."[30]

What Smith saw as inhumane and foolhardy, reducing wages to starvation level, becomes in the nineteenth century the theoretical under-
pinning of how to motivate workers without using government policy,

---

29   Smith, *Wealth of Nations*, 94–95.
30   Smith, *Wealth of Nations*, 95–96.

laws, or policing, as we saw in Chapter One. Wacquant argues that, under twentieth-century neoliberalism, the predominant mode of disciplining workers shifts from starvation threats to prison terms. In reality, though, liberalism was never able to fulfill an anti-government ideology. Deregulation and the preservation of self-regulating economy has *always* required state involvement and punitive violence.

Further reading

Angela Y. Davis, *Are Prisons Obsolete?* (New York: Seven Stories Press, 2003).

Michelle Alexander, *The New Jim Crow: Mass Incarceration in the Age of Colorblindness*, tenth anniversary edition (New York: The New Press, [2010] 2020).

Danielle Sered, *Until We Reckon: Violence, Mass Incarceration, and a Road to Repair* (New York: The New Press, 2019).

Ruth W. Gilmore, *Abolition Geography: Essays Towards Liberation* (London: Verso, 2022).

Chapter Five

Nothing but Clowns

On Media Melodrama

"Happy look, Thomas Wayne's on TV!" Arthur shakes out the last two pills from the emptied medicine bottles. Wayne is on the Good Morning Show. *Wayne has been invited to "make sense of the brutal triple murder" because, with the swelling anti-rich sentiment, Gotham's "less fortunate residents are taking the side of the killer." It was Arthur who killed the three stockbrokers on the train, and he watches in astonishment as the effect hits the media. Wayne dampens praise for the killer by dividing the city. On one side, there are "those of us who have made something of our lives." These include the dead brokers, who worked for Wayne Investments. They are "good, decent, educated." Though Wayne doesn't "know them personally, like all Wayne employees past and present, they're family." Penny, former Wayne house staff, feels vindicated: "Did you hear that. I told you we're family!" And on the other side are the clowns. The first is the killer. He wore a clown mask, Wayne argues, because he was hiding, a "coward" who was "envious of those more fortunate." Wayne then broadens "clown" into an entire class of jokers who don't make it in a modern economy: "And until those kind of people change for the better, those of us who have made something of our lives, will always look at those who haven't, as nothing but clowns." Disdain for these people and wariness of anti-rich sentiment motivate Wayne's calling to politics: "It's one of the reasons why I'm considering a run for mayor. Gotham's lost its way" (38:15–39:38).*

Two scripts are flipped in these scenes. The first, the scene of the brokers being shot, is flipped by Wayne. Fleck didn't wear a clown mask when he killed the three men. He was wearing his work clothes, which included his clown makeup and clown wig. And Fleck didn't kill out of class envy. He killed the first two men in explosive self-defense after being harassed and viciously beaten. The third man Fleck murders after stalking him down, partly, it appears, for the pleasure of revenge, and partly, one assumes, out of raw self-interest: because he witnessed the other two being shot. The killings were not those of a freeloading coward intending to spark a political movement with criminal violence, as Wayne alleges. The killings were spontaneous acts of an unstable clown on the subway defending himself, then exacting revenge.

Wayne mobilizes sympathy for the brokers for political reasons. Their deaths provide him a media spectacle to remind voters that political interference in the economy is not heroism but criminality. He challenges middle-class voters to take sides: choose a meritocratic system, where the heroes are "good, decent, educated" and, conspicuously, white men. Or side with the clowns who have made nothing of themselves, and whose desire to meddle in the economy—from striking to protesting—leads them naturally to resentful murder. Wayne doesn't like people being political. But the godfather of finance is compelled, reluctantly and out of duty, to put aside the business of running Wayne Enterprises, and to run for office to rein in Gotham: a city becoming political. He goes on TV because he realizes that a politician must steer the media's stories of heroes and villains, not to get people to vote, but to get them to vote for leaving the financial economy untouched.

The other person flipping the script in these scenes is the director, Todd Phillips. Arthur's subway shootings turn on its head a famous incident from New York. In December 1984, a white guy named Bernhard

Goetz shot four unarmed Black men on the subway.[1] Unlike in Arthur's case, Goetz was not assaulted, only feared he would be, and though one of the four he shot ended up paralyzed, all of them lived. Goetz was initially treated by tabloids as a vigilante hero. Many people were fed up with crimes of precarity. Like Arthur, Goetz had been attacked once before, and gotten himself a gun. But as more information came out in subsequent months, people slowly turned against Goetz. He had a record, according to neighbors, of racist outbursts at community meetings: "The only way we are going to clean up this street is to get rid of the spics and niggers."[2] When interrogated, Goetz struggled to explain how he knew the men intended to assault him. One of the men asked "how are you?" and another, Goetz said, demanded five dollars. "It wasn't a joke," Goetz told the police. "These guys say they were joking and laughing . . . His eyes were shiny . . . and then he had a big smile on his face."[3] Afterward, Goetz told a neighbor, sounding much like Randall, "those guys I'm almost sure are vicious savage people. What I did, I responded in a vicious savage way."[4] "My intention was to murder them, to hurt them, to make them suffer as much as possible."[5] Though Goetz served some months for possessing an illegal gun, he evaded criminal conviction for the shootings, using self-defense laws that permit deadly force if one *reasonably* believes doing so would avoid grievous bodily harm or death. The case is canonical in criminal law because objectively the men

---

1   Thank you to University of Alabama student Jackson Alsup for pointing us to the Goetz case.

2   Quoted in Myra Friedman, "My Neighbor Bernie Goetz," *New York Magazine*, February 18, 1985, 38.

3   Kirk Johnson, "Goetz Account of Shooting 4 Given on Tape," *New York Times*, April 30, 1987, Section B, 1.

4   Friedman, "My Neighbor," 38.

5   "You Have to Think in a Cold-Blooded Way," *New York Times*, April 30, 1987, Section B, 6.

were unarmed, but the court also allows for a subjective view of what is "reasonable." (In lower courts, the Goetz defense successfully argued that subjective view was all that was needed, but the appellate court preserved the requirement for objective views too—what would an average person think reasonable). But as one line of legal criticism of this case runs: what if "the reasonable person *is* a . . . racist?"[6] What if feelings are deemed objectively reasonable because a racist culture and a melodramatic media have long demonized minorities, Black men in particular?

In a stunning counterfactual, *Joker* posits what if, rather than the intentions of Black men, people in Gotham were paranoid about the intentions of white men in finance capital? Do those guys not cause harm to particular communities in the city? Would it be reasonable to feel scared of *them* and their entitlement? Would advocates for vigilante justice feel the same way if the men shot and killed were "good, decent, educated" white men? Wayne's media blitz and political campaign, and the support of the tabloids, gives the answer: even were the script to be reversed, the blame would still be melodramatically channeled through the same class and racial patterns. When white brokers are shot, even though Arthur was *objectively* assaulted and had no need to rely on Goetz's *subjective* reasonableness, the lesson to be drawn is that Gotham's "less fortunate residents" are resentful, and therefore criminal. When Black men are shot by a white man, the response is also that such less fortunate residents are resentful, and therefore criminal. *Joker* flips the script, to show how the media story stays the same. For the likes of Wayne, what matters is that capital be put beyond suspicion. Capital is always innocent, never intentionally harmful, sexist, or racist. The real villainy is found among the clowns who seek to regulate it. With the clowns lies intentionality and criminality. Naturally, such melodramas say little that is truthful

---

6   Stephen P. Garvey, "Racism, Unreasonable Belief, and Bernhard Goetz," *Cornell Law Faculty Working Papers* (2007), 34. Emphasis in original.

about Arthur or the brokers. But in this chapter, we show that media melodrama can be more important than the truth.

Gotham has lost its way

Wayne's political strategy emerges from the paradox that neoliberalism needs citizens to give up political power over an economy, even as people like Wayne still must garner votes and win elections. How can citizens be encouraged to sit out voting? Or how can they be encouraged to vote for their own depoliticization? We answer these questions by showing how *Joker* implicates the media. *Joker* critiques the media in two ways. The first chimes with observations by Neil Postman: TV appears as a medium that transforms news analysis into entertainment, which leads to civic passivity.[7] Second, to become entertainment, news increasingly adopts a melodramatic approach to narrative, relying on emotion and outrage as the index of truth and fashioning tidy moral oppositions, good guys and bad guys. This simplification harmonizes with the neoliberal political aim of demonizing or criminalizing democratic power that seeks to regulate the economy. Set in the 1980s, *Joker* grounds this in TV and newspapers, but even as our own media now threads through X, Facebook, and Instagram, the dynamic persists.

Media isn't the only agent of depoliticization. In *Send in the Clowns!* we have already identified other ways neoliberalism prevents people from becoming too political. Chapter One reminded us that poverty keeps people trained on work, not politics. This nineteenth-century method of motivating industry through precarity persists today, even in a country as wealthy as the US. Chapter Two showed that flexible labor depoliticizes workers. Gig workers, by definition, are excluded from decision-making connected to an organization's planning and vision. Their jobs are bound

---

7   Neil Postman, *Amusing Ourselves to Death: Public Discourse in the Age of Show Business* (Harmondsworth: Penguin, 1985).

narrowly by task and time. The gig worker has no prospect of sharing in governance or profits. This suits the "rapidly changing demands of a high-tech economy," but it demands compliant workers, willing to labor without security, promotion, or stable benefits. It also demands what Sheldon Wolin calls "pliable" citizens: people willing to live in a society that withholds such protections.[8]

Chapter Three showed how welfare insecurity depoliticizes. By itself, welfare can provide autonomy and dignity for individuals as well as stability for political regimes. But welfare provision can also be manipulated to prevent political engagement.[9] Introducing erratic tests for disability, as we have seen, or complicating procedures for requesting benefits clot these systems with the people who flow through them. A "time tax," Anne Lowery calls this maddening bureaucracy.[10] But the ill effects go deeper. When people cannot rely on a social safety net, they can become wholly preoccupied with present needs. In these circumstances, their ability to plan the future—their economic rationality—is hobbled and their political horizon narrows. Having the capacity and confidence to influence our future is at the core of politicalness.[11]

Neoliberalism's iron fist—the growing security state discussed in Chapter Four—also depoliticizes. In most US states, incarcerated felons lose voting rights and, in many states, fail to regain them even after serving time.[12] Recent efforts by Republicans to suppress popular

---

8   Sheldon S. Wolin, "Democracy and the Welfare State," in *The Presence of the Past: Essays on the State and the Constitution* (Baltimore: Johns Hopkins University Press, 1989), 158, 160.

9   Sheldon S. Wolin, "What Revolutionary Action Means Today," in *Fugitive Democracy and Other Essays*, edited by Nicholas Xenos (Princeton: Princeton University Press, 2016), 373–374.

10   Annie Lowery, "The Time Tax," theatlantic.com, July 27, 2021, np.

11   Wolin, "Revolutionary Action," 374.

12   National Conference of State Legislature, "Brief: Felon Voting Rights," ncsl.org (June 6, 2024), np.

participation in voting, disproportionately affecting minority groups, should be understood as part of this same strategy.[13] As should the unwillingness of Democrats to muster the votes to counter these anti-democratic machinations.

Even when we can vote, that civic ritual hardly guarantees the meaningful participation in political power that election fanfare suggests. Gerrymandering is rife in US politics, diminishing choice. And candidates legally take vast contributions, open and hidden, from lobbyists who steer their agendas and frequently write their bills. There's a revolving door between K Street, where lobbyists congregate, and Congress. More, the very structure of the US political system, where power is allocated across federal, state, local, and municipal levels, often means that what you vote for at the federal level, even when passed in a bill, doesn't show up when funds are allocated at the state, local, and municipal levels.[14] In Alabama, to give one example, federal COVID funds slated for health mitigation and economic protections for the vulnerable were used instead to fund the construction of more prisons. These gaps between voter expectations and actual outcomes needn't be understood as the result of a vast conspiracy. Instead, they reflect the self-interest of different groups and levels of power: a structural dimension of the US political system. But they feed age-old mistrust of so-called Washington elites, and as a result, people become cynical about the political process. All of these effects combine to depoliticize a population, even when the population tries to engage the system politically.

The present chapter shows how the media, too, is a powerful depoliticizing agent. In *Joker*, Wayne's appearance on TV reveals a paradox central to neoliberal governance: "anti-government" politicians must run for

---

13   See the Brennan Center for Justice, brennancenter.org, which tracks legislation that makes it more difficult for Americans to vote.

14   Loïc Wacquant, *Punishing the Poor: The Neoliberal Government of Social Insecurity* (Durham: Duke University Press, 2009), 45.

government. Wayne may want to discourage political interference in business, and he may wish to discourage civic involvement through protest, but he still needs some of the clowns to vote for him. The United States is not Chile, after all. When Chile tried to establish a neoliberal utopia, General Augusto Pinochet saw fit to eviscerate worker protections, privatize national banks, and open the country to floods of cheap imports. He was taking the economic advice of Milton Friedman, of the Chicago School of Economics, whose ideas we discussed in Chapter Three. Friedman did not counsel politically. He stuck to economic recommendations. But Pinochet could only gut hard-won economic protections for the working and middle classes through massive political shock: a military coup, followed by torture and police repression.[15] Such brutally efficient means are not available to those seeking neoliberal revolution in the US. We say this even though the dismantling of American democratic institutions is well underway. Fully 147 members of Congress, the so-called Sedition Caucus, voted against authorizing the legitimate 2020 election of President Joe Biden. They did so even after supporters of Biden's predecessor, President Donald Trump, staged a violent attack on their own institution and its authority. Moreover, the flow of corporate money to these politicians, initially withheld in outrage, has resumed.[16] This illiberal turn is the subject of later chapters. But such developments owe also to long-standing features of the US media.

Who do you talk to?

In *Joker*, when the Flecks are at home, they spend most of their lives watching television. TV is Penny's window onto the world. TV is where

---

15   Naomi Klein, *The Shock Doctrine: The Rise of Disaster Capitalism* (London: Picador, 2007), 70–80.

16   Andy Kroll, "Big Law Firms Promised to Punish Republicans Who Voted to Overthrow Democracy. Now They're Donating to Their Campaigns," rollingstone.com, December 9, 2021, np.

they get their news and their entertainment. *Joker* joins the familiar critique of TV as producing pliable citizens. TV has long been called the idiot box for this reason. It's not just for what's on it. TV is ridiculed because we sit passively before it. Few of us consider ourselves couch potatoes; but most of us know what it means to decompress in front of the tube. It's why TV is regarded as the world's best babysitter. But it's also why we worry when our first child watches too much. TV is a form of "speech without response," says Jean Baudrillard. It "fabricates non-communication," he adds. ("Thank God!" says the exhausted parent of the second and third child.) You don't need to think of television as a "state periscope" prying into our lives to distrust it, says Baudrillard. What matters is the "certainty that people are no longer speaking to each other." TV diminishes communication by its very form. This silencing is how it performs its function of "habitual social control."[17] When the Murray Franklin show begins, in *Joker*, TV is shown to have this power of silencing.

But for *Joker*, it's what happens before the Flecks fall quiet that also tells us how the media works. The movie script tells us TV is "*their nightly ritual.*"[18] We know it's a ritual because Arthur shakes medicine from bottles to put beside the foil TV dinner that he carries to his mother where she sits up in bed. He cuts her meat into smaller pieces, as if she were a child or in his medical care. Similarly, the local news is segmented into digestible bits. The last feature spins the story of "the city . . . under siege by scores of rats; and not just any rats but super rats . . . Sounds like the city needs to find the Pied Piper" (10:55–11:28). For Penny, the solution lies with Thomas Wayne:

---

17   Jean Baudrillard, *For a Critique of the Political Economy of the Sign* (London: Verso, 2019), 181, 182.

18   Todd Phillips and Scott Silver, *Joker: The Official Script Book* (New York: Insight, 2022), 32.

SEND IN THE CLOWNS!

PENNY

He must not be getting my letters.

ARTHUR

It's Thomas Wayne, Mom. He's a busy man.

PENNY

Please. I worked for that family for years. The least he could do is write back.

ARTHUR

Here. Don't get all worked up. Eat. You need to eat.

PENNY

You need to eat. Look how skinny you are.

TV ANCHOR

Both victims were taken to Gotham General. Sounds like the city needs to find the Pied Piper.

PENNY

He'll make a great mayor. Everybody says so.

ARTHUR

(playfully)

Oh, yeah. Everybody who? Who do you talk to?

PENNY

Well, everybody on the news. He's the only one who could save the city. He owes it to us.

(Live! With Murray Franklin begins. She pats the bed.)

Come sit. It's starting.

ARTHUR

Yay, Murray.

(11:00–11:48)

Penny's worldview is mediated in deluded "conversation" with the media. Even Arthur sees it. Foil dinners, pills, and TV news: all three are linked as kinds of consumption. In our role as consumers, says Baudrillard, we are banished from the political sphere.[19] *Joker* points out, however, that TV makes sure this banishment does not *feel* like banishment.

Media can do this by fostering what we call an *intimacy delusion*: the illusion that our feelings are a guide to objective reality, a source of political insight, and a mode of participation in public life. The most obvious intimacy delusion in *Joker* is Penny's misreading of her relationship with Wayne: she takes seriously his lie that Wayne Enterprises treats employees like kin. She accepts Wayne's assurance that corporate culture is family. She'd rather implicitly blame the postal service—"He must not be getting my letters"—than revise her judgment of Wayne's decency (11:01). *Joker*, of course, calls bullshit. Even as Wayne claims family ties, he admits he never met the dead men who worked for him. More, Penny did work for him, yet Wayne ignores her. Penny holds to the myth of the caring patriarch for personal reasons: in her account, when she worked for Wayne's household, she and Wayne were in love, and Arthur is their son. Arthur shows us proof: a signed photograph that says, "Love your smile, TW" (1:25:37). But Wayne neither cares for Penny as literal family, the ostensible mother of his child, nor as symbolic family, his employee of old.

Penny misjudges her intimate understanding of Wayne; this is his political strategy, a strategy the media enables. Gotham *Nightly News*, case in point, does not diagnose the city's economic problems by presenting an objective analysis of the cause of labor unrest. Instead, it offers a

---

19 Baudrillard, *For a Critique*, 180.

sensational narrative that elicits an emotional response to the symptom: *rats*. Rats are attacking people. That's horrific! It's scary! This outrageous narrative spurs a political conversation for the Flecks. But it prepares Penny to accept the TV's political cure: a Pied Piper. "He'll make a great mayor. Everybody says so."

Arthur is not taken in by Penny's intimacy delusion when it comes to politics: "It's Thomas Wayne, Mom. He's a busy man." But as the Murray Franklin show begins, Arthur takes off his shoes and gets into bed with his mother, a visual indication that TV induces a regression for him too. Murray's show takes the cue from late night news and pushes politics further away from objective analysis into late-night comedy: "what we need for superrats are supercats!" he quips. Within seconds, Arthur is off in his own intimacy delusion: that Murray admires him personally, that he recognizes that living at home is not arrested development, but filial responsibility, helping his ailing mother. Absorbed in TV, his actual mother forgotten beside him, all political conversation ends, replaced with gratifying personal validation. In this compressed way, *Joker* suggests that TV replaces news analysis with entertainment, geared toward validating and pacifying emotional responses to news events.

Superrats and Supercats

When American conservatives turn to TV to launch their counterrevolution in the 1970s, they do so because they recognize this emotional connection that TV fosters. They also recognize that the melodramatic narratives of entertainment culture can advance a neoliberal worldview. "Television is dramatic," says Milton Friedman. "It appeals to the emotions. It captures your attention."[20] The media revolution aimed to

---

20   Milton and Rose Friedman, *Free to Choose: A Personal Statement* (New York: Harcourt Brace Jovanovich, 1980), xi.

build "an ideological infrastructure that would help [conservatives] dominate political debate for decades."[21] A fine example of the kind of people who made it happen is Roger Ailes. From the 1960s, Ailes spent years persuading conservatives of the importance of television. When he met Richard Nixon on the latter's second presidential campaign, in 1968, Ailes famously told him: "Television is not a gimmick. And if you think it is, you will lose again." Impressed, Nixon hired him as his campaign media advisor.[22] After that, Ailes was involved in many of the defining campaigns that shaped the neoliberal age. He was closely affiliated with the Heritage Foundation, funded by Joseph Coors and Richard Mellon Scaife. The Scaife Foundation spent $650,000 making a TV series of Milton Friedman's *Free to Choose*.[23] Ailes was also Rudy Giuliani's media consultant when he first ran for New York City Mayor in 1993.[24] He finally ended up moving to *Fox News* where he gained unprecedented power due to his spectacular success in raising the network's profile, gradually eclipsing CNN.

Ailes understood the power of television and was ruthless in deploying it. His formula for electoral victory was simple: "Candidate + Money + Media = Votes." Lee Atwater, who drafted Ailes into George H. W. Bush's 1988 presidential campaign, noted that he had two speeds: "Attack and destroy."[25] Ailes also knew how to unsettle people: how to exploit racial and ethnic tensions, how to convince people that there were superrats

---

21 David Brock, Ari Rabin-Havt, and Media Matters for America, *The Fox Effect: How Roger Ailes Turned a Network into a Propaganda Machine* (Milwaukee: Anchor Books, 2012), 26.

22 Brock et al., *Fox Effect*, 21–22.

23 Mark Blyth, *Great Transformations: Economic Ideas and Institutional Change in the Twentieth Century* (Cambridge: Cambridge University Press, 2002), 159.

24 Brock et al., *Fox Effect*, 34.

25 Brock et al., *Fox Effect*, 32.

threatening America. And he would champion political Pied Pipers who promised to put things back in order, always with the support of supercats.

When Wayne describes the subway murders on TV, he follows Ailes's script. Wayne fashions a neoliberal melodrama. In melodramas, as noted above, individuals represent moralized versions of wider societal struggles in stark binarisms: good and bad, them and us. Standard superhero films work as melodramas. A man, constrained by unbearable forces, finds himself pushed into anti-social behavior or heroic revolt, even if that means, as so often it does, that he sacrifices himself. Think of *Armageddon*, *District 9*, *Star Wars*. In movies where the hero does not die, as with *Batman*, life is reduced to an ascetic devotion to higher values: justice, truth, fighting evil. Ideological conflicts are simplified, and characters become myths. *Joker* makes us aware that melodrama is not just a type of movie, but a political strategy that borrows a narrative and emotional structure familiar from the news and the movies. When Wayne characterizes the street protestors as a bunch of clowns headed by a murdering criminal, he writes a melodrama in which he stars as the reluctant hero, come to rescue Gotham. Admittedly, melodrama is low fruit for the picking: the killer was dressed as a clown after all, a familiar bogeyman. But Wayne exploits the clown trope to indict the losers in Gotham's economy. Clowns are those who haven't "made something of [their] lives," he says, recasting structural inequality as individual failure. Wayne sharpens the difference between those who accept the neoliberal cult of personal responsibility and those who fail, grouse, or revolt against it.

Wayne's melodrama has been prepared by the TV news's focus on the symptoms—rats—rather than the causes—the political struggle over the economy. Wayne mirrors this approach himself: he takes a symptom (a spectacular subway crime), abstracts away the cause, and redeploys the spectacle to ignite his political rise and criminalize those who would regulate the economy. Ailes adopted similar strategies when media advisor to political campaigns. The classic case is the story of Willie Horton, habitually cited as a turning point in the 1988 Bush campaign.[26] Horton was a Black convict who committed multiple crimes while on temporary release from prison, including armed robbery and rape. Ailes, Bush's media advisor, gleefully harnessed the spectacle to the Bush campaign: "The only question is whether we depict Willie Horton with a knife in his hand or without it." Ailes was not directly responsible for the infamous ad that stoked fears of Black violence.[27] Ailes's former employee, Floyd Brown, produced it, giving the campaign needed distance. But Ailes strategized behind the scenes and his fingerprints were all over the ad. The Bush campaign expertly exploited fears of Black violence with the melodrama of Horton, then recontextualized the fear to link Democrats to prison releases. The power of TV did the rest.

As Ailes transformed *Fox* into the formidable propaganda machine that it remains today, the strategy was the same: create a group of criminal superrats so that it always seems "like your values are under attack."[28] Wayne shows the division: the hardworking, law abiding citizen versus the layabout and criminal. President Bill Clinton adopted the same tactics, announcing crackdowns on Hispanic gangs. He even announced his own superrats, so-called superpredators, repeat offending criminals, as discussed in Chapter Four. President Donald Trump cashed in on this legacy like no other, opening his 2016 presidential campaign by declaring, "Mexicans: they are rapists."[29] Trump exaggerates the script, but

---

26   Brock et al., *Fox Effect*, 182–196.

27   Brock et al., *Fox Effect*, 33. On Willie Horton, see David C. Anderson, *Crime and the Politics of Hysteria: How the Willie Horton Story Changed American Justice* (New York: Random House, 1995).

28   Brock et al., *Fox Effect*, 157.

29   Jake Miller, "Donald Trump Defends Calling Mexican Immigrants 'Rapists,'" cbsnews.com, July 2, 2015, np.

he didn't write it; fostering class and race anxiety has been central to the neoconservative media project from the beginning. As in the Goetz case, even the objectively reasonable subject of self-defense law is further habituated as a racist. And structural harms, from urban violence to the violence of precarity, are melodramatically isolated into individual criminality, so that unregulated capitalism is let off the hook.

In Gotham, we see the same trends. Gotham newspapers coin *Kill the Rich* as a headline, reducing the class-based power struggle roiling the city to a movement of murderers. When Gotham TV networks report the protest, they narrow in on one clown in makeup, clearly a Black man, and ask him "what's the point of all this?":

> CLOWN PROTESTER (ON TV)
> Fuck the rich. Fuck Thomas Wayne. That's
> what this whole fucking thing is about. Fuck
> the whole system.
>
> (1:01:42)

The selective reportage omits a practical purpose and political agenda. Instead, it gives us Black rage with the threat of revolution. This flimsy reporting, echoed in Wayne's melodramatic formulation, tells us how neoliberals view the prospect of politics from below. The poor do not produce politics, they produce chaos: riot. People like Wayne do not recognize the clowns' grievances as valid politics. Wayne's goal is to "help them. To lift them out of poverty" (1:02:03). But they are to be lifted out of poverty by free market capitalism, certainly not by engaging the political process to shape a fairer economy.

When Trump had crowds chant "Lock her up" about his political rival Hillary Clinton, the slogan is pure melodrama. When, at his rallies, fans parade posters with Trump's head glued to the body of Rambo or Superman, this is superhero melodrama as well. But Trump is not alone in desiring to criminalize opposition; liberalism already imagines political regulation as criminality. The political theorist Carl Schmitt noticed this contradiction in liberalism (even as, in the 1930s, Schmitt resolves it himself by aligning with fascism). Liberalism, remember, preaches an economy where people make voluntary contracts to exchange goods and labor. Instead of violence, there is consensual, contractual competition. Yet, for Schmitt, this economy comes with hidden baggage. Competition, even voluntary competition, does not preclude the possibility of exploitation. Just because you agree to a wage doesn't mean you are not getting screwed. In capitalism, the disadvantaged compete to their disadvantage all the time. Most have to work, one way or another, and many in exploitative conditions. If such people want to defend themselves from exploitation, Schmitt writes, "they cannot do so by economic means." After all, if you are being exploited, it's likely because your employer has more economic clout than you. The employer can wait you out, sue you, or hire someone else (or, if you are a small country, destroy your currency, freeze your bank accounts, refuse trade, and so on). Political agitation is another means available to the exploited to contest their exploitation. But, according to Schmitt, the "possessor of economic power" considers all attempts to redistribute power "by extra-economic means as violence and crime," and seeks to hinder them.[30] Here, Schmitt puts his finger on the pulse of men like Wayne and the system he represents. Political interference within the economy—striking, blocking the roads, even democratic agitation for reform—is quickly interpreted as illegality. This is the point where neoliberalism resents democratic meddling and opens up to autocratic solutions.

Penny's whole-hearted acceptance of Wayne's media and political strategy links to her gullible desire to imagine herself living in a melodrama: not the villain and superhero kind, but the domestic melodrama,

---

30 Carl Schmitt, *The Concept of the Political*, expanded edition (Chicago: University of Chicago Press, [1932] 2007), 77–78.

where a servant is saved by a loving relationship with her employer. She even writes longhand letters in that tradition. Penny's hopes for her family and her hopes for her city are wrapped up in her hopes for one man: Thomas Wayne. Penny's psychological pacification, that is to say, is a plot line that illuminates how neoliberalism urges corporate paternalism instead of democratic involvement.

Penny longs for an employer-savior who masters melodrama, who divides evil from good, who commands the media, who holds the key to Gotham's success. Her desire allegorizes our modern attachment to political strongmen. It's true that Wayne lacks many of the characteristics of the strongmen of recent history: the performative virility of a Putin, the corrupt violence of an Erdogan or Duterte, the oversized machismo of a Bolsonaro or a Trump.[31] But the tendencies are there. Penny is not sophisticated enough to recognize her leverage. She will not be hushed with money, as will Stormy Daniels or Karen McDougal. She can give her story no hashtag. But this pre-political space matches the willful unawareness of a financial class that needs to win elections while hindering democracy; a class which cannot admit that championing plutocracy produces political strategies that first imagine the opposition as clowns before then construing them as murderers. For neoliberals, discovering the enemy within one's own society solves the contradiction between economic freedom and democracy. In doing so, it lays the foundation in democratic societies for a fascist turn.

Joker is set in 1981 and, by 2024, this critique of TV as the reigning form of media social control appears quaint. Hasn't TV gotten better? Penny isn't watching *The Wire*, a TV show that exposes urban decay and the sociology of drug crime. She's not tucking into *Last Week Tonight*—which still uses the news as joke, but focuses steadily on one problem,

---

31   Ruth Ben-Ghiat, *Strongmen: Mussolini to the Present* (New York: W. W. Norton, 2020).

rather than segmenting it. Anyway, is TV the proper model of media analysis these days? Contemporary social media and internet news is hardly designed to produce the calm and quieted. Upvoting comments, muting troll attacks, sparring in counterargument with counterlinks. Does contemporary news still create passive subjects? Or would we not better say that people are more critically engaged and maybe even downright agitated?

Digital media can indeed produce agitated subjects, but, like TV, new forms of media also depend upon a passive consumerist model—with a couple of tweaks. First, with digital media, the intimacy delusion is reinforced by algorithms that tailor content to personal tastes, recorded through data harvesting and mass surveillance. Second, digital media accelerates sounds and video to give the impression of immediate truth, even when what's shown is false. We have greater media choice now. But it turns out that more choice means more confirmation bias. Faced with a flood of information, we more readily absorb material that reinforces our previously held beliefs.[32]

Most importantly, even when we consume fact-based news, we mistakenly assume that keeping up with politics is the same as producing political power. Eitan Hersh calls it "political hobbyism":

> I refresh my Twitter feed to keep up on the latest political crisis, then toggle over to Facebook to read clickbait news stories, then over to YouTube to see a montage of juicy clips from the latest congressional hearing. I then complain to my family about all the things I don't like that I have seen.[33]

---

32 Gad Allon, Kimon Drakopoulos, and Vahideh Manshadi, "Information Inundation on Platforms and Implications," *Operations Research* 69.6 (2021): 1784–1804.

33 Eitan Hersh, *Politics Is for Power: How to Move Beyond Political Hobbyism, Take Action, and Make Real Change* (New York: Scribner, 2020), 3.

Getting agitated by the news, Hersh says, is not the same thing as engaging in politics. Wolin puts it more sharply. For Wolin, political involvement is more than agitated awareness. It is about "constituting power."[34] In the same way, citizenship is "more than a matter of being able to claim rights. It is about a capacity to generate power, for that is the only way things get established in the world. And it is about a capacity to share in power, to cooperate in it, for that is how institutions and practices are sustained."[35] The promise of democracy is that ordinary people develop their capacities by having access to power, which "is crucial to human dignity and realization."[36] This includes making mistakes and accepting responsibility for them.

Arthur gets physically agitated when Wayne comes on TV to politicize the murders: at this point *Joker* visualizes how agitation splits away from anything to do with political power. The word "agitation" means physical discomfort—to be agitated. It also means conscious political activity. Fleck's agitation is the physical kind: his legs shake, he hauls on his cigarette, he laughs in his quizzical way. Wayne rails against the "coward," who "hides behind a mask," and Arthur's legs tremble violently. Arthur, we know, until this moment, is fully depoliticized. He did not kill the brokers as a revolutionary political act, but in self-defense. Arthur is, in fact, a hapless adult with a mental illness still living at home with his mother. But Wayne characterizes Arthur as the symbolic head of class resentment. When Arthur laughs at Wayne's melodramatic analysis, Penny tells him: "it's not funny" (39:44). Arthur's agitation indicates his relationship with TV as a pacifying agent is shattered. This plotline expands across the entire movie. Next, his comedy routine will be mocked by his hero Murray. Then on a fantasy date with Sophie he sees the monstrous Clown

---

34 Wolin, "Democracy and the Welfare State," 154.
35 Wolin, "Revolutionary Action," 376.
36 Wolin, "Democracy and the Welfare State," 154.

face on the front of the news. Arthur takes his revenge on media itself by killing Murray. The end result of agitation without political process is violence.

Further reading

Neil Postman, *Amusing Ourselves to Death: Public Discourse in the Age of Show Business* (Harmondsworth: Penguin, 1985).

Nir Eyal, *Hooked: How to Build Habit-Forming Products* (New York: Portfolio, 2014).

Shoshana Zuboff, *The Age of Surveillance Capitalism: The Fight for a Human Future at the New Frontier of Power* (London: Profile Books, 2019).

Chapter Six

Can I Help You with Something, Pal?

On Capital

Fleck disappears briefly, then reappears wearing his clown nose. He's out-side the walls of Wayne Manor. Bruce, playing alone, walks to the other side of the gate to join him. Fleck first amuses the boy with magic tricks. A collapsing wand turns into a feather duster. When this doesn't work, Fleck reaches through the bars and stretches the young boy's cheeks into a smile: "That's better." Alfred, Wayne's loyal family servant, interrupts them. Fleck remains calm: "It's okay, I'm a good guy." When Alfred threatens to call the police, Fleck introduces himself: "My mother's name is Penny, Penny Fleck. She used to work here, years ago." Alfred remembers what happened and refutes Fleck's claim: "Your mother was delusional. She was a sick woman." Again, Fleck presents his credentials: "Thomas Wayne is my father." When Alfred laughs in his face, Fleck reaches in through the gate, grabs Alfred by his throat, then leaves off choking him to run away (51:11–55:03).

Two brothers happen to find themselves on different sides of the gate. They both wear the same color pants and jacket. But on one side, the clothes are tatty; on the other, fine wool. On one side of the gate, the signs of adult poverty, a man who travels on foot; on the other, wealth and splendor, a monopoly-house inheritance, complete with a loyal servant. For the audi-ence, the split is visually dramatic, marked by a gate we can see through but not cross. Poverty is not without its resources, it's true. If the brother with everything has his own playground, the brother with nothing has imagination and magic. The brother with everything is isolated, lacking friends or siblings; the brother with nothing offers human contact. What's more, the brother who fends for himself can joke that he's more of a man than the brother who has everything handed to him by their father. When Arthur passes the wand to Bruce, it falls limp. But in the hands of the clown, the flaccid wand stiffens to a sizable erection.

Despite this raillery, the scene stages the frustration and danger that follow from inequality. Arthur's magic tricks are not powerful enough to open the gate; the wealthy protect their property with legal walls and the threat of police. Alfred implies it is crazy for Arthur to imagine he has a claim on the house or the family. But is it crazy if they really are brothers? Is it fair that one child should inherit everything while the other child goes unrecognized and abandoned?

More profoundly, the scene also asks whether these questions about family justice and inheritance pertain even if they are not brothers. *Joker* leaves it unclear whether Arthur is, in fact, Wayne's child, with Bruce his biological brother. Wayne may have disavowed and exiled a pregnant Penny, avoiding the trouble of his bastard child. Or maybe Arthur has just inherited Penny's delusion. This ambiguity remains not because the film takes place before Jerry Springer and paternity tests. Rather, *Joker* leaves the question open because the drama between legitimate and illegitimate siblings poses more difficult questions about liberalism and fairness that are roiling all of Gotham.

Politically, liberalism establishes everyone as political brothers, equal under the law, a fraternity. But economically, liberalism allows for astonishing economic inequality: for political brothers to live on different sides of the gate. Economic liberalism calls this outcome fair because economic freedom, devoted to allocating capital efficiently, rests on the basic compact that those who work harder legitimately deserve to get more. This is the language of merit that Wayne speaks. It's as old as the philosophy of John Locke, who famously argued that we create individual private property from what belongs to everyone in common through our own labor. But as the protesters in Gotham know, the actually existing system of creating property and protecting wealth is rigged. After all, some brothers, like Bruce, won't have to work at all, and still, they will inherit the earth. Fleck's appearance through the gate dramatizes an unequal family inheritance, then. It also asks whether liberalism's claims about fairness and merit can be believed. As fewer believe those claims, so grows popular indignation at the social arrangements they underpin. And as indignation grows, well, so grows the threat of violence.

In this chapter, we look at some ways that wealth inequality forms under capitalism and answer why the family is the visual center of this fraternal fissure. One obvious reason is inheritance. Inheritance gives the lie to *meritocracy*: the story that liberalism tells about hard work leading to just reward often overlooks the leg-up of family money. Another reason is that family is the language Wayne himself employs to express corporate loyalty: we are all family at Wayne Enterprises. This linkage between family and corporation, in fact, points to a deeper commonality between Wayne Manor and Wayne Enterprises. The law that forms Wayne Enterprises as a corporation owes to early trust law, which first allowed wealthy families to pass to their children—without the interference of creditors or state taxes—their manors and land.

The law's *coding*—how law itself transforms assets into capital—helps those with good lawyers to shield assets, shift losses, and make wealth durable. These attributes, according to Katharina Pistor, explain one of the great mysteries of modern capitalism.[1] Capital consistently grows at a higher rate of return than growth in the economy as a whole.

---

1   Katharina Pistor, *The Code of Capital: How the Law Creates Wealth and Inequality* (Princeton: Princeton University Press, 2019), 54–67.

Those who start with capital—whether gotten by theft, inheritance, luck, or entrepreneurial skill—widen their wealth advantage over time. Thomas Piketty captures this phenomenon in a formula, $r > g$: the rate of capital growth (r) is higher than growth in general economic output and wages (g). When gross domestic product (GDP) rises 1 percent over time, say, capital—which includes agricultural land, housing, stocks, and so on—will give a consistent rate of return of 4–5 percent. Working as it should—without crises or corruption—capitalism concentrates ever more wealth into the hands of the already wealthy. The rich get richer as the "the past devours the future."[2]

Wayne Enterprises is, like all corporations, legally encoded with the same three purposes: asset shielding (keeping assets behind gates), loss shifting (capturing the upside of profit but shifting losses downward to employees, creditors, or the public at large), and immortality (making the wealth creation durable through time). Arthur imagines he's on a family quest for recognition from his father Wayne. But what he encounters are the defenses of Wayne Enterprises, of corporate law that sees him as a threat to shielded assets, that ignores him because he and his mother have been a target for loss shifting, and that will outlast him, because, like Batman, the corporation aims to exist in perpetuity, to become immortal.

You lookin' for money or something?

We can better see why *Joker* dramatizes a conflict with corporate law if we first notice how the Batman franchise celebrates corporate law as giving rise to and immortalizing Batman. *Batman* has traditionally celebrated corporate and trust law because they normalize the kinds of legal loopholes that vigilante justice—by definition a loophole in the law—also

---

2   Thomas Piketty, *Capital in the Twenty-First Century* (Cambridge, MA: Belknap of Harvard University Press, 2014), 571.

depends upon. Take Batman's fancy outfits. In Christopher Nolan's *The Dark Knight Rises* (2012), the final movie in his *Dark Knight Trilogy*, the billionaire Bruce Wayne can suit up in nifty gear and military gadgets because of canny corporate accounting.[3] Fox, Wayne's right-hand-man inside Wayne Enterprises, hides the Applied Sciences division that makes Batman's kit by means of familiar legal maneuvers:

> FOX
>
> After your father died, Wayne Enterprises set up fourteen different defense subsidiaries. For years I've been shuttering and consolidating all the different prototypes under one roof. My roof.
>
> (38:07)

Traditionally corporations set up subsidiaries—child companies that a parent corporation owns—to shield assets from taxation, limit liability, and shift losses. Subsidiaries can be bought and sold without shareholder approval. And subsidiaries select the most business-friendly legal code by incorporating in whichever state or country best protects assets and avoids regulatory burdens, worker rights, environmental protections, or tax obligations. (Lehman Brothers, which collapsed in the 2008 Great Recession, had 209 registered subsidiaries, tied together with a web of debt that eventually helped to bankrupt the corporation.)[4] Fox's Applied Sciences division is literally embedded in a hidden floor of the Wayne Enterprises skyscraper in Gotham. Though "under . . . [his] roof," this child corporation legally is based anywhere—not off the books, exactly, but masked. In *Dark Knight Rises*, the murkiness of corporate accounting, much like the hideaway under a billionaire's mansion, is the dark

---

3   *The Dark Knight Rises*, directed by Christopher Nolan (Warner Bros, 2012).

4   Pistor, *Code of Capital*, 50.

cave from which a superhero can emerge. Fox is a surrogate father to Bruce. But in these movies, the real family structure that enables a child to become a man, and a man to become the superhero, is the parent corporation and its child subsidiary.

Arthur stands before Wayne Manor to remind us that more than one bastard is begotten in this corporate lovefest. A grown Bruce Wayne in *The Dark Knight Rises* will charitably entrust Wayne Manor to Gotham's orphans. But Arthur's presence before the gate in *Joker* suggests that capitalism's profit structure rests upon an initial exclusion, creating a class of disinherited such as Fleck. Capitalist profit first owes, that is, to legal barriers that shield assets by limiting responsibility, whether to employees (Penny), to children outside of the marital contract (Arthur), or to the public at large and nature in general. *Batman* responds to this criticism in advance: corporate leaders and the wealthy must try to be good people—*melodrama!* The wealthy must compensate those they dispossess through voluntary charity, with technological advancements, and by taking out bad guys rather than arresting them, whether through Batman or good cops like Robin. Everyone from Selina Kyle—who moonlights as Catwoman—to Bane—a formidable Batman foe—knows that Gotham is corrupt and grossly unequal. But the Batman franchise steers the critique of capitalism into a conservative defense of vigilante justice and catastrophist fear of revolution. Its solutions are antidemocratic: justice beyond the law and corporate capital beyond democratic regulation. The people cannot be trusted. What we need are wise, wealthy leaders who know how to employ corporate law for good.

But here stands Arthur, outside the legal gates designed to shield inheritance and capital from the likes of him. When Arthur walks along the wall of Wayne Manor, the visual recalls the oldest way manorial lords acquired wealth: by literally walling and fencing off land to keep commoners out. In England, powerful families began to enclose common land in the early 1500s. Before enclosure, nobody held title to land. The use of it was shared by commoners and nobles alike. But by 1600, the best land was all captured, long before the *Enclosure Acts* of Parliament between 1720 and 1840.[5] Initially, peasants ripped up the hedges and fences, so they could still plant their crops. The commoners also took the battle to courts, to defend their own claims to the land. But eventually, over two centuries, the wealthy prevailed. They argued for exclusive property title on the grounds they used the land first: *first usage*. They stereotyped the peasants as rioters.[6] And they claimed everyone, the whole nation, would benefit from their ownership and efficient use of the land. (Capital today makes the same arguments for individual privatization of public assets, just as right-wing media still characterize popular protest as riot.) The smallholders were ruined, left with nothing to sell "except their own skins," in Marx's memorable phrase.[7] By the early nineteenth century, these legal brawls finally produced a new legal concept: "absolute private property rights."[8] These property rights allow a person to own and sell and borrow against a property. As the British empire sailed the globe, this concept of private property was emblazoned on its bow. To this day, the concept still informs World Bank policies and still displaces communal use rights across the world.

But how could English people claim "first usage" in colonies, where indigenous peoples obviously lived before them? The answer is that, when abroad, European settlers advanced private property rights on different grounds. Property rights, they now claimed, go to those who "discover"

---

5 Pistor, *Code of Capital*, 29.

6 See E. P. Thompson, "Custom, Law and Common Right," in *Customs in Common: Studies in Traditional Popular Culture* (New York: The New Press, 1993), 99.

7 Karl Marx, *Capital: A Critique of Political Economy, vol. 1* (Harmondsworth: Penguin, [1867] 1990), 873.

8 Pistor, *Code of Capital*, 33.

the land and "improve" it. US law deployed these same arguments to grab communal land from Native Americans. By 1823, the US Supreme Court ruled that:

> *discovery* gave an exclusive right to extinguish the Indian title of occupancy either by purchase or by conquest; and gave also a right to such a degree of sovereignty, as the circumstances of the people would allow them to exercise.[9]

This law instantly turned Native Americans into squatters, and cut a path for the *Indian Removal Act* of 1830. That law forced Native Americans onto reservations and carved their territory up into plots, turning the land "into capital."[10]

Arthur naively imagines magic is on his side of the fence. When he flicks the wand, a final trick to impress the young Bruce, a feather duster springs forth. The magic duster recalls that his mother, Penny, cleaned the enormous house behind the gate. Penny was a member of the Wayne household, not unlike Alfred himself. The wand also suggests that labor itself is magic. After all, the labor of "improvement" provides a basis for claiming property as one's own. In philosophical liberalism, if you work the commons for yourself, the goods produced become your property: labor is its own kind of magic.[11] Arthur is no philosopher. But by invoking his mother's labor, he evokes a contradiction in liberalism's account of property. If labor and cultivation justify the formation of private property, Arthur's feather duster asks: why does the *servant's* improving labor not confer a moral basis for property? Why does the *servant's* labor profit the

---

9   Our emphasis. Quoted in Pistor, *Code of Capital*, 34.

10   Pistor, *Code of Capital*, 34.

11   John Locke, *Two Treatises of Government*, edited by Peter Laslett (Cambridge: Cambridge University Press, [1689] 1988), 289.

aristocratic family, as it does in Locke's writing,[12] but not the servant herself? Does Penny's hard work maintaining the house not give her some claim on it?

The answer, it turns out, is simple: Wayne's side of the wall boasts stronger magic. One name for this magic is *contract law*. Penny, we have to assume, once signed a contract that exchanged her labor for the Wayne household for a certain wage—she likely wouldn't have received property or stock as part of her agreed compensation. Similarly, Penny has signed another contract, one that apparently relieves Wayne of obligation to the fruit of Penny's biological labor, Arthur. Contract law defines obligations between private parties. Alfred treats claims made outside of contractual obligation as irrational: "Your mother was delusional. She was a sick woman" (54:29). Under obligations set out by contract law, Arthur is not simply beyond obligation; his claims appear like very insanity. Contract law assumes that property rights are settled in advance, or merely residual, to be discussed only after contract terms are fully executed. Contract law couldn't care less whether property was originally acquired by theft, inheritance, or entrepreneurial skill, and it certainly isn't interested in wealth inequality as a general condition. It is, literally, entitlement. (Blockchain, like the bitcoin ecosphere more generally, imagines this same fantasy: that all business interaction can be solved by unbreakable contracts between private parties, with no role for the government. This fantasy ignores how property was initially allocated. It also ignores that property itself is titled against all other claims by the full power of the state—by the threat of state violence, a background condition that contracts take for granted.)[13]

For these reasons, *Joker* makes viewers uneasy about contracts. The contract Penny signed, as well as Alfred's nasty critique of her sanity, look

---

12   Locke, *Two Treatises*, 289.
13   Pistor, *Code of Capital*, 107.

like intimidation, bullying. Treating a child's claims as already settled or residual also leaves us wondering whether Wayne isn't ignoring other obligations that go beyond the contract. If you were to sign away parental rights, for instance, you would still have an obligation to pay child support. Were you to renounce parental rights, your child still stands to inherit your estate, unless a will states otherwise. Obligations to children are not so neatly resolved by contracts! Arthur's presence makes Wayne uneasy for this reason. He mistakenly assumes that he just needs a new contract to get rid of him, again: "What do you want from me, money?" (1:06:05). But without a lawyer to help her, Penny resorts to mere sentimental letters, appeals to a rich man's humanity: *melodrama!* And Arthur can only threaten feeble violence before running away.

Maybe it seems like disputes over communal property are just long-dead history. Who cares about sixteenth-century England? But the effects are still with us. Today, nearly half of England is owned by less than 1 percent of the population.[14] And Pistor reminds us that these legal strategies persist: indeed, that we are living through a second great enclosure. With help of patent law, corporations now claim nature's DNA as their private property. They patent it on the same basis that they have "discovered" and "improved" it, generally with some minor genetic modification.[15] The coding and produce of nature, in usage common to all, as well as to other life forms, turns into private property for the few.

The rich don't even go broke the same as the rest of us, huh

Anyway, Wayne has other tricks in his bag than contract law, tricks that allow him to shield his assets and to limit his losses. Foremost is the family *trust*. As with the shell company, or subsidiary, the legal coding of the

---

14   Simon Fairlie, "A Short History of Enclosure in Britain," *The Land* 7 (2009): 16.

15   Pistor, *Code of Capital*, 108–131.

trust also creates space for the superhero. Near the end of *The Dark Knight Rises*, when Alfred thinks Bruce has died, he sobs at his funeral: "I'm so sorry. I failed you. You *trusted* me, and I failed you" (2:32:58). Alfred was scared that Bruce would get killed by Bane, the better-trained fighter. He complained that Bruce was exposing himself to too much personal liability. So, in protest, Alfred leaves Bruce. Now he thinks Bruce has died. By "trust," Alfred means that Bruce relied on him as a father figure, trusting him that Alfred would support his ambitions.

But as with Fox and corporate law, Alfred's parental function is also legal-financial. He is something like a *trustee* to Wayne family wealth, ensuring that it endures and passes undisturbed to Bruce and his future heirs. (No wonder Alfred takes such interest in Bruce's dates!) Trusts are designed to shield family wealth from liability—debt or taxes—so that capital stays in the family. Alfred administers the will after the funeral and entrusts Wayne Manor to the state as an orphanage. But, in a way, Alfred has failed, since the main purpose of trust is to pass the estate to someone in the Wayne family.

It helps here to know the history of trusts. After English aristocrats won title to what was common land, that title allowed them to borrow against the land. They could get mortgages, i.e., use the land as collateral to borrow money. In this way, legal title transformed a mere landed asset into capital. But those same aristocrats wanted to ensure that, even if their estate was indebted, they could still pass the manor and grounds to their children, protected from creditors' claims. The method used was the legal trust. In this period, the trust was called "entailment," a legal concept that remained in operation until the late nineteenth century. Entailment guaranteed that the manor and land went to the oldest male. Though entailment granted this inheritance, the eldest son was also forbidden from selling the land or house. Entailment law had roots in feudal codes, and it allowed the rich to borrow against their estates, yet never lose them to the bank if they didn't pay their debts.

The Dark Knight Rises makes trust a punch line. When Batman (briefly) loses all his money because of Bane's financial chicanery, Wayne confesses to Selina: "actually, they're letting me keep the house." She retorts: "The rich don't even go broke the same as the rest of us, huh?" (1:06:07). The provision that protects Wayne Manor is left unclear, but it's probably a reference to the power of the trust, the legal mechanism that first allowed the wealthy to pass on their property unscathed. This also matters because the trust is an early basis for the corporation—another legal entity that, like a family estate handed down, aims to exist forever. Wayne Enterprises binds together these two distinct mechanisms that together generate extreme inequality: inheritance and legal shielding.

Just like a family trust, a corporation aims to shield assets from, and shift losses to, those outside of the corporation: consumers, creditors, taxpayers, the general population, and nature at large. Pistor explains how this works. A trust allows an owner (called the settlor) to transfer an asset into a legal shell. The rights of the asset are then divided into those of the trustee, who holds formal title (someone like Alfred), and the beneficiary, who receives the future economic interest (someone like Bruce). Since the settlor no longer owns the asset, his creditors cannot seize it to satisfy their claims. The trustee holds formal title but cannot profit or receive economic benefit from the assets. As Pistor puts it: "by insulating assets from various groups of creditors, the trust works magic in enhancing their durability."[16] Durability—the ability to preserve capital through time—is the magic of the trust. Because they are legally owned by someone else, the trustee, the assets cannot be repossessed. But the trustee cannot benefit from the assets, only pass them on to the beneficiary. Wayne gets to keep his house! Just as the wealthy use trusts this

---

16   Pistor, *Code of Capital*, 43.

way to shield assets slated for inheritance, so corporations use trusts to protect assets from their creditors. Bruce entrusts Wayne Manor to the state as an orphanage, a charity that ostensibly recognizes his political brothers excluded from inheritance. But like so many family charities and trusts, which are notoriously murky in their finances, this trust also hides Bruce's private interests, preserving the array of Batman technology and military toys lurking beneath.

Every character in *The Dark Knight Rises* is obsessed with "trust," showing us how central the management of trusts is to the myth of the superhero. Can Bruce trust Gotham with a fusion reactor Wayne Enterprises developed? It produces emission-free power, but it might be turned into a thermonuclear bomb. (Melinda: "Bruce, if you want to save the world you have to start *trusting* it" [1:02:19].) Can Bruce trust Catwoman? (Catwoman: "Still don't *trust* me, huh?" [1:10:30]) Can he trust Melinda Tate, who masquerades as a green-energy philanthropist, but turns out to be the child of Ra's al Ghul bent on destroying Gotham? (Bruce: "I'm choosing to *trust* you" [1:02:28].) Can Gotham be trusted with the truth that Commissioner Gordon lied about Harvey Dent dying as a hero, a lie that enables police overreach to be legalized and legitimated? (Bane, reading Gordon's letter: "It is time to *trust* the people of Gotham with the truth" [1:38:11].)

All of these trust issues, though, are secondary to the central message: Bruce must learn to employ the *legal* trust. By trusting or incorporating Batman itself, he can make Batman immortal, pass on the role to Robin, and shield his own body from personal liability. By this legal mechanism, Batman's legacy endures even as he retires to Paris with Selina. The movie ends with this solution: Bruce has not died when flying the fusion bomb so it can explode away from Gotham. Rather, he allows people to believe he's dead, so he can entrust his mansion to the city of Gotham, and at the same time entrust the batcave, and the "idea" of

Batman, the intellectual property, to Robin (1:05:19). The trust and corporate structure allow Bruce to limit his own liability and ensure Batman lives forever. The message of these movies is, if you want a superhero, learn to use corporate and trust law! The legal mechanisms that protect the wealthy from paying taxes like everyone else does, or from paying their creditors like everyone else does, are the same cheat codes that, over time, generate the Waynes and the Flecks—that create systemic inequality. And the message is that the corporation, which acquires "legal personality"—the rights of a person to "own assets, contract, sue, and be sued in its own name"—is the first step toward not only entity shielding and loss shifting, but also "the prospect of immortality."[17]

I'm Gotham's reckoning. Here to end the borrowed time you've all been living on

Bane's reckoning comes to Gotham in the language of a financial crisis. A financial crisis is when the future—borrowed time—appears in the present demanding payment now. Borrowing from the future—taking on debt—is capitalism's greatest magic trick. Debt lets us have now, what we can only afford later. You get to live in a house you cannot afford today, because you convince the bank you will make enough money over the next thirty years to reliably pay the mortgage. The interest rate covers the risk that some borrowers won't pay, covers the time value of money, and also supplies the bank a handsome profit. The home forms collateral for the loan: if you don't make payment, the bank keeps full title to your home and evicts you (you are not, alas, a nineteenth-century English aristocrat protected by entailment). By taking out mortgages, houses get built, tradesmen get work, and builders make money. The economy grows: a miracle.

---

17   Pistor, *Code of Capital*, 55.

But when a debt crisis comes—when a crisis appears in what Bane calls "borrowed time"—money borrowed from the future suddenly all comes due today; it is no longer spread over the future (1:04:48). Think of it this way. If you have a mortgage, a car payment, or credit card debt, you have been lent that money on the promise of your future earnings. But if you face a crisis—you lose your job today—and you are unable to make payment, your creditors will fight for priority to get back whatever they can of all the money they lent. The future comes rushing back into the present wanting everything now; they repossess the car, they take the house, and the credit card company (which has nothing to take, since the debt is unsecured) ruins your credit score, raising your rates in the future. If they had just waited six months, when the recession passed and you got work again, it could have all been fine! Bane's revenge on capitalism is to create crises on purpose: to bring the future (borrowed time) back to the present. This is how he temporarily bankrupts Wayne: he has the stock price of Wayne Enterprises plummet. You see, the price of stocks also has a relationship to earnings in the future. If those earnings appear in doubt, the price in the present plummets. When Bane hacks Wall Street to make it seem that Bruce Wayne has sold future puts of Wayne Enterprises (contracts which imply he's betting that the future price of Wayne Enterprises will drop), the stock collapses, temporarily bankrupting Wayne.

Bane makes it sound like all debt is evil and that he is there to avenge this mechanism of capitalism, even as he secretly aims to destroy Gotham itself. Debt certainly *can* be evil: poor people get locked in debt traps with outrageous interest rates. Think of payday lenders, mostly owned by the large banks, who set rates so high that desperate borrowers can never escape them. And debt is used to plunder. Think of vulture capitalists and corporate raiders—now called "private equity"—who buy companies, only to gut their quality, cut jobs and pension benefits, sell their assets, drain their cash flows, and even have the company itself issue debt to pay back its own purchase—only then to resell the company five to seven years later once all money has been sucked away.[18] These versions of capitalism are vampiric, employing debt not to make an economy grow or create jobs, but to suck value from some people (employees, pensioners, sustainable growth) just so they can funnel it to others (private equity management and investors). Even ardent capitalists criticize these debt mechanisms because they imagine such abuses fully explain the yawning gap between the rich and everyone else.

They don't. As we've seen, inequality is endemic to unregulated capitalism, even without such egregious abuses. What explains $r > g$—what explains the fact that capital grows faster than wages and the economy as a whole—are legal structures that limit corporate liability, shift corporate losses to the general public, and shield corporate capital from tax and obligation. It's certainly true, as Piketty points out, that the gap between wage and capital growth can close in periods that protect higher wages.[19] The postwar compromise from 1945 until the 1970s saw a smaller gap between the increase in return on capital and the growth in wages. Neoliberal policies, as we have seen, purposefully dismantled the unions, destabilized welfare programs, and depoliticized the masses for this reason: to widen that ratio again to capital's benefit. And it's also true that the gap in wages between the lowest and highest paid has widened dramatically in the last fifty years, even as the uber wealthy secure loopholes to pay lower tax rates than regular people. Massive inequality in capital has always been the norm, but massive inequality in wages is a more recent phenomenon.[20] Present wage disparities in the United States are at the greatest levels seen anywhere at any time. Between 1977 and 2007,

---

18   Gretchen Morgenson and Joshua Rosner, *These Are the Plunderers: How Private Equity Runs—and Wrecks—America* (New York: Simon and Schuster, 2023).

19   Piketty, *Capital in the Twenty-First Century*, 326–329.

20   Piketty, *Capital in the Twenty-First Century*, 329–333.

the richest 1 percent appropriated nearly 60 percent of the total increase in US national income.[21]

But a debt crisis lets us see that capitalism's inequality grows inexorably even *without* vultures, because law and politics are structured to shield those with capital, while foisting losses onto the general public. The debt crisis of 2006–2009 illustrates how this works. When individuals couldn't pay their mortgage, the bank possessed their home, and they had to start their lives over, with their credit ruined. But something quite different happened to the banks. The debt crisis was precipitated because private companies bought up mortgages, sliced them up by risk, placed them within legal trusts, then sold them as securitized debt. This created an enormous market for mortgages, so banks supplied that market by extending mortgages to people who couldn't really afford them (subprime), sending house prices soaring. When it became clear that the future didn't support these inflated house prices (a market correction), and that many people issued mortgages wouldn't be able to repay the loans, the value of those loan portfolios collapsed. The losses were so vast that they threatened the entire financial system. They were therefore shifted to the public: President George W. Bush and Congress bailed out banks and insurance companies to the tune of $700 billion in loans. Most of the money was eventually paid back, just as one imagines it would have been if individuals were given leeway on *their* mortgages for a few years, rather than evicted. But individuals were instead left to fend for themselves. What's more, taxpayers (the government) did not take shares in these companies at the time (did not take assets, like the bank repossessing your house). So, taxpayers failed to profit from bailing out the companies when stock prices recovered.

This glaring double standard rips apart neoliberal ideology. The same private lenders who reap profits in the good times, who seek to

---

21   Piketty, *Capital in the Twenty-First Century*, 297.

avoid regulation and taxes, and who shelter assets in trusts to avoid liability, then beg for government help when a crisis comes. It sounds like
corruption. But crises are common in capitalism. What matters more is to
notice that individuals are treated differently. Neoliberal ideology holds
to the line with individuals, that they should be judged by whether they
"make something of themselves" or are "nothing but clowns," as Wayne
puts it (39:38). When the Great Recession of 2006–2009 arrived, ten million Americans were displaced from their homes.[22] Regular people take
it on the chin so that markets can be more efficient. Eviction becomes
their own responsibility, and they are scorned as losers. Even neoliberal
economic theory is clear about losers. Here is Friedrich Hayek, perhaps
the leading neoliberal economist of his age, comparing free markets to
gameplay. Think of *Monopoly*:

> It proceeds, like all games, according to the rules guiding the
> actions of individual participants whose aim, skills, and knowl-
> edge are different, with the consequence that the outcome will
> be unpredictable and that there will be regularly winners and
> losers. And while, as in a game, we are right in insisting that it be
> fair and that nobody cheat, it would be nonsensical to demand
> that the results for the different players be just.[23]

Hayek insists we abandon the aim of "just" economic outcomes. Brothers
end up on different sides of the fence not because anyone has cheated, and
not because the game is rigged. They end up there because one brother
has different aims, better skills, and more knowledge than the other. But
real life isn't like Hayek's monopoly. Sure, people make contracts based

---

22 Investopedia, "How the 2008 Housing Crash Affected the American
    Dream," investopedia.com, September 28, 2021. np.

23 Friedrich A. Hayek, *Law, Legislation and Liberty: A New Statement of the
    Liberal Principles of Justice and Political Economy* (London: Routledge,
    [1973] 2013), 234–235.

on their skills and abilities, and while not everyone buys property and collects rent, most get $200 for passing go (going to work). And some people roll bad dice through nobody's fault at all. But Hayek's vision of an economy is a contract fantasy that, like all contract fantasies, puts aside the question of how property was formed in advance. It puts aside history. In real life, some people inherit money and others inherit poverty. Who wants to play monopoly in a game where some keep their winnings from the last round, letting them buy up everything, even as we're all to pretend the game is fair, winners winning and losers losing according to their aims and abilities? In real life, property has a history that includes theft. In real life, the law protects wealth, individual and corporate, through trusts that shield assets and shift losses, and corporate immortality that ensures wealth endures.

It matters that Fleck feels "abandoned" by the system rather than excluded from it (1:45:05). Neoliberalism has restored Gilded Age levels of inequality but combined these with hyperinflated individual expectations and internalized demands. Arthur has internalized meritocratic ideals and is being humiliated in pursuit of them. And we know it is not just him who feels this way, because his rationale for killing Murray Franklin quickly spreads to the streets outside. There, it finds and targets Thomas Wayne: "Hey Wayne! You get what you fucking deserve" (1:49:48). Fleck's rage is spreading, and it is spreading because it reflects the violent underpinnings—the big lie—of the meritocratic ideal: that clowns always have the same chance as everyone else.

Further reading

Thomas Piketty, *Capital in the Twenty-First Century* (Cambridge, MA: Belknap of Harvard Press, 2014).

Katharina Pistor, *The Code of Capital: How the Law Creates Wealth and Inequality* (Princeton: Princeton University Press, 2019).

Chapter Seven

Does He Have Sexual Problems?
On Bros and Incels

Arthur has been fired at work after his gun flopped out at the children's hospital. Riding the subway home, he is joined by three "Wall Street guys," returning from a failed night on the pull. They debate their escapades. An attractive woman across from them reads her book and minds her business. Ryan, the drunkest broker, pesters her, trying to foist on her his fries. She signals to be left alone. The broker bros take umbrage at this: "He's being nice to you." She looks around, pointedly at Arthur. It is an appeal. She is assessing the threat level. Fleck just bursts out laughing. Sensing insult again, the Wall Street guys turn on Fleck, and the woman departs. "Bitch." Arthur laughs louder. He is about to get another kicking. They pounce. He goes down. The lights flicker off and on. Arthur shoots the face off one broker, then shoots another in the chest. The third won't escape (29:33–33:56).

In earlier chapters of this book, we would have read this scene as an economic and political allegory. Wall Street guys want to treat women with the same entitlements they expect to run high finance: without regulation. When rebuffed—when someone refuses their fries—they pretend not to understand, then get aggressive. Laugh at their plans and they roll out the disdain: "Send in the clowns," one sings. Should the laughter persist: time for systemic violence.[1] In turn, Fleck's response could be allegory.

---

1   Slavoj Žižek, *Violence* (London: Picador, 2008), 9.

When he fires back from the carriage floor, he demonstrates inevitable resistance, the spontaneous eruption of those at the breaking point. This is how Polanyi reads working-class resistance in the nineteenth century. Treat workers to wages so low they cannot feed and clothe themselves, forbid regulation that might allow young children time for school or religion, and just wait. Movements spontaneously erupt. Workers organize and strike. They demand the vote. They win legal protections for labor and trade. Otherwise, Polanyi argues, human society would not be able to reproduce; it would have been "annihilated."[2] A mentally ill loner with a loose gun is a melodramatic metaphor for the manic necessity—the compulsory aspect—of the defensive political reaction Polanyi describes. It is paranoid as well as melodramatic because it conflates outrage, which can be directed to political change, with individual rage and violent revenge.

That's how we would have read this scene before. But in this chapter, we put aside political allegory to think about sex. We ask: what is the relationship between broker bros, in the business of contracting and accumulating capital for others, and sexual capital? Why, when politely rejected, is harassment on the dance card? Is there a relationship between economic deregulation and toxic masculinity? What sexual psychodynamics does neoliberal capitalism produce?

And what about Arthur? He inadvertently provides the woman an escape in this scene by drawing their aggression onto himself. In one way it makes him appear more haplessly decent; certainly, it fosters that delusion in himself. But as he learns how to handle his gun, it also supercharges his testosterone. After the killings, Arthur tomcats tai chi before the mirror, he strides the tenement corridor losing his limp, he boldly knocks on his neighbor Sophie's door, and kisses her in a rapture of self-confidence, as her arms fold round him. Is this the same man who

---

2   Karl Polanyi, *The Great Transformation: The Political and Economic Origins of Our Time* (Boston: Beacon Press, [1944] 2001), 79.

climbed into bed with his mom each evening to watch TV? The loner who, when it comes to sexual capital, was completely broke? We're led to think so. But it turns out that Arthur's self-idealization only gives him the confidence of the involuntary celibate, who would kill to preserve his fantasy.

The woman on the train is trapped between two variants of contemporary toxic masculinity: the broker bro and the incel. Between them, they offer a bleak portrait of masculinity in two of its contemporary modes.

She was in love, Bro. . .

Joker wants us to see how the logic of capital suffuses the logic of sexual relations in ways that affect both women and masculinity. Sex turns into a transaction, writes Rebecca Solnit, and men "rack up" transactions to "enhance their status."[3] Yet, not all transactions are of equal value. One of the comedians showcased in *Joker* has a routine about sex and parking. Women treat dating like buying a car, he says. Men treat dating like trying to park one: "There's a spot. There's another one; that would work. Oh, you have to pay? Never mind" (42:31). In the logic of accumulation, sex with prostitutes doesn't count. Women should want men freely and for free. The same routine knows that accumulation of sexual capital is often for show: bro one-upmanship. Confronted with the possibility of parking in a "handicapped" spot, the comedian quips, "I hope no one sees this" (42:42). It is not *all* sex—not sex *per se*—that secures the man's status: only sex with women that other men deem desirable. Men want to be wanted by women, yes, but only such women as other men want. Hence the intense bonds of solidarity and recrimination that sustain this kind of masculinity. It is a cult of frustrated entitlement, and also the glue of male bonding.

---

3   Rebecca Solnit, "The Problem With Sex Is Capitalism," in *Whose Story is This? Old Conflicts, New Chapters* (Chicago: Haymarket Press, 2019), 93.

SEND IN THE CLOWNS!

The scene on the train demonstrates these dynamics. The bros initially jockey over whether a woman on the dance floor "loved" one of them. If she did, the bro accrues cachet. But his friends mock this as a delusion to take him down a peg.

> WALL STREET #1
> I'm telling you, she wanted my number. We
> should have just stayed.
>
> *The train starts moving again . . .*
>
> WALL STREET #2
> You're dreaming, man. She wasn't interest-
> ed—at all.
>
> WALL STREET #1
> Are you nuts? Did you see how close we
> were dancing!? She was in love, Bro.
>
> Ryan. Ryan. Am I crazy? Tell him what you
> saw.
>
> *Arthur's watching them closely, impressed by their
> confidence and easy-going camaraderie.*

With the new woman before them on the train, the scene has a chance to replay. Only now, we see that when men preen their sexual potency, it is for other men. And when the woman doesn't play her part as admirer: look out.

> WALL STREET #3
> *Drunkenly leaning forward to the woman in
> front of him*
>
> Hey, you want some French fries?
>
> *Wagging bag*
>
> Helloooo. I'm talking to you, hey.

136

WOMAN

No. Thank you.

The other two guys crack up at this apparent blow-off. The third Wall Street guy shakes his head, embarrassed, and starts softly flinging fries at the young woman.

WALL STREET #3

You sure? They're really good.

She just buries her face deeper in her book—

WALL STREET #2

Don't ignore him. He's being nice to you.

(30:02–30:23)

For the first broker it just doesn't make sense that a woman would not be "in love" with him; for the third, even polite refusal is an "apparent blow-off." First embarrassed, then hostile, he throws food and shade, yet she is the one guilty of an affront. She is either on call or in defiance of his dignity. When a woman doesn't accept the basic rules, the bros put aside their earlier competitiveness and line up in fraternal solidarity: "don't ignore him. He's being nice to you."

Sexual entitlement is an old possessive logic that comes with a newer psychological dimension as well. It would be nice to think that liberal democratic revolution, which overturned monarchy with the patriarchal law of the father to champion instead "liberty, equality, fraternity," as they put it in the French Revolution, would have also dismantled the sexual subjugation of women. But the keyword was "fraternity," not "sorority." Modern freedom was reimagined as a brotherhood: for men. When civil liberties were established and society became governed by consent through contracts, as Carole Pateman reminds us, the new realm of liberal political freedom was made possible by cordoning off private life, where married women of a certain class were kept. They were beyond politics and deemed naturally inferior, subjugated.[4] The marriage contract was available, a profession of a kind. But within this contract, women couldn't be legal owners of money they earned or inherited until 1870 in England (a few decades earlier, in the US); whatever money they had belonged to their husbands by law. And women had to wait another hundred years, until the *Joker* era in fact, for marital rape to be made illegal. Even today, some US states treat spousal rape differently than other rape. In this long era of liberty, then, the marriage contract included "sex right" for men: entitlement to sex without consent. This right, this entitlement, was a silent assumption attendant on the original revolutionary political freedom: liberty, equality, and bros.

Maybe such political stuff seems passé today. You no longer need a penis to possess property. Women can become stockbrokers. Sex right is no longer legal in the west. Women have won legal equality. And, in WAP, Cardi B and Megan Thee Stallion turn the trope of male sexual capital to women's (bank) account: "swipe your nose like a credit card."[5] But *Joker* knows the most lucrative and powerful professions are still fraternities: that rewards still trace gender outlines. Even today, 85 percent of brokers are bros. Ask why. What's more, the culture of sexual entitlement persists as a possessive function in the logic of capital: there's a lingering expectation that men make contracts, women want those men, and if he's being nice, a woman ought to accept his Harvey-wiener and fries, even when he flings them at her.

Arthur bursts out laughing at this french-fry masculinity, throwing your symbolic dick at a woman who has already refused it. Arthur's

---

4   Carole Pateman, *The Sexual Contract* (Stanford: Stanford University Press, 1988), 1–18.

5   Cardi B and Megan Thee Stallion, "WAP." Track 2 on *WAP*. Atlantic Records, 2020.

laughter picks up the movie audience's uneasiness with such phallic masculinity. But Arthur's laughter is murkier than solidarity with women, even though it has that practical effect by drawing the bro's aggression to Arthur himself, and even though Arthur, just fired, is also victimized by contracts that exploit him. Arthur's no feminist. But his laughter puts him beyond the band of brothers. After all, if he's not brokering contracts, he must be a clown. If he's laughing at the male code—the fraternity of sex right—then he's a threat to be brought into line.

Arthur's laughter also exposes the fragility of the bro's self-possession ("I'm telling you, she wanted my number"). It's more threatening than the woman's "no, thank you" in saying, maybe she didn't. It's not just toxic men who are sensitive to humiliation and humiliation's rage, though. Anyone with ideals is. We all experience a contradiction between our ideals about how we think we should be treated and how we experience the world. In part, this is structural. Modern liberty (*liberté*) tells us freedom means autonomy. We are all laws unto ourselves, able to do what we want. Except that we are not autonomous—and cannot be—since our rights are grounded externally in a body of law that legislates for all (*égalité*). And equality itself can require solidarity (*fraternité*) to secure entitlements based on identity. There is always an uneasy tension, Adam Phillips argues, between "an individual's sense of what he is due" and "the so-called rights of man." There is also an uneasy tension, we add, between an individual and their group identity. This makes modern identity fretful; it is grounded in individual possession but also founded in the impossible ideal of self-possession. We're never fully self-possessed because self-possession also involves the judgment of both the law and wider society to keep individual rights secured. To never achieve self-possession, in a society that elevates self-possession into an ideal, is a kind of humiliation. "That we can feel humiliated," Phillips argues, "reveals how much what matters to us matters to us."[6] Polite refusal triggers anger because rage is one face of a frustrated sense of entitlement.

Joker shows these psychoanalytic readings of humiliation and rage can often be distinguished by gender or subject position. The woman on the train, though treated to humiliation, does not become enraged, for instance. The men do. She may be indignant or outraged, but she acts non-aggressively to change the situation, by leaving the carriage. One way to understand this difference is to ask: why do phallic men uphold the fantasy that women must be into them? The fraternity is invoked to guarantee this manic need: "She was in love, Bro. Ryan. Ryan. Am I crazy? Tell him what you saw!" This ideal is necessary because it squares the bro's investment in a fraternity that celebrates lingering sex-right, now reduced to notching women on the bragging belt, with his other ideals: that he be thought of as a decent man who respects liberty and equality. "When you're a star, *they let you do it*. You can do anything," Trump said about being able to grab women's genitals.[7] He marvels that sex right persists for celebrities such as himself. If women are actually *into* it, if a polite "no" really means "yes," then the glaring contradiction produced by feeling entitled to another's liberty disappears. John Stuart Mill, in *The Subjection of Women* (1869), said men did not only want the obedience of women, but also their affection: "not a forced slave, but a willing one, not a slave merely, but a favorite." Mill knows most men of his era are not "brutish," looking to rape their wives, even if sex right had legal protection until just a few decades ago. Instead, men want—and educate women to believe—that women naturally want their own submission.[8]

---

6   Adam Phillips, "Just Rage," in *The Beast in the Nursery: On Curiosity and Other Appetites* (New York: Vintage, 1998), 127, 123.

7   Dylan Matthews and Dara Lind, "Vox Sentences: 'When You're a Star, They Let You Do It. You Can Do Anything,'" vox.com, October 8, 2016, np.

8   John Stuart Mill, *The Subjection of Women*, in *On Liberty, Utilitarianism and Other Essays*, edited with an introduction and notes by Mark Philp and Frederick Rosen (Oxford: Oxford University Press, [1869] 2015), 422.

Men are afraid that women will laugh at them, says Margaret Atwood. And women are afraid that men will kill them.[9] Atwood's observation suggests that what people fear from humiliation differs by gender. It implies something else, too: that gender conditions how we treat the object of our humiliation. Perhaps those whose ideals are grounded in a desire for mutual autonomy, rather than entitlement to someone else's body, are more likely to laugh than to lash out; are more likely to experience outrage than rage. Amia Srinivasan puts it this way: "women who protest against their sexual marginalisation typically do so with talk not of entitlement but empowerment. Or, insofar as they do speak of entitlement, it is entitlement to respect, not to other people's bodies."[10] But men who feel entitled to women's bodies, and then confront a request for bodily respect, either blow off the reality of that rejection, or lose their self-possession and displace their frustration onto the source-object of their desire: women. "Bitch," the broker calls out (30:56). More, their insecurity demands the rousing mutual support of men who are either part of the fraternity or asking for a beatdown.

Am I crazy? Tell him what you saw

At his best, Fleck offers a poignant counterpoint to the phallic masculinity of the Wall Street guys. At his worst, he stalks a woman and kills two others. In his head, he has an attractive girlfriend who likes his jokes; in reality, he has an austere social worker who barely listens. His gratuitous murder of the one, the social worker, is fueled by his humiliated desire for the other, Sophie. If Arthur is an incel—and he does share some incel traits (being bullied, financial insecurity, isolation)—is incel just a more extreme variant of phallic masculinity, as Rebecca Solnit asserts? Or is

---

9   Margaret Atwood, "Writing the Male Character," in *Second Words: Selected Critical Prose, 1960–1982* (Toronto: House of Anansi, [1982] 2000), 413.

10   Amia Srinivasan, *The Right to Sex* (London: Bloomsbury, 2021), 90.

it something else? *Joker* poses this question by making the viewer fully complicit in Arthur's perspective, as if we're his bros and he's asking the same question to us: "Am I crazy? Tell him what you saw." And what do we see? Arthur kissing, going on dates, Sophie laughing at his jokes. The movie invites us fully into Arthur's desires for himself, deep into complicity with the structure of his fantasy, before we realize our mistake. If we're his bro, we're in for a wakeup about what being a bro asks of us.

Movies, especially melodramas, often work this way: they light, stage, and set our perspective from a character's deluded view, only to clobber us with our complicity. The scene that absorbs us into the delusion is where the beautiful Zazie Beetz, who plays Sophie, raps on Arthur's door to confront him about his stalking her:

> SOPHIE
> Hey. Were you following me today?

> ARTHUR
> *(sheepishly)*
> Yeah

> SOPHIE
> *(sternly)*
> I thought that was you.
>
> *(Pause and the camera switches to Arthur's face)*
> I was hoping you'd come in and rob the place.

> ARTHUR
> Wh . . . I have a gun. I could come by tomorrow.

> SOPHIE
> You're so funny Arthur.

ARTHUR
Yeah. You know, I do stand-up comedy. You
should maybe come see a show sometime.
(27:07–27:42)

Artfully acted, this scene begins as reprimand but turns into dating. It starts as chiding and turns to flirting. By all accounts, Sophie should be enraged: she's confronting an odd neighbor who, hooded, follows her to her child's school and then to her workplace. But strangely, as the camera fixes on Arthur's face, Sophie veers into a joke: "I was hoping you'd come in and rob the place." Maybe Sophie is relieving a legitimate fear with dark humor? But the camera, trained on Arthur's face as he hears this line, suggests we are switching to how Arthur actually imagines himself, the very moment his fantasy kicks in. Sophie's joke, after all, is a thinly veiled rape invitation: "come in and rob the place." Arthur, missing the humor, responds in the same symbolic register by offering the service of his male phallus because it's just been confirmed that's what she wants: "I have a gun. I could come by tomorrow." It looks like dark humor, but it turns out to be mental illness. It looks like mental illness, but it expresses an internalized phallic fantasy that comes from the culture itself: sure, it's stalking and violation, but that's *what women themselves really want*.

Why, even in the teeth of red flags, do we go along with Arthur's fantasy?—and we admit we did when we first saw *Joker*. As movie goers we tend to believe what we see: Sophie herself starts the dark humor, and Arthur's dark retort seems plausible. But there are other reasons for our mistake. We feel bad for Arthur: he deserves a break, maybe some dignity and empowerment, solidarity at work, medicine for his illness, a therapist who listens, a relationship with someone other than his mother. But from that empathy, we become complicit with the movie's quick fixes. Maybe Arthur just needs a good woman! The movie will take our hope that women can redeem men—better them and stabilize them—and show that this kind of thinking has a common origin in thinking women are *for* men. Or the flipside, another gender fix: maybe Arthur just needs to be a better man and learn to use his gun! Maybe the problem is not deteriorating social, medical, and economic conditions, but a deficiency of masculinity? Maybe Arthur should just man up and possess his birthright. You don't have silver? Better get some brass. Lastly, we go along with this five-second scene because *Joker* reckons we'll be seduced by another sentimentality: that in a city constructing a penal state based on the fantasy of whiteness, as we saw in Chapter Four, Arthur is keen to date a poor, Black, single mother. But just as Arthur's heroism on the train is not feminism, his interracial desire is not progressive solidarity either. *Joker* weaponizes our investment in such romance, so that, when the curtain drops, we see our liberal condescension lingering here too: because someone is a single Black mother, they should risk sexual violence to help a poor white man get better? Please. But that is what we see and go along with.

To be fair, we don't know for sure that Arthur is incel at this point. In theory, the term "incel" describes anyone who is involuntarily celibate, writes Srinivasan, but in practice it identifies "a certain kind of sexless man: the kind who is convinced he is owed sex, and is enraged by the women who deprive him of it."[11] It is because these men feel entitled to enjoy women as property that celibacy feels like an outrage, not merely a disappointment. Women-as-bodies are treated as "sex waiting to happen," says Solnit, so women-as-people become their annoying gatekeepers.[12] Women are both the commodity to be enjoyed and the obstacle to its enjoyment. Does this describe Arthur? There are signs: his social worker is disturbed by the cut-out porn stars in his therapy journal. These dismembered pin-ups experience in fantasy the evisceration Fleck feels— for real—every time he is ignored. Fleck also acts out symbolic violence

---

11   Srinivasan, *The Right to Sex*, 73.
12   Solnit, "The Problem With Sex," 92.

against imaginary rivals, as when, in another scene, he shoots his gun at some invisible man in his mom's living room. On this fantasy date, Fleck dances with gun in hand:

> ARTHUR
>
> Hey, what's your name?
>
> Arthur.
>
> Hey Arthur. You're a really good dancer!
>
> I know . . . you know who's not? Him! *(Bang!)*
> (22:59–23:09)

Fleck is menaced by the part of himself that knows he is not who he wants to be: an attractive romancer, an admired dancer, a man who can use his gun. Freud calls this fantasy version of ourselves our ego-ideal. Everyone has one. And, as Adam Phillips argues, we feel humiliation and anger when our ego-ideal is contradicted by reality. "Tell me what makes you enraged—what makes you feel truly diminished—and I will tell you what you believe or want to believe about yourself."[13] One difference between an incel and a regular bro, though, is that bros are not isolated. They social-ize and mock each other's self-regard, adjusting their ego-ideals to real-ity: "You're dreaming, man. She wasn't interested—at all." Typical incel, Arthur has no friends to check him: he's isolated. Arthur uses a fantasy phallus—a real gun—to kill a fantasy rival—with a real bullet—so that no bro can question how he wants to imagine himself. Incel rage is the rage of the man-who-is-not-a-man, as seen through his own eyes. Fleck wants to believe he has what it takes. But no one seems to believe him, least of all himself. Arthur tries to kill off his humiliation and doubt, threats to his self-possession. He starts out the scene by pointing the gun to his own head, but then learns to point it outward, at the voices who get in the way

---

13   Phillips, "Just Rage," 123.

of the ideal of himself he's trying to embrace. For Fleck, the gun means manliness: it is an index of potency. His veneration of the gun allegorizes the incel's turn to violence in pursuit of masculine redemption.

The curtain drops when Arthur enters Sophie's apartment. *Joker* brings incel back into the fantasy marriage, where sex-right originates, and it leaves it there on the couch, where no means yes, and Sophie looks on bewildered, unsure how to get this pathetic and dangerous man out of her apartment. From Fleck's fantasy life with Sophie, we learn what he wants. It is not that unusual. He wants a girlfriend, someone to come home to. He wants someone to see the good in him and cherish it. His ideals for himself are the conventional stuff of family life: the nurturing side of manliness affirmed in fatherhood and provision. Against a background of torrential rain, Fleck enters Sophie's apartment as if it were their own: a homecoming. He caresses the walls, touches her daughter Rocco's artworks. He is trying to touch the life he cannot have, but also to feel something in himself: he needs help. He has "had a bad day" (1:18:05).

As an incel, Fleck's desiring life is split between vain fantasies of potency and vengeful acts of reprisal. The more Fleck deludes himself with fantasy, the more reactive he becomes. What he does not get in fantasy, he re-enacts for real in perverse form: his kiss with Sophie is inflicted on the TV sex therapist (1:38:00); his botched dance is re-enacted catastrophically with his mom (47:00); his shooting of a rival bro in his apartment becomes the real shooting of Murray on TV (1:45:10). When Fleck pretends to shoot himself in Sophie's apartment, he is signaling the death of a version of himself: the naive self, given to fantasy, foolish enough to believe the world held a place for him. What he touches in Sophie's apartment—her life, her modest possessions, her child's gifts of care—will always be out of reach. She does not want to be around him. Nobody does. He does not even want to be around himself. And this unbearable reality is resolved into rage.

We don't know if Fleck kills Sophie or Rocco, but his rage has a familiar pattern. In 2014, Elliot Rodger went on a shooting rampage in Santa Barbara. His target was sorority women: those "spoilt, heartless, wicked bitches." Rodger was an incel. Sexual rejection had made his life hell, he suggested, and it was women, the "hottest" he could find, who would pay the price: "All I ever wanted was to fit in and live a happy life," he explained, "but I was cast out and rejected, forced to endure an existence of loneliness and insignificance, all because the females of the human species were incapable of seeing the value in me."[14] Arthur, too, feels unrecognized: "Until a little while ago, it was as if nobody ever saw me" (40:35). From the perspective of the incel, the logic is implacable, the necessity for revenge self-evident: "If they are intent on denying me life, I will have no choice, but to deny them life," said Scott Paul Beierle, hours before he shot up a hot-yoga class in Tampa in 2016.[15] In this scenario, manliness is what happens when incels get a life, when man takes back control. It is a rape a minute. A thousand corpses a year.[16] Neoliberalism humiliates with false meritocracy and women pay a murderous price for the compensatory fantasies of phallic men.

Further reading

Audre Lorde, *Sister Outsider: Essays and Speeches* (London: Ten Speed, [1984] 2007).

bell hooks, *The Will to Change: Men, Masculinity, and Love* (New York: Washington Square Press, 2004).

Rebecca Solnit, *Whose Story is This? Old Conflicts, New Chapters* (Chicago: Haymarket Press, 2019).

Amia Srinivasan, *The Right to Sex* (London: Bloomsbury, 2021).

14   Quoted in Srinivasan, *The Right to Sex*, 74.

15   Maya Yang, "'Incels' Are a Rising Threat in the US, Secret Service Report Finds," *Guardian*, March 16, 2022, np.

16   Rebecca Solnit, "A Rape a Minute, A Thousand Corpses a Year," *Guernica*, January 25, 2013, np.

Chapter Eight

Smotherhood

On Mother Blaming

Arthur Fleck goes to see his mother in hospital for the final time. He is alone. No Sophie, this time. No fake girlfriend. He sits and smokes. Everything he has been told about himself is a lie: "Happy! I haven't been happy a single moment in my entire fucking life." Stubbing out his cigarette, he goes to Penny's bedside: "Do you know what's funny? Do you know what really makes me laugh? I used to think that my life was a tragedy. But now I realize, it's a fucking comedy." Grabbing her pillow, he brings it down on her face and smothers her with grim satisfaction. We feel her spasm. We hear her heart monitor sputter and go silent. Fleck goes to the window and stands in a shaft of sunlight. It is over (1:19:53–1:21:44).

Arthur Fleck feels abandoned by "the system," and rightly so. Certainly, he has been abandoned by his father. But it is his mother—Penny—who will pay the price. Most of Fleck's murders in this film are spontaneous. They are outbursts. But his first premeditated murder comes close to home. We do not kill the person we hate the most, Ernest Jones observed. We kill the person who creates in us the most unbearable conflict.[1] And for Fleck, beholden to her as he is, that person is his mother. Penny will be his most satisfying (but also most devastating) victim. When it is over—when he

---

1   Quoted in Adam Phillips, "Just Rage," in *The Beast in the Nursery: On Curiosity and Other Appetites* (New York: Vintage, 1998), 121–122.

has smothered the only person he has ever loved with her own hospital pillow—Fleck stands at the window. Everything is made to look how Fleck suddenly feels: relieved. He is bathed in the light of liberation from a nightmare.

Smothering Penny allows Fleck to make sense of himself. There was never anything wrong with him. The problem was his mother, or so he tells her as he kills her: "Penny Fleck. I always hated that name" (1:20:04). Blame is inevitable in a world structured by accountability, an essential aspect of life as well as politics. We find it easier and more satisfying to blame someone else, to offload accountability, than to find solutions to our problems. Early in *Joker*, Fleck sees past this dynamic. When mugged, he reminds Randall it was "just a bunch of kids" (16:04). Gradually, however, he falls into the blame game. Multiple beatings and humiliations contribute their share of outrage. When he finally learns the truth about his origins at Arkham Asylum, mounting indignation finds an available, all-too-easy target: mother.

Blaming mothers is widespread and foundational in capitalist societies. Multiple social institutions reinforce it. Maternity is idealized as a vocation while actual mothers are vilified, and vilify themselves, for failing to attain that ideal. In *Mothers: An Essay on Love and Cruelty*, Jacqueline Rose traces the history of this simultaneous resentment and veneration of the maternal function. She wonders why we ask mothers to carry the burden of "everything that is hardest to contemplate about our society and ourselves."[2] Why, this chapter asks, is it okay to blame mothers? What contradictions in capitalist society do mothers have to bear?

I take good care of my mother

Psychoanalysts know all about blaming our mothers. Being helpless and dependent, children, Freud discovered, often feel slighted by both their

---

2   Jacqueline Rose, *Mothers: An Essay on Love and Cruelty* (New York: Farrar, Straus and Giroux, 2018), 1.

parents. Daddy is more easily venerated, however, when he avoids the day-to-day raising of the child: the frustrating, disciplining, and feeding. A mother's proximity breeds deeper conscious attachment but also deeper, more or less unconscious, resentment.[3] In short, children tend to scapegoat their mothers. When society joins in to blame them too, it exacerbates this dynamic. To the extent that we depend on our mother, we risk blaming her when things go wrong.[4] Freud describes such scapegoating as fundamental to the Oedipus complex. The child wants the mother, but the mother wants someone else, and the child gets frustrated. *Joker* keeps the same psychoanalytic structure. When Fleck returns empty handed from his big date with Sophie, he tries to dance with his mother instead (47:06). In psychoanalytic terms, this substitution indicates a regression: rejected in the world of adult desire, the child returns to desiring its mother. But Penny brushes Arthur off, preoccupied with her latest pleading letter to Wayne. When Arthur opens her envelope, all hell breaks loose. Penny utters the prophetic words: "you are going to kill me" (49:08).

Fleck smothers his mother for several reasons. He wants to be a comedian, and she sees the unlikelihood. Stand-up fulfills Fleck's mandate as a man. He will do what Murray Franklin did: overcome all the obstacles—his father's disappearance—and become a star. This fantasy makes Fleck's life bearable. He may gig-work as a clown, but he also works on his material (17:43). Unfortunately, his jokes aren't funny, and he learns this truth from his mother. She tells him—straight out—in the bathing scene (21:48). The mother frustrates the child because he must see himself differently through her familiar eyes. What Fleck sees is a truth

---

3   Sigmund Freud, "Family Romances," in *On Sexuality: The Penguin Freud Library, vol. 7* (Harmondsworth: Pelican, 1977), 221–225.

4   Paula Caplan, "Mother Blaming," in Molly Ladd-Taylor and Lauri Umansky, eds. *"Bad" Mothers: The Politics of Blame in Twentieth-Century America* (New York: New York University Press, 1998), 127–144.

he cannot bear to face: he does not have what it takes to be a comedian (and, thus, to be a man). The situation is ripe for scapegoating.

Another reason for Penny's untimely demise links to this first: Arthur is tired of pretending to be Happy (1:20:49). (Happy Fleck, recall, is Penny's nickname for her beloved boy.) But Penny knows he is not happy. She says so in her letter to Wayne: he's "a good boy, perhaps a little sad" (48:50). Calling Arthur "Happy" encapsulates Penny's impossible demand of him: "smile and put on a happy face" (14:00). "Put on" is the giveaway. Arthur cannot be himself, feel sad for example, and still be seen as lovable by his mother. Worse, she demands something of him she admits he cannot give. "She tells me I was put here to spread joy and laughter" (14:00). This is not easy to do, if you aren't all that funny.

Donald Winnicott calls it *compliance*. The child appeases their caregiver in order to gain love and recognition. As a boy, Fleck had little choice but to comply with Penny's wishes for him, however frazzled and unfitting they may have been. Her psychiatric file documents neglect, which Fleck's fantasy dramatizes: "I never heard him cry" (1:15:15). Presumably, Fleck did cry: all children do. But Penny didn't respond and, gradually, Fleck went silent. He adopted a mask: Happy. For Winnicott, the solution quickly becomes the problem.[5] Compliance makes life difficult, finally unbearable. Fleck's search for a father signals his need to grow up—move out of home—and escape compliance. For Freud, children who fail to liberate themselves become "neurotic." Arthur Fleck is one such case, visibly trapped in his relationship to his mother. He needs liberation and, Freud would say, "the whole progress of society rests upon" him getting it.[6]

---

5   Donald W. Winnicott, "Ego Distortion in Terms of True and False Self," in *The Maturational Processes and the Facilitating Environment: Studies in the Theory of Emotional Development* (London: Karnac, 2006), 140–152.

6   Freud, "Family Romances," 221.

But Wayne has reneged on his duties to the Fleck branch of the family tree, as his shoddy treatment of both Penny and Arthur reveals. Wayne's rejection of both is brought rudely home in the cinema bathroom scene. Fleck shows up to confront his father, determined this time to put him before his responsibilities: "Maybe a hug, Dad? How about some common fucking decency?" (1:06:36). We must read this scene against Fleck's prior TV fantasy with Murray Franklin. In dramatic counterpoint, we see Fleck getting in fantasy from Franklin everything denied to him in reality by Wayne. Franklin, we have said, is Fleck's dream Daddy. At the most banal level, the Franklin fantasy gives Fleck what he wants most: recognition. He has been a good boy, and he needs his Daddy to say so. On TV, he does not need to ask for a hug but gets one, the spontaneous affection he craves. Where Franklin reassures Fleck about his family situation—"There's nothing funny about that" (13:38)—Wayne blithely insults it. Where Franklin compliments Penny's efforts as a mother—"she must love you very much" (13:58)—Wayne calls her "crazy" (1:06:42). Finally, as befits a dream come true, Fleck's TV fantasy ends with Franklin renouncing his patrimony to adopt Fleck ("I'd give it all up in a heartbeat to have a kid like you") (15:03), whereas the real encounter ends with Wayne stoutly defending his patrimony *from* Fleck: "You touch my son again, I'll kill you" (1:07:02). The real Thomas Wayne is the antithesis of everything Fleck needs and hopes for.

We've been through this, Penny

But the person who bears the brunt of his rage is Penny. She pays the ultimate price for the disintegration of Arthur's family romance. Fleck's decision to murder his mother comes after his visit to Arkham Asylum to read her psychiatric file: "We went over this Penny, you adopted him" (1:14:14). When the file appears to corroborate Thomas Wayne's version of events—he is adopted, she is crazy—Fleck buys in immediately. First, we see the state and its institutions colluding with powerful men to invalidate vulnerable women. Then, we see vulnerable men corroborating their story. Both Penny and Arthur are trapped in frustrated codependency. Neither has ever *really* had a chance. But in the absence of a political grammar with which to grasp the structures that shape their lives, it feels as if they only have themselves (and each other) to blame. Fleck scapegoats his mother because he cannot grasp the truth of his position in the tangle of half-truths and lies that is their life.

A more dispassionate reading of the evidence might have stayed his hand. Fleck's fantasy interview with Penny condenses the evidence of her file with his own experiences and projections of their relationship. The hospital records feel objective in ways that lead him to indict his mother on all counts. Penny was committed to Arkham at the age of twenty-five, not for the first time. The file contains committal reports, adoption papers, and newspaper articles that document Arthur's abject condition, all of which point to one thing: Penny's guilt. Keywords flash up on the screen: "extremely bizarre," "abandoned," "adopted" (1:13:56). Fantasizing himself present at her committal, Fleck stares grimly down on his young mother. The evidence is damning: "your son was found tied to the radiator in your filthy apartment, malnourished, with multiple bruises across his body" (1:15:01). Fleck laughs, hysterically. If he does have "a condition," it may be the result of brain damage, a horrific discovery. All his life, he has struggled to make sense of himself. Now, he knows. He has learned what he takes to be the truth: Thomas Wayne was right. Penny is crazy. He's adopted. She has abused and neglected him: not been a "good-enough mother."[7]

However, Fleck doesn't read the evidence very carefully. If Penny's file is to be believed, she is a vulnerable young woman with a significant history of mental health issues: drug abuse, narcissistic personality disorder, and delusional psychosis. She has been in the system since age

---

7   Winnicott, "Ego Distortion," 145.

fifteen, and is swept up again after the scandal of abusing her adopted baby. But there are reasons not to believe the file. Would a woman with Penny's past have been allowed to adopt a baby? Legally, she would have been deemed incapable of the responsibilities entailed by the right to adopt. As we saw in Chapter One, it is a longstanding liberal principle that you cannot validate a contract if you do not have your wits about you. Penny claims she worked for the Wayne family, got pregnant by her employer, and was then abandoned to the system. She says Arthur's adoption was a cover story—to protect Wayne and his business interests—and she consented because she was vulnerable and afraid. She feared both damaging his reputation and hurting her boy's chances. Wayne called in a few favors. He got her to sign "some papers"—denial of paternity, maybe—and she was incarcerated at Arkham Asylum (50:01). She got knocked up and locked up.

Kimberlé Crenshaw has shown how criminal charges made by vulnerable women are often dismissed out of hand. Their stories resist telling. The stigma of mental illness is a common sticking point. Women with mental health problems are more readily discounted as unreliable witnesses of their own experience.[8] Penny's incarceration—her unanswered letters—allegorize this truth. Fleck asks the clerk at Arkham Asylum how people end up in there: "Have all of them committed crimes?" "Some have," he is told, but others "just got no place else to go" (1:10:52). On admission, Penny says that she has "done nothing wrong" (1:13:47); that Wayne "made all that up so that it [the baby] stayed our secret" (1:14:23). Arthur has a photograph of Penny signed by Wayne at the time of the affair: "Love your smile" (1:25:37). After he kills her, he burns it. The truth—whatever it was—goes up in smoke. It is the stuff of cliché, but

---

8   Kimberlé Crenshaw, "Mapping the Margins: Intersectionality, Identity Politics, and Violence Against Women of Color," *Stanford Law Review* 43.6 (1991): 1241–1299.

also of terror. First, Penny is left holding the baby. Then, she is murdered for her failings. Physical abuse, mental illness, and underemployment—but also hope, love, and the audacity to dream—intersect, brutally, in her maternal body.

One detail, in particular, suggests that Penny never stood a chance. In the fictionalized interrogation scene, Fleck's fantasy interviewer—a man who embodies both the criminal justice and mental health systems—lays the charge: "You also stood aside while your boyfriend repeatedly abused your adopted boy and battered you" (1:14:29). For the bureaucrat's story to make sense, Penny must be in two places at once: both victim and accomplice. She must stand aside *while* being battered *and* neglecting her son. This is not a personal failing; it is a structural problem: a *two-body problem*. Can a woman really stand aside while being battered? Can she really take a beating and still be expected to protect her child? The scene is defined by smoke and mirrors, but the implication is clear. In the system, you can be a mother or a victim, but not both. The record first acknowledges Penny's victimhood (as woman) but then indicts her neglect (as mother). Gotham's newspapers chime in to seal the verdict: "Mother of adopted child allowed her son's abuse" (1:14:39). Compelled by his own indignation, and a certain residual trust in the workings of the system, Fleck sees none of these inconsistencies. He sides with Wayne, though he has ample reason to suspect him too. This allegiance tells us how patriarchal societies apportion blame. We cannot know what really happened. But we *can* see who pays the price. Penny Fleck is in an impossible position. And that, Jacqueline Rose would say, is the point: Penny is a mother. She is destined to be blamed whatever happens.

He's the only one that can save us

Freud helps us to analyze the dynamics between individual characters in *Joker*. But we must go beyond psychoanalysis if we are to understand the broader structures that bear down on them. To understand why Fleck scapegoats his mother, it is not enough to know that she frustrates him. Almost everything does. We need to study how social institutions and interpersonal dynamics collude to point her out as a deserving victim: as a worthy scapegoat.

Penny Fleck's fate is a particularly cruel allegory of the impossible position of women in late capitalist society. Women, we have said, have a two-body problem. The two-body problem originates when the labor of childcare fails to count, a devaluation that is the gendered root of women's oppression. Marx understood that capitalism needed to reproduce itself to survive, but he overlooked the labor of its biological reproducers, i.e., mothers and their children. He ignored the links between labor for pay and the labor of family. Childcare is an indispensable precondition of social health and viability that, even today, is routinely excluded from political calculations. Women, it turns out, are not just laborers like men. They are also central to another kind of labor—the labor of family. Work is needed in the outside world. Work is also needed to produce future workers at home. By debasing the labor of care, capitalism renders *itself* unsustainable, effectively swallowing its own tail: Nancy Fraser calls it cannibal capitalism.[9]

Fraser sees three things every woman deserves from the social contract: equality of rights, state support for the work they do in the home, and equitable recompense for the work they do outside it. Historically, she argues, the most women have received is two of three. When the industrial revolution dragged women from their homes into the factories, women had neither rights nor recompense for childcare. In the postwar New Deal (1945–1979), state intervention dragged them back home again.

---

9   Nancy Fraser, *Cannibal Capitalism: How Our System Is Devouring Democracy, Care, and the Planet—and What We Can Do About It* (London: Verso, 2022).

The solution was the family wage model, which re-domesticated women based on a strict division of labor. Middle-class women would work at home, and married men would earn more to support them. Maria Mies called it "housewifization."[10]

Penny Fleck is a product of the vulnerability of this bygone model of the family wage. She stays at home while Arthur takes up the substitute position of the father. Penny has internalized a paternalist model in which women cannot prosper without a man. *Joker* believes this too, making the trope of the missing father decisive to the decline of the Fleck's family fortunes. In fact, everywhere we look, fathers are missing: from the single mother on the bus to Sophie and Rocco. Women do the work of childrearing alone, and everyone suffers as a result. Even Murray Franklin's dad walked out on him as a boy: "went out to get a pack of cigarettes and never came back" (13:40). The film styles a crisis of patriarchal accountability, that women and childcare are vulnerable to the honor of men. When fathers disappear, children try to take their place. Arthur boasts: "I've been the man of the house as long as I can remember" (13:47). This is a recipe for dysfunction. No child can be everything to a parent. Whenever they try, or are made to try, the result is psychic havoc.[11]

The final demise of the Fleck family, however, owes less to this abandonment by the father than to the dismantling of the welfare state under neoliberalism. Happy's descent into psychopathy tells the story. We see a mentally ill young man visiting his social worker, holding down a job, caring for his mother, getting by. Then, his social supports are kicked away, and everything falls apart. Losing either parent matters, but what matters more is whether the one left providing the care finds a safety net. Rhetorically, neoliberals privilege family to diminish the state welfare agenda. When Thatcher dismissed the idea of society, she highlighted

---

10   Quoted in Fraser, *Cannibal Capitalism*, 36.
11   Phillips, "Just Rage," 130.

individuals and their families instead.[12] Protecting family, in this view, meant leaving individuals alone—in person and in property—to go about the business of sustaining themselves responsibly. Families sink or swim on a case-by-case basis. Wayne, as we have seen, sentimentalizes his workers as family, but he nevertheless abandoned Penny when she got pregnant under his care. Her pleading letters try, literally, to underline his responsibilities: "<u>your son and I need your help</u>" (48:31). But he ignores them all.

Rejecting this dependence on men, women—Fraser argues—emancipated themselves from family wage dependency by joining the workforce. But men and women both lost the family wage so that, in effect, workers were no longer paid to raise children. Progressives pursued political equality through work equality. A new era of gender-blind egalitarianism left women free to embrace the professional world and have a family if they wished. Finally, women were free to choose. But for those who did want a family, there would be no additional wages for childcare. If women worked, who would be left holding the baby? Arlie Hochschild sounded the warning bell in *The Second Shift*.[13] The new woman could have it all. But how could she *do* it all?

Here we find a new version of the woman's two-body problem based on the contradictory demands of leaning in and being leaned on. "Lean in" was Sheryl Sandberg's message of empowerment to women as Chief Operating Officer of Facebook. Published in 2013, *Lean In* sold four million copies and carries a powerful message: the limits of a woman's world are the limits of her ambition. In particular, women should not let pregnancy be a barrier to professional advancement. In Sandberg's paradigm,

---

12   Iain Dale, ed. *Margaret Thatcher: In Her Own Words* (Hull: Biteback, 2010), 260.

13   Arlie Hochschild with Anne Machung, *The Second Shift: Working Parents and the Revolution at Home* (New York: Viking, 1989).

a woman can have a family life and enjoy the experience, while also embracing the public sphere and working a fulfilling job. "Lean on," by contrast, is a psychoanalytic term for the situation of the newborn child in relation to their mother. They lean on her for support, love, and sustenance.[14] This demands of the mother an initial period of total preoccupation that precludes her from other tasks, including self-care. It is a crazy time, and she also needs support: a caregiver puttering around in the background.[15] In the era of the family wage, the ideal solution was paternalist: husbands would earn more money in the world so that wives could focus their efforts at home. The wife was left to herself, unless her husband decided to help when his working day was done. It was a solution, albeit an oppressive one. In the neoliberal era, this family wage model was replaced by a new ideal: empowerment as personal choice. Sandberg said women should lean in at work. This begged the question: would men lean in at home?

In the neoliberal view, individual women should choose their own solutions.[16] If it makes financial sense to work *and* be a parent, do so. If not, you need to earn more or dream less. Yet this view ignores biological differences between individuals—such as the ability to bear children— alongside differences of class—such as the ability to afford childcare. It also ignores structural wage inequality: among full-time workers in the US, women still earn only about four-fifths of what men do.[17] If two earn

---

14 Jean Laplanche, "Interview: The Other Within," *Radical Philosophy* 102 (2000): 35.

15 Donald W. Winnicott, "Primary Maternal Preoccupation," in *Through Paediatrics to Psycho-Analysis: Collected Papers* (London: Routledge, [1975] 1992), 300–305.

16 Friedrich A. Hayek, *Law, Legislation and Liberty: A New Statement of the Principles of Justice and Political Economy* (London: Routledge, [1973] 2013), 226–260.

17 Carolina Aragão, "Gender Pay Gap in U.S. Hasn't Changed Much in Two Decades," pewresearch.org, March 1, 2023, np.

in a family, and one must stay home, who should it be? On balance, the lower earner. What looks like pragmatic choice functions as structural oppression. For most mothers, the age of neoliberal empowerment has meant combining paid work with the unpaid labor of childcare. They are not free to choose. Sandberg's corporate ideals are not generalizable. She addresses women at the top—"C level jobs"[18]—who are exceptionally well paid. She recasts the phallic ideal of capitalism for the one percent of women able (and willing) to join the fray. Her guidance cannot serve as a social ideal for the 99 percent. Or it can, but only as a source of structural humiliation. Arthur's love interest, Sophie, is a good example. She works. She has a daughter. She is exhausted but getting by. What happens when school's out? Or when Rocco needs to stay home? Then Sophie will be in an impossible two-body position. If raised to internalize meritocracy as her self-ideal, she will be left with an unsettling question: "Why can't I *do* this?"

More recently, Sandberg has admitted problems with her model and called for men to step up at home.[19] This request is reasonable, but as a solution, it relies on individual decency. Many men contribute meaningfully to the work of raising their children. Many more are less engaged.[20] The *structural* problem, in any case, is unaffordable childcare. The real solution is to make childcare affordable. To her credit, Sandberg has been a passionate advocate for both maternity and paternity leave. She oversaw the introduction of four months paid leave at her parent company, Meta. But in the absence of socialized childcare for all, class-based concessions

---

18   Sheryl Sandberg, "Why We Have Too Few Women Leaders," ted.com, December 2010.

19   Gabrielle Chung, "Sheryl Sandberg Opens Up About Family Leave, Says Women Can't 'Lean In' Without 'Right Corporate Policies'," people.com, December 10, 2020, np.

20   Nancy Fraser, *The Old Is Dying and the New Cannot Be Born: From Progressive Neoliberalism to Trump and Beyond* (London: Verso, 2019), 44.

of this kind merely cement inequality. Penny is devoted to the corporate myth that counts everyone as family. Yet not everyone counts as family, not even a former housemaid such as herself. The United States has lagged in provisioning support for parents, the only developed country in the world without mandatory paid maternity leave.[21] A woman like Sandberg can lean in while also being leaned on. More pragmatically, she can forget about being leaned on and hire someone else to take her place. Fraser calls it the "care chain." One class of woman goes out to work—or lunch—while another class of woman picks up the slack at home. But who looks after the childminder's children? The problem of childcare can only be displaced, often to the neglect of poorer children, such as Rocco and Arthur. This is *Joker*'s message. By exploiting women as mothers as well as workers, neoliberalism has undermined the social basis of childrearing as well as its own viability as a system. Fleck turning on his mother allegorizes the system turning on itself: smotherhood.

Fraser calls for an expanded conception of capitalism that accounts for the ways it "free-rides" on mothers and their labor.[22] She adds a further twist to liberalism's story of hidden hands. Adam Smith imagined a hidden hand behind the processes of exchange. Karl Marx turned our focus to the hidden hands of the workers that made exchange possible. Nancy Fraser looks to home, and the hidden hand that rocks the cradle: the various institutions of mothering, childcare, and community that sustain society by reproducing it. Mothers have been the perennial scapegoats of late capitalism: indispensable victims of their own propensity for care. They have been oppressed by men, other women, their desire for a family, even the terms of their own liberation. Childcare is the lynchpin of this system of oppression. Capitalist society requires it, but then abuses its

---

21 Findlaw Staff, "Paid Parental Leave in the U.S. vs. Other Developed Countries," findlaw.com, January 31, 2023, np.

22 Fraser, *Cannibal Capitalism*, 54.

providers. Tasked with the extraordinary labor of birthing and socializing the young, mothers have been forced to grapple with a cruel variant of the Peter Parker problem: with little power comes great responsibility. Ultimately, this impairs mothers, their children, and, finally, society itself.

Further reading

Donald W. Winnicott, *The Child, the Family, and the Outside World* (London: Pelican, 1964).

Nancy Fraser, *Cannibal Capitalism: How Our System Is Devouring Democracy, Care, and the Planet—and What We Can Do About It* (London: Verso, 2022).

Helen Hester and Nick Srnicek, *After Work: A History of the Home and the Fight for Free Time* (New York: Verso, 2023).

Chapter Nine

Is It Just Me?

On Conspiracy

He is silhouetted before a motley curtain awaiting his entrance to Live! With Murray Franklin. *As the audience laughs at a rerun of Arthur's failed stand-up set, Joker channels his humiliation into his careful, buckled dance. Announced, he shimmies out the curtain, flicks away his smoke, then pirouettes across the set like Fred Astaire, accepting the delight of the crowd. He shakes hands with Murray. He plants an unsolicited kiss on Dr. Sally's face. This is his moment. Everything is as he imagined it: the lights, the cameras, the applauding crowd. But things take a turn. The jokes bomb and Joker gets defensive. "I'm not political," he tells Murray Franklin, when asked if his clown makeup is a "political statement." When he admits he killed the three stockbrokers, Murray presses the point: "I think I might understand it: you did this to start a movement, to become a symbol?" Joker responds coyly, but honestly: "Come on Murray, do I look like the kind of clown that could start a movement?" (1:37:44–1:42:53)*

This is a fair question. All film long Arthur demonstrates no understanding of government; he is not motivated by any program for how society's laws, economy, or institutions could be shaped differently to provide a better future. His personal grievance intersects political grievance at axes of accident, convenience, or self-interest. When he encounters a political protest by demonstrators in clown masks, he doesn't join or seek to lead it, but rather uses it as cover to sneak into the cinema to confront his father (a scene we discuss in Chapter Eleven below). Similarly, on *Live! With Murray Franklin*, Arthur rages at Wayne. Wayne runs for mayor, employs the stockbrokers, and has become the target of political resistance. This confirms to Murray that Arthur is an activist. But for Arthur, the constellation is personal. True, Arthur talks about the "system that knows so much," that decides "what's right or wrong" (1:42:27). But his theory of political conspiracy mostly allows him to allocate blame for why no one laughs at his bad jokes: "you decide what's funny or not." Even his punk warning *we're not going to take it!* is coded in psychoanalytic language, no longer wanting to be "good little boys." This is classic Oedipus: fathers and their rebellious sons. He defends violence in terms that, by definition, are pre-political: to "werewolf and go wild" (1:44:03).

Despite this, shortly after, in one of *Joker's* most visually striking images, Arthur is symbolically born as the acknowledged legislator and symbol of a political movement. In a gothic cesarean, he is lifted gently from the womb of a police car, placed on the cruiser hood, where he gasps his first breath as a cough of blood and rises to the crowd's adulation (1:50:14–1:51:09). Here, Phillips deliberately conflates Joker with his Marvel counterparts. He reenacts the scene, "Careful, he's a hero," from *Spiderman 2* (2004).[1] But in Phillips's version, we are witnessing the coronation of a clown. How does a clown become the figurehead of a political movement?

One answer is that Arthur publicly embraces conspiracy theory. He does so to legitimize his personal desire for revenge with public appeal. Conspiracy theory embraces him because he convincingly expresses systemic grievance and, more importantly, his dramatic killings of the stockbrokers simplify structural contradictions into violent targets for blame. Arthur is convincing because those who have humiliated him are also public figures: Murray and Wayne. On the talk show, Arthur first critiques

---

1   *Spiderman 2*, directed by Sam Raimi (Columbia Pictures and Marvel Enterprises, 2004).

the system: the system decides what violence is legitimate, whose lives matter and don't: "if it was me dying on the sidewalk you'd walk right over me" (1:43:21). But then he narrows his target. "You're awful Murray" (1:44:18). He first blames systemic neglect: "nobody thinks what it's like to be the other guy" (1:43:46). He then narrows it to Wayne: "you think men like Thomas Wayne ever think what it's like to be someone like me?" (1:43:50). For Arthur, who is wounded by Wayne and Murray, his lament is mere individual psychology. For those who will later take to the streets, however, Arthur's conviction validates conspiracy thinking, and cultivates legitimacy for violence against supposed conspirators. Conspiracy thinking is what catalyzes rioters, who burn down parts of the city. And Arthur's own narrative is echoed by the man who murders not just Wayne but also Wayne's wife: "you get what you fucking deserve" (1:49:51).

Conspiracy theory has a natural place in superhero films because conspiracy narratives make good melodramas. Melodramas, remember, are morally Manichean, eliciting sympathy for victims and feelings of ill-will against evildoers, to steer our political sympathies. Melodramas compel us through style, not analysis. They express political feeling, not rational insight. In superhero melodramas, social problems are caused by a conspiracy of evil individuals, and justice is protected by heroes who operate boldly beyond the law. Yet *Joker* knows that melodrama and conspiracy theory are not just book or movie genres, but also types of political discourse. Wayne uses melodrama, for instance, to exploit the killing of the stockbrokers and elicit sympathy for his business and political career. As discussed in Chapter Five, their deaths allow him to advance the neoliberal ideology that those who do not succeed have only themselves to blame: they are clowns. As a political discourse, conspiracy theory also draws upon feeling, but it jams neoliberal melodrama's emotional currents and reverses the flow. It says there *are* systemic problems that explain victimhood. But it preserves melodrama's desire to identify specific evildoers, imagined as primal agents, as omnipotent, whether or not they actually exist. It is not just that there are systematic problems in law or economy, supported by ideologies held by certain groups; there are also individual agents of evil who conspire—breathe together, as the etymology has it. It points to the Waynes of finance, the Murrays of the media.

Joker also aligns formally with the flow reversal against Wayne's melodrama. The film prepares us to see conspiracy theory as the inversion of neoliberal melodramatic political discourse by taking *all* of the genres Arthur is caught up in—joke telling, late night skit, and tramp comedy—only to darken or invert them. On *Live! With Murray Franklin*, Arthur's knock-knock joke dead-ends into a policeman knocking at the door to explain to a mother that her son has been killed by a drunk driver. It is not funny. But it is clever: it collides the genre of knock-knock with realistic knocking whose traumatic revelation destroys the joke itself.

The film communicates how bad things are by inverting genres of movies too. The story of the stand-up comedian hoping to make it on a late-night show—Arthur's original fantasy—belongs to *The King of Comedy* (1982).[2] The upstart, played by Robert De Niro, wants to do a set on the late-night show of his idol, Jerry Langford. But with no break coming, he resorts to kidnapping Langford and goes on his show, to comic success. His crime lands him in prison, but the stunt makes him famous. After serving time, he reappears to a book contract and a late-night show of his own. De Niro's success at the end of *The King of Comedy* is Scorsese's joke that the kind of individual demanded in an era marked jointly by neoliberalism and monopoly capitalism must be both exceptional *and* criminal to compete. When Arthur shoots De Niro in the head (01:45:12), he puts an end to this joke too.

---

2   *The King of Comedy*, directed by Martin Scorsese (20th Century Fox, 1982).

The last inversion is *Modern Times* (1936), a Charlie Chaplin film which famously concludes with a tramp wiping a smile with his fingers on his face to remind his girl to cheer up.[3] They are unemployed, chased by the law—but look on the bright side, Chaplin's smile says, before they walk to the distance, hand-in-hand; we can persevere with humor. Standing on the hood of the police car, Arthur wipes a smile on his face. But it is from his own blooded lip which coats his teeth grotesquely. The scene pays homage to Jack Nicholson in *Batman* (1989), who claims he has died and been reborn as Joker, as well as to Heath Ledger in *The Dark Knight* (2008), who explains his wound-smile, cut into his face by an abusive father: "why so serious[?]" (30:58).[4] But here, at the end of *Joker*, Phoenix's blooded smile supplants Chaplin's, and shows that chin-up humor after violence is just bloody make-up. Todd Phillips empties clown films, make-it comedian films, and even jokes. For some people, there is so little to laugh at anymore that the impulse to joke itself becomes the joke. This is the tragedy that makes Arthur laugh. His laugh signals not only the birth of the cruel anti-hero, but the insight of the anti-genre.

I think the guy who did it is a hero

So how are we to understand conspiracy theory: as legitimate critique of the system, as cover story for the wounded subject, or as perversion of melodramatic genre? *Joker* combines all three explanations. What's more, the movie implies that conspiracy theory is initially the expression of the apolitical and disgruntled, who fumble for a narrative to explain their unfreedom. But with enough TV time, shock, and charisma, these genres drawn from fiction can give a political movement narrative shape. This puts conspiracy theory in a dangerous position: of both truth telling and fraudulence, of resisting government melodrama while being susceptible to fascist scapegoating.

---

3   *Modern Times*, directed by Charlie Chaplin (United Artists, 1936).

4   *Batman*, directed by Tim Burton (Warner Bros, 1989).

Melodrama and conspiracy theory are among the founding political genres of democracy, employed to manage the revolutionary violence needed to create democratic states and to allocate blame for that violence in a way that quells it. Superheroes appear in even the most rational political philosophy because they can regulate blame. The philosophical text most central to the theorization of the ideal modern democracy is probably Jean-Jacques Rousseau's *Social Contract* (1762). Rousseau is an early advocate for direct democracy based on a social contract. Contract theory purports to reject hereditary privileges and the divine right of kings. Instead, it grounds the legitimacy of government in rational choice. Everyone agrees to give up some rights to the community in exchange for a stable, well-governed society: that's the social contract.

For Rousseau, democracy presents a catch-22: a new democratic government will give people the civic skills they lack so they can govern without arbitrary, illegitimate, and coercive rule. But a people without civic skills cannot fashion a new government to begin with. Rousseau leaps this impasse with a superhero. He calls him "the legislator." Here is someone not from the people, but who cares deeply about their success. He is someone who gives the gift of the law, but will not have any command in the new Republic. The legislator is "an individual and superior function" that has no power, no command over men, or else his laws would be biased: would be "ministers of his passions" or "serve to perpetuate his injustices." Without worldly power over others, all the legislator has to recommend him is genius and wisdom. No, that's not all. He also has snap and style: "unable to appeal to either force or reason, [the legislator] must have recourse to an authority of a different order, capable of constraining without violence and persuading without convincing."[5] Rousseau describes this style as religion, not because the legislator is

5   Jean-Jacques Rousseau, *On the Social Contract*, translated by G.D.H. Cole (Mineola: Dover Thrift Editions, [1762] 2003), 26, 27.

religious, but because in the eighteenth century, religion is the spandex and cape of wisdom. It's the only way to convince people without force or reason.

For Rousseau, religion is costume. Others can put on "idle tricks" and caped disguises:

> Any man may grave tablets of stone, or buy an oracle, or feign secret intercourse with some divinity, or train a bird to whisper in his ear, or find other vulgar ways of imposing on the people. He whose knowledge goes no further may perhaps gather round him a band of fools; but he will never found an empire, and his extravagances will quickly perish with him.[6]

Not so our caped legislator. He is a wise loner with a genius for justice. He is, we might fancy, Batman.

"There is surely something too neat about this script," says Bonnie Honig about Rousseau's legislator.[7] Steven Johnston agrees: "it is too neat in that it denies the violence, thus the tragedy, it enacts."[8] What they mean is that when a new political system is formed, it often requires revolutionary violence. This superhero melodrama neatly covers up the messy violence of a political revolution. It also infantilizes the populace. The people are cast as unable to devise their own laws, undermining the logic and purpose of "social contract." Honig suggests that maybe Rousseau's infantilization is not descriptive of what happens, but proscriptive of how democracies should narrate their founding. Maybe Rousseau urges us to tell this story for its benefits, even if it is untrue. Melodrama offers a

---

6   Rousseau, *Social Contract*, 28.

7   Bonnie Honig, *Democracy and the Foreigner* (Princeton: Princeton University Press, 2001), 23.

8   Steven Johnston, *American Dionysia: Violence, Tragedy, and Democratic Politics* (Cambridge: Cambridge University Press, 2015), 122.

simplified moral narrative of the good and wise prevailing over the way-ward and corrupt. It establishes governmental legitimacy and channels focus away from foundational violence. Law is secured by the virtuous hero. Since the hero can be symbolically banished afterward, society is allowed to preserve unity and transfigure the impulse to revenge by those who have experienced the uneven sacrifices demanded by revolution and a new constitution. With the legislator conveniently disappeared—Rousseau does not say whether he is ousted—Rousseau tacitly acknowl-edges that melodrama can be reworked to localize and dispel blame. The legislator is a foreigner, after all, not one of the people, so his disap-pearance is easy enough to accept. From its theoretical inception, then, Rousseau implies that democracy's foundational genre is not romance, as some have argued,[9] but melodrama. And the way to make sure the melo-drama is not questioned is to get rid of the superhero at the movie's end.

This is the story of Batman. At the end of *The Dark Knight* (2008), Batman convinces Commissioner Gordon to preserve district attorney Harvey Dent's image as a hero. He urges him to blame Dent's rampage of violence on Batman himself: "You either die a hero or you live long enough to see yourself become a villain" (2:22:02). As *The Dark Knight Rises* (2012) opens, we learn that, by sacrificially absorbing blame, Batman has allowed Gotham to keep their hero in Dent and to blame the violence on Batman, even though, like the legislator, Batman is both hero and out-cast. Batman retreats from public life completely. Doing so establishes peace in Gotham. Even his butler Alfred knows the plot: "I never wanted you to come back to Gotham. I always knew there was nothing here for you except pain and tragedy" (17:34). Superhero stories replay the founda-tional story of the violence required to establish democracy; melodrama and superheroes take the blame for violence that new laws effect. In this way they establish the legitimacy of the new state. Melodrama secures

---

9   See Honig, *Democracy*, 109.

the myth that the unbiased legislator has provisioned a state for equality, not to advance a conspiracy of interests by those who fashioned the laws.

You people, the system

But conspiracy theory calls bullshit. Are you really so stupid that you do not see that you are being duped? A foreign philosopher who speaks to birds? What kind of a children's story is this? Next you'll believe that munchkins are liberated by a girl's house that lands from the sky. Or that a man communes with bats. Conspiracy theory unmasks interests. It says that the powerful hatch melodramatic scripts to conceal abuse and accrue power. The first language of conspiracy theory is affront. For the conspiracy theorist, common purpose is sentimental. It disbelieves before it believes. Conspiracy theory is the brother of melodrama. It is *Batman*'s Joker.

Conspiracies proliferate because melodrama persists as the main governmental mode of transfiguring violence. After the terror attacks of 9/11, Elisabeth Anker argues, the US government scripted the global war on terror through the melodrama of good and evil:

What I call *melodramatic political discourse* casts politics, policies, and practices of citizenship within a moral economy that identifies the nation-state as a virtuous and innocent victim of villainous action.

This script fostered "*felt legitimacy*" for the invasions of Afghanistan and Iraq.[10] Rousseau knows this resource too: the legislator's legacy can be gauged by whether the government can "found an empire."[11] That is, he suggests that melodrama can manage the theoretical conflict between a

---

10   Elisabeth R. Anker, *Orgies of Feeling: Melodrama and the Politics of Freedom* (Durham: Duke University Press, 2014), 2, 27.
11   Rousseau, *Social Contract*, 28.

democracy, premised on equality, and an empire, which, in most forms, explicitly rejects equal political participation.

Empire is another site of tragic violence that democracies hope to dispel through melodrama. Conspiracy theories provide the means to block such emotional manipulation. They rewrite the scripts. 9/11 is a good example because it spawned popular conspiracy theories that the US government either permitted or fabricated the attacks against Americans to achieve long-held objectives by neoconservatives in power, such as regime change in Iraq. Though these claims were proven false, conspiracy theories, like melodrama, are not truth-dependent. Instead, they function to block the state's melodramatic strategies of felt-legitimacy, a symbiosis integral to their power.

Conspiracy theories also proliferate because they are ideologically free-floating. Frank Mintz, who coined the term "conspiracism," argues that it does not "typify a particular epoch or ideology." Rather, it "identifies elites, blames them for economic and social catastrophes, and assumes that things will be better once popular action can remove them from positions of power."[12] Conspiracism also proliferates, as Kathryn Olmsted argues, because there *was* genuine government overreach and secrecy during the Cold War. The US government spied on dissenters. There was Watergate, an actual conspiracy of the Nixon administration to cover up the crime of breaking into Democratic National Committee Headquarters. There was the Tuskegee Syphilis Study, conducted by the Centers for Disease Control and Prevention (CDC) and the United States Public Health Service (PHS), which studied Black men with syphilis to monitor its effects, even as the government refused to provide the men treatment when it was available for more than thirty years into the study. There was MKULTRA, a CIA-funded program to develop chemical mind

---

12   Frank P. Mintz, *The Liberty Lobby and the American Right: Race, Conspiracy, and Culture* (Westport: Greenwood, 1985), 199.

control, and other programs besides.[13] There are more recent government conspiracies, such as when members of the US government formulated a conspiracy theory that linked Saddam Hussein to the attacks in Washington and New York on September 11, 2001. And as we saw in Chapter Three, according to Adam Smith, there are inherent conspiracies among manufacturers to keep wages low.

If some conspiracy theories are true, others deny uncomfortable realities, evade contradictions, or avoid more obvious explanations. A paranoid aesthetic, conspiracism scapegoats malefactors: a sinister group of people controlling things from the center. This is Arthur's "system." Fredric Jameson calls conspiracy theorizing the "poor person's cognitive mapping."[14] He has in mind someone who holds fast to the ideology that working hard will get you ahead, who believes the creed of individual responsibility. But when their job is exported despite their hard work, this person, unable to mount a critique of the economic ideology they still believe in, externalizes the blame. The targets are easy and many: immigrants or Muslims, Black people or Jews. Fleck does not console his ego by scapegoating other groups. He careens between blaming himself or general behaviors—"Nobody is civil any more" (01:43:45)—and blaming figureheads, who are literal and symbolic father figures of the system that has rejected him. Conspiracy thinking makes it possible for him to point the gun away from his own head and instead point it outward at Murray. But without a rational critique of institutions, laws, or economic systems, Arthur's conspiracy offers only one mechanism of satisfaction: violence.

---

13 Kathryn S. Olmsted, *Real Enemies: Conspiracy Theories and American Democracy, World War I to 9/11* (Oxford: Oxford University Press, [2009] 2011), 8, 156–160, 186–187, 174–175.

14 Fredric Jameson, "Cognitive Mapping," in *Marxism and the Interpretation of Culture*, edited by Cary Nelson and Lawrence Grossberg (Champaign: University of Illinois Press, 1988), 356.

We are all clowns

If Rousseau is correct—that the superhero legislator is the narrative device that best manages the founding of a new constitution—then melodrama and conspiracy persist culturally as dominant modes to contend with systemic violence. Slavoj Žižek distinguishes *systemic* violence from *subjective* violence. Systemic violence is "the violence inherent in a system"; the daily, background violence of institutions functioning normally. It is the "often catastrophic consequences of the smooth functioning of our economic and political systems,"[15] such as offshore tax havens, unrestricted campaign funding, selective overpolicing, and so on. Subjective violence is the disruptive, conspicuous violence of actors outside or opposing the dominant system—street protest, for instance, or the sacking of the US Capitol. When Fleck shoots the "Wall Street guys," this is read by his followers as a subjective assault on the allegorical embodiment of the systemic violence of finance capitalism.

Theoretically, democracies aim to prevent subjective violence by encouraging civic involvement—ballasted by an independent judiciary and electoral participation—and by an education system that fosters "habits of mind which secure social changes without introducing disorder."[16] Yet in the United States, at least, each of the pillars of civic participation—what Sheldon Wolin calls the "constitutional imaginary"—have been under attack.[17] The judiciary is politicized; pervasive gerrymandering sustains minority rule; corporations write laws and fund campaigns; and the systematic privatization, vocationalizing, and defunding of

---

15   Slavoj Žižek, *Violence* (London: Picador, 2008), 1.

16   John Dewey, *Democracy and Education: An Introduction to the Philosophy of Education* (New York: The Free Press, [1916] 1944), 99.

17   Sheldon S. Wolin, *Democracy Incorporated: Managed Democracy and the Specter of Inverted Totalitarianism* (Princeton: Princeton University Press, 2008), 19.

education erode it as a public good. The combined effect is to demobilize the public, creating widespread voter apathy and disaffection.

What's more, according to Wolin, the "constitutional imaginary" has been crashed into by an opposing force in modern societies: the "power imaginary." The power imaginary is an expansive force. Hobbes—a philosophical favorite among neocons—had envisioned a dynamic rooted in human nature and driven by a "restless" quest for "power after power" that "ceaseth only in death."[18] For individuals, this power quest dies with them. For societies, the quest takes political form. Hobbes developed a constitutional imaginary that could enfold an expansive political imaginary. But that constitutional imaginary by nature has to be anti-democratic. Here is Wolin:

> The individual members of society, driven by fear and insecu-
> rity, agree to be ruled by an absolute sovereign or chief executive
> in exchange for assurances of protection and domestic peace.
> He becomes the custodian of the power imaginary, "the great
> Leviathan," as well as the final interpreter of the constitutional
> imaginary.[19]

By increasing fear and insecurity in the populace, governments can transform the constitutional imaginary to admit this Hobbesian power imaginary. Practically, this means expanded military and surveillance power, imperial adventure, and curtailed democratic rights.

Wolin is also aware of the imaginative dimension. "Fear and insecurity" in this period were driven by the narrative of terrorism: terrorism presented as a ghoulish, decontextualized specter of evil that threatens daily life. The United States then styled *itself* as a "superpower," a

---

18   Thomas Hobbes, *Leviathan*, edited by Richard Tuck (Cambridge: Cambridge University Press, [1651] 1996), 70.

19   Wolin, *Democracy Incorporated*, 19.

superhero, to justify an illegitimate war, indefinite detention, mass surveillance, and assassinations. To accrue Hobbesian power within the state requires such mythmaking: "a perverse strategy that thrives on chaos." The consequence is "the blurring of the lines separating reality from fancy and truth telling from self-deception and lying."[20] Empire and myth compensate for insecurity. Wolin calls this transformation of the constitutional imaginary into a Hobbesian form "inverted totalitarianism." It is inverted because, in practice, no charismatic or otherwise awe-inspiring leader is required any more: President George W. Bush was no great Leviathan.

Wolin's account needs to be updated in three ways. First, Wolin, along with other theorists influenced by him, ignores how conspiracism functions as a counterimaginary to state mythology. Wolin is correct that myth, or what might be more precisely called melodrama, enabled—first during the Cold War and then after the attacks in September 2001—an enormous US military build-up globally, at the cost of supporting higher standards of living at home. But myth also spurs conspiracy theories that block melodrama's emotional impact. That blocking confronts state melodrama with indiscriminate mistrust, a critique of the systemic violence wrought by empire as well as by inequality. We will return to this theme in the next chapter.

Second, conspiracism attempts to represent "inverted totalitarianism" by recasting Hobbes's dictator as back-room decision makers with exaggerated capacities and agency: "the government," pedophile democrats, and so on. Conspiracism, that is, functions as a demotic political imaginary, which, like state melodrama, breaks the individual free from their function as citizen. Conspiracism depoliticizes. Conspiracy theory *poses* as critical theory. It *looks* like critical thinking. But it isn't. Wolin argues that education has become positivist: data driven and narrowly

---

20   Wolin, *Democracy Incorporated*, 14, 11, 20.

rational, but without the capacity to evaluate the direction of society as a whole. Conspiracy theory rejects positivism. It appeals to the intelligence of those who know, through feeling, that surface reality has another meaning behind it.[21] But conspiracy theory is pseudo-theory and lacks the analytical resources that might activate citizenship or reimagine democratic constitutionality.

Third, a new political imaginary has emerged in the years since Wolin wrote his last book. Because President Donald Trump largely eschewed military interventionism abroad, and therefore no longer required imperial melodrama to the same extent, he could afford to fully empower conspiracy grievance as a political force at home. Normally, conspiracy theory provides a melancholic critique of government: it channels mistrust and grousing and generates a sense of individual (but *only* individual) agency, without much political effect. Trump's geopolitical isolationism allowed him to cast aside the mythology of American goodness and righteous empire, and to legitimize those conspiracy theories—such as QAnon—which oppose that mythology. The millions of Americans who long employed conspiracism to navigate mistrust of US propaganda, economic change, and patriotic anti-war sentiments, suddenly found their views validated at the highest level of the state. By abandoning empire rhetorically, while keeping military expenditures high, Trump repoliticized conspiracy and made available a new mode of fascist politics.

Further reading

Mahmood Mamdani, *Good Muslim, Bad Muslim: America, the Cold War, and the Roots of Terror* (New York: Doubleday, 2004).

---

21 Jacques Rancière, "The Fools and the Wise," versobooks.com, January 21, 2021, np.

Sheldon S. Wolin, *Democracy Incorporated: Managed Democracy and the Specter of Inverted Totalitarianism* (Princeton: Princeton University Press, 2008).

Elisabeth R. Anker, *Orgies of Feeling: Melodrama and the Politics of Freedom* (Durham: Duke University Press, 2014).

Luc Boltanski, *Mysteries and Conspiracies: Detective Stories, Spy Novels and the Making of Modern Societies* (Cambridge: Polity Press, 2014).

Michael Mark Cohen, *The Conspiracy of Capital: Law, Violence, and American Popular Radicalism in the Age of Monopoly* (Amherst: University of Massachusetts Press, 2019).

Chapter Ten

Punching Out

On Violence

After a colleague, Randall, gives him a gun, the weapon slips out Arthur's pocket while he's entertaining children in hospital. Fired from his job as a result, Arthur is back at Ha-Ha's agency to collect his gear. The clowns ready their faces for work, as the song My Name is Carnival *plays from the radio. Gary says he's sorry Arthur got fired. Another clown is mystified that Arthur brought a gun to a children's ward. A third enquires mockingly whether the gun is now part of Arthur's act: if the dancing doesn't work, he can shoot himself. Walking away, Arthur turns brightly: "Why don't you ask Randall about it. It was his gun . . . I still owe you for that, don't I?" Randall protests that Arthur is talking "out his ass" to which Arthur responds by honking a horn, then leaving. "Oh No! I forgot to punch out!" He reappears and violently punches the punch-out clock until it collapses from the wall. Skipping downstairs, he stops to graffiti the sign: "Don't* forget to *Smile." The anthem becomes louder: "King of all, hear me call, hear my name: Carnival." (37:04–38:03)*

Joker resurrects the spirit of carnival, and this scene crowns Arthur carnival King. We all know something of carnival from New Orleans Mardi Gras, Rio samba floats, or Venetian masquerade. Cities cede the streets to dancing, to joyful boozing, to breasts bared and beaded, to parades where regular people float as motley royalty. Carnival derives from old medieval traditions, older still, and often lasted for months (from after Christmas to Lent). In its original form, it was a period when a second world appeared alongside the first, to mock and oppose it. It was a world of uninhibited jokes and laughter, a world in which all the hierarchies of power, privilege, and prohibition are leveled and inverted, when the poor confront the rich and scoff, when authority and reason see the anarchy and madness bubbling beneath, when societal norms are suspended. In carnival, the needs of the sensual body trump the seriousness of the rational mind. People "talk out of their ass"—honk! And clowns, dwarves (Gary), and giants (Randall) reign supreme and anoint their king. In this period of feasting and revelry, festival becomes "the second life of the people, who for a time entered the utopian realm of community, freedom, equality, and abundance."[1] It is a utopia because people are free to behave without discretion, food and drink abound, and those in power must confront laughter that says they hold their positions by chance. They should be more humane. Someone else could take their place.

Arthur's clown name is Carnival, but his firing does not strip him of this title. Rather, it ushers in his reign as king. Arthur works as a clown all year long, but *Joker* begins the season of carnival. In the medieval period, too, clowns preserved carnival spirit outside of carnival time. The most famous philosopher of carnival, Mikhail Bakhtin, says that clowns were not actors, or dolts, or eccentrics. Instead, they represented a form of life which was "real and ideal at the same time. They stood on the borderline between life and art, in a peculiar midzone." Punching the punch-out clock inaugurates this new double-time in the film. This physical joke, which retaliates against the punch clock in kind, shows carnival taking revenge against time in the regular world, regulated by employers and jobs. With time suspended, Arthur's delirium ushers us further into carnival's "two-world condition."[2] In carnival, a loner living with his mother

---

1   Mikhail Bakhtin, *Rabelais and His World*, translated by Helene Iswolski (Bloomington: Indiana University Press, [1965] 2009), 9.

2   Bakhtin, *Rabelais*, 8, 6.

is equal to an attractive neighbor. A man beaten up at work by some kids can raise the streets in a manic riot against hierarchy. An unemployed gig worker measures up before the richest man in the city—indeed, claims himself his son.

Carnival finds joyful liberation in laughter, revealing laughter's "indissoluble and essential relation to freedom." Carnival laughter, like Arthur's laugh in *Joker*, is not the laughter we all know when we laugh *at* something or someone and feel superior to it. It is not an individual reaction to some isolated "comic" event. Carnival laughter is aimed at the entire social structure in which we *all* live. It is the laughter of the people. It even targets those doing the laughing. This laughter is Arthur's disability— which most people fail to understand—just as they misunderstand the universal equality upon which it is based. He tries to choke it back, so as not to be misunderstood. The stockbrokers on the train think he is laughing *at them*, rather than a social order that has turned gender relations into male entitlement. It is Arthur's laughter on the bus where, because the world is so dysfunctionally racist, a white man making a Black child laugh appears to their mother as a nuisance or threat (07:54–08:22). Carnival laughter mocks the social categories that lump people into hierarchy, class, race, and gender, long before we see them as individual humans. Arthur is the emissary of this laughter. Carnival "laughter is ambivalent: it is gay, triumphant, and at the same time mocking, deriding. It asserts and denies, it buries and revives. Such is the laughter of carnival."[3] Here is the inscrutability of Arthur's laugh, a laugh that also laughs at laughing, and so chokes.

But *Joker* also suggests that carnival laughter and carnival logic are inadequate to the task of reinventing the world or even of humbling those in power in order to restore their humanity. So, Fleck turns, instead, to violence. When a Ha-Ha's clown asks Arthur if this is now part of his act—"if your dancing doesn't do the trick you just gonna shoot yourself?"

---

3   Bakhtin, *Rabelais*, 89, 89, 11–12.

(37:42)—he establishes classic carnival themes. During carnival, the carnival King symbolically dies—not, like medieval Jesus, so that everyone can live forever, but to remind us we all will die. And just as winter death renews the world for bounteous spring, so we are to be reminded that we too have a claim on goods and power in a renewed world, here and now. The King of carnival dances, as Arthur dances down the stairs, to contest social order, to subvert hierarchies, to escape the police. But this carnival King will not shoot himself. In Gotham, to do so would merely be Arthur Fleck committing suicide. Arthur does point the gun at his own head, considering it (1:23:56). But, on reflection, he decides to point the gun outward instead: he shoots the brokers, chokes Alfred, stabs Randall in the eyes, likely rapes Sophie, and certainly shoots Murray in the face on live TV, a broadcast which inspires the city to riot. Arthur transforms clowning under these demands—"*Don't* ~~forget to~~ *Smile.*" He keeps the medieval fool's transgression of normal boundaries: he talks back to the king (Wayne), confronts Murray, kisses Dr. Sally. But unlike the medieval fool, Arthur's joking turns to literal violence: punching the punch-out clock is only the beginning.

We know carnival laughter won't work for two reasons. First, in modern times, medieval logic—that people hold their station in life largely by chance—has been usurped by the modern ideology of meritocracy—that you have earned your place. Wayne is meritocracy's chief exponent in *Joker*, but Murray Franklin also advocates this view. When Wayne is invited on TV to explain the murders, he labels the poor as "clowns": here he is the voice of "you get what you deserve." In response, Gothamites protest his ideology that blames the poor for their inequality. But even after clown protests, Wayne continues to mock the clowns ("there's something wrong with those people") and announces he is their "only hope" (1:02:10). Murray Franklin, secure in his individual merit, also refuses to be humbled. He ridicules Arthur's performance on TV. It offers evidence that Franklin is the late-night comic because he's better at it, deserves it: "In a world where everyone thinks they can do my job" (59:40).

The other reason carnival logic is less effective is because modern governments based on popular will don't rely on carnival to prod social justice. Instead, modern democracy theoretically grants everyone a chance to share in the formation of political power so as to address social ills: rather than laughing at those in office to humble them, you can run a different candidate or run for office yourself. If inherited wealth is producing an aristocracy, or capital accumulation an oligarchy, we can dwindle the rich with taxes, as the United States did after World War II.[4] If Arthur has his medical benefits cut, he can vote for those who will restore them. But what if the gears of democracy themselves are jammed and the prospect of checking an economic system has become impossible? What if election, the modern form by which the people find representation and hold politicians to account, has been subverted by the interests of the wealthy donor class who can afford to fund them? And what if the modern way to root out corruption—a free media—has also been captured by monied interests? Does the threat of violence, as Steven Johnston argues, have a part to play in preserving the common good in democracies? "Violence is endemic to democracy," says Johnston, but "what happens when official institutions of accountability fail to perform, when they fail to hold those responsible to account? Does democracy rely on its citizens to take matters into their own hands, including using violence, when the state disappears?"[5]

In this chapter we seek to answer that provocative question. To do so, we will reflect on how democracies, even when functioning smoothly,

---

4   Thomas Piketty, *Capital in the Twenty-First Century*, translated by Arthur Goldhammer (Cambridge, MA: Belknap of Harvard University Press, 2014), 493–499.

5   Steven Johnston, *American Dionysia: Violence, Tragedy, and Democratic Politics* (Cambridge: Cambridge University Press, 2015), 172.

inflict violence. When Johnston writes that the "state disappears," he has in mind how, when the market is given free reign, it rewards "winners" and punishes "losers." But, as we saw in earlier chapters, the state often piles on, advocating sadofiscalism for those already punished, and it gloves the invisible hand of the market in the iron fist of the carceral and police state. Fleck is not just disciplined for his lack of talent in comedy; he's punched in the mouth by the richest man in Gotham and humiliated on national TV. When the market and the state become sadistic, should citizens take matters into their own hands? Does the threat of violence help renew capitalist democratic systems that have ceased to work? Is the threat of violence a necessary catalyst to repairing social dysfunction and inequality, necessary to preventing actual violence?

Or is violence always to be rejected because violence outside of the law is unpredictable? The stakes are high, not least because the state, which has a near monopoly on the use of violence, legitimizes its own violence against anyone else who employs it. What's more, not everyone who threatens violence cares about the common good. Rampant misinformation, conspiracy theories, racist resentment, ethnonationalism—these also furnish ideals for those who risk violence to improve things: storming the capitol to "save democracy," hammering the head of Nancy Pelosi's husband in an imaginary attack on "the system," or raging into a DC pizza parlor armed to the teeth in search of a non-existent pedophile ring. Our superheroes are a bit crazy.

Some people get their kicks stomping on a dream

When Arthur spurns carnival comedy for carnival violence on TV, shooting Murray in the head, he does so because he's upset about everyday violence. Systemic violence, remember, is the name that Žižek gives to background violence that ensures the smooth running of a political economy. Think police violence; think debt traps; think the vast for-profit prison complex. Systemic violence is the material as well as ideological violence that holds the system in place, at the cost of occasional "outbursts" of more-or-less irrational, inarticulate, impulsive resistance. These rage incidents, in Žižek's formula, express systemic violence in its "inverted true form."[6] Žižek worries that when we take a moral stance against all violence—"from direct physical violence (mass murder, terror) to ideological violence (racism, incitement, sexual discrimination)"—we tend to drown out analysis of systemic violence and thus actively participate in it.[7]

Arthur comes to this same realization. When Murray asks Arthur to tell a joke, Arthur lingers over a journal entry that exemplifies his own encounter with systemic violence, unrecognized and preventable, an entry recounting when Arthur witnessed paramedics called out to check on a dead homeless man (1:40:20). Moved by the man, Arthur worries for himself:

Can you imagine that??? dead on the sidewalk with peeple steppig over you. Maybe he's happier but I don't want to die with peepl just stepping over me. I want people to see me.

(06:22)

Though himself upset, Arthur's journal transforms this moving encounter into one of his bad stand-up jokes. The joke works by first imagining himself in the plight of a homeless man, to then adopting the voice of reason that blames the homeless themselves, in effect washing the audience's hands of responsibility:

What? We're supposed to take care of every drunk who can't hold a job??? Its about time we start getting realistic about what we're doing here people.

(1:40:20)

---

6   Slavoj Žižek, *Violence* (London: Picador, 2008), 10.
7   Žižek, *Violence*, 9.

It's not a good joke. On *Live! With Murray Franklin*, Arthur stares at this joke as a sonorous bass saws over the scene, indicating his dark realization: "Take your time. We've got all night" (1:40:27). Arthur apparently no longer agrees with this joke's approach. Instead, as an unemployed Joker, he casts himself the emissary of such homeless men, of the excluded and unnoticed:

> If it was me dying on the sidewalk, you'd walk right over me. I pass you every day and you don't notice me. But these guys [the stockbrokers], what because Thomas Wayne went and cried about them on TV?
>
> (1:43:18–1:43:29)

Arthur feels disposable. He allies himself with those who experience neglectful violence, sustained by the moralizing rhetoric of meritocracy and enabled by the media's selective attention to violent outbursts. The question asked, in Arthur's melodramatic and unsophisticated way, is whether killing by slow and impersonal violence deserves any less attention than violent crimes?

Of course, Arthur is not the best spokesman for this analysis. He embraces private violent revenge, which even Arthur knows is the outcome of crossing "a mentally ill loner with a society that abandons him and treats him like trash" (1:45:08). In this scene, he attacks the media with the only form of violence the media's attention economy appears to care about: an outburst of crime. "You get what you fucking deserve," he says, like a good meritocrat. Despite the outrageous spectacle and outburst of vendetta murder, *Joker* still asks whether the regular running of neoliberal capitalism also kills people. And why, if we care so much about eliminating violence, do we not examine this lethal violence of the system?

Arthur's intuition—that neoliberal capitalism kills—should not shock our sensibilities. The claim falls in line with how even Pope Francis, the head of the Catholic Church, straightforwardly describes our modern neoliberal economy:

> Just as the commandment "Thou shalt not kill" sets a clear limit in order to safeguard the value of human life, today we also have to say "thou shalt not" to an economy of exclusion and inequality. Such an economy kills.[8]

The Pope has in mind victims similar to those Arthur Fleck notices and identifies with:

> How can it be that it is not a news item when an elderly homeless person dies of exposure, but it is news when the stock market loses two points? This is a case of exclusion ... [T]hose excluded are no longer society's underside or its fringes or its disenfranchised—they are no longer even a part of it. The excluded are not the "exploited" but the outcast, the "leftovers."

Modern political theorists also agree with the Pope's view of what happens to leftovers. Johnston puts it this way:

> The effects that neoliberal capitalism produces take time to unfold and enjoy a certain effective invisibility. Not that neoliberalism doesn't kill. It kills slowly, often imperceptibly—and legally. Impoverishment, including forced homelessness, lack of nutrition, and limited access to medical care, shortens individual life spans and increases infant mortality rates. In times of economic crisis, suicide rates surge.[9]

---

8   Pope Francis, "Apostolic Exhortation Evangelii Gaudium of the Holy Father Francis to the Bishops, Clergy, Consecrated Persons and the Lay Faithful on the Proclamation of the Gospel in Today's World," vatican.va, November 24, 2013, 53.

9   Johnston, *American Dionysia*, 171.

It is true that the deathly effects are noticeable everywhere particularly after a recession. In Europe from 2007–2009, suicide rates shot up by twenty percent.[10] Gotham is moving into recession too, and Arthur fears his life drifting from disenfranchised or exploited to what the Pope calls leftovers or Arthur calls trash: healthcare access limited, suicide a possibility, and the street or prison a slip away.

We could argue that systemic violence is simply an exaggerated, regrettable byproduct of the cycles of boom-and-bust capitalism, with the bust leading to efficient reallocation of capital to companies that are better run, more profitable. But the decision to target a bust's violence downward to the poor and tilt the economic rescue upward to the wealthy is political. After the speculative property collapse of 2006–2008, for instance, many bondholders were not asked to accept their losses, as meritocratic capitalism would demand. Instead, their debt and risk were socialized. Entire national populations were compelled to accept fiscal austerity so that international bondholders could be made whole. According to the political economist William Davies, this transfer of blame after the Great Recession marks a new phase of neoliberalism, organized around an ethos of punishment:

> Under punitive neoliberalism, economic dependency and moral failure become entangled in the form of debt, producing a melancholic condition in which governments and societies unleash hatred and violence upon members of their own populations. When debt is combined with political weakness, it becomes a condition for further punishment.[11]

---

10   David Stuckler and Sanjay Basu, *The Body Economic: Why Austerity Kills* (New York: HarperCollins, 2014), 86.

11   William Davies, "The New Neoliberalism," *New Left Review* 101 (2016): 130.

The EU was more punishing than the United States, where fiscal stimulus, though restricted, was still doled out in tax breaks and other forms. In the US, moreover, when a state such as Florida or Nevada's economy is decimated from a bursting property bubble, federal wealth transfers—Medicare, Veterans benefits, Social Security—automatically continue to flow. Built into the structure, these are mostly beyond political debate. Europe, united by a currency and market, lacks a federal government and automatic transfer system. After Greek, Irish, and Spanish property bubbles burst, the citizens of those countries shouldered capital collapse entirely by themselves. Locked in the euro, they couldn't even find relief by devaluing their currencies. Bad property debts for investors became austerity for the masses. Systemic violence follows. In the three years after 2006–2008, Greece witnessed a 40 percent rise in infant mortality and a 47 percent rise in unmet healthcare needs. Disability and welfare support rules were rewritten to disqualify people. James Galbraith called austerity for the Greeks a form of "collective punishment."[12] Yanis Varoufakis called it "fiscal waterboarding."[13] Neoliberal policies, then, do not simply punish so-called losers; they create scapegoats.

Arthur feels humiliated by the threat of becoming such a scapegoat. Initially he interprets his experience not as sadism but as neglect: that he lacks basic *recognition* on the street and that he has been *abandoned* by society. But the truth is that Arthur has been recognized by his employer—to fire him; and recognized by the state—to cut his benefits; and recognized by the media—to bring him on TV and mock him. "You just wanted to make fun of me" (1:44:33), he tells Murray. Arthur is learning that neoliberalism is not just a market mechanism that asks customers to politely leave the bar at closing time; they are also kicked to the street. True, neoliberalism finds vulnerability wherever it lies;

---

12   Stuckler and Basu, *Body Economic,* 90–91, 93.
13   Davies, "New Neoliberalism," 122.

in the US, for example, overall life expectancy has actually reversed in the neoliberal era, led by those without college degrees, an astonishing fact after a century of progress.[14] But we don't have to wait until recent times to witness a punitive liberalism that targets "violence and hatred" toward its own populations, as Davies argues. Sadofiscalism was part of Reaganomics and Thatcherism from the beginning, as we saw in Chapter Three. Moreover, in the US, racism has long been a principle of selection for sacrificial victimhood. Police brutality is one obvious example. So is the contemporary self-wounding by Southern states that reject federal funding for expanded healthcare, despite the cost in economic activity, in closed hospitals, and in lives.[15] And *Joker* knows an older sacrificial victimhood that founded the very conditions for US capitalism: after Joker shoots Murray and grabs the camera to deliver a signature sign off, the TV cuts him off with the black-and-white still, which includes a Native American head in profile.

Arthur's outburst dramatizes how humiliation and self-blame transform when the story of merit, which replaced the humility of chance, is unveiled as raw class power. When that happens, *Joker* warns, humiliation and melancholy curdle into rage. According to Adam Phillips, humiliation confronts us—at a personal and political level—where justice lacks resources: where we lack the means to do what's right.[16] Arthur's violent outburst owes to his personal humiliation. He idealizes a comedy career and seeks a father who loves him—Murray and Wayne. But both see him as a failure. Humiliation is exacerbated because Wayne clearly

---

14 Robert H. Shmerling, "Why Life Expectancy in the US Is Falling," health.harvard.edu, October 20, 2020, np.

15 Madeline Guth, Rachel Garfield, and Robin Rudowitz, "The Effects of Medicaid Expansion Under the ACA: Studies from January 2014 to January 2020," kff.org, March 17, 2020, np.

16 Adam Phillips, "Just Rage," in *The Beast in the Nursery: On Curiosity and Other Appetites* (New York: Vintage, 1998), 127.

has plenty of resources, and even if Arthur is not Wayne's son, Penny was surely his long-term employee. Humiliation operates similarly at the level of politics. It is naturally exacerbated in a recession, when personal and business resources dry up. If struggling people realize that government policy rescues the wealthy, while targeting austerity at the impotent, this psychological tinderbox can easily spark into rage.

Davies tells the first part of the story—where humiliation becomes a "melancholic condition." But the other half of the story recognizes that governments did come to the economic rescue after the Great Recession, albeit mainly with monetary stimulus. Central banks lowered official borrowing rates, then lowered them further by opening up floodgates of money to purchase and guarantee mortgage and other bond debts. Monetary stimulus rescues an economy by inflating assets. Those who already own assets—whether houses, stocks, bonds—become further enriched as values soar. Newer asset classes foam in the froth: crypto, NFTs, and so on. Just as the "have nots" are punished by an economic downturn, first by the market layoffs and again by government austerity, the "haves" see their wealth expand with monetary rescue. None of these outcomes—neither the punishments nor the rewards—has anything to do with merit, hard work, or even in many cases the efficient allocation of capital. It is simply class politics that doles out both stimulus and systemic violence based on the calculus of power.

Of course, *Joker* is only a movie. It keeps to carnival's *symbolic* level as spectacle: though Murray's brains are splattered on the wall behind him, Robert De Niro is not hurt in the making of the film. But it raises a pertinent question: is carnivalesque violence useful or viable as a corrective to the sadistic distribution of economic violence in modern economies? Or is such violence to be seen as unpredictable, irrational, and pathological? Rage might be a just response to certain types of humiliation, but raging violence, which restores some dignity to the humiliated ego, can as easily target a harmless neighbor whose crime is to be uninterested in a relationship, as a colleague who advocates self-protective violence, as a parent who rejects you, or a TV idol who mocks you.

You gotta protect yourself

To answer those questions, we should first remember that democracies and republics, in their own telling, do not reject violence, but aim instead to minimize it by transforming revenge into justice, or by creatively employing the political process to defuse mass discontent before it explodes. The reasons to contain revenge through a judicial process are clear enough: if you kill someone in revenge for a harm they have done you, someone in turn might take revenge by killing you, which in turn could lead to someone else killing on your behalf, and so on, into ruthless feuding. To put an end to this reflex, the ancient Greeks instituted a trial by a jury of peers with the presumption of innocence for the defendant. It may not fully quell a victim's fury (or the perpetrator's guilt), but it stops the vengeance cycle on society's behalf and weakens the urge to revenge violence.

Second, republics commit in theory to minimizing violence by being responsive to the people's needs before they erupt into riot, or what Niccolò Machiavelli calls "tumults." Nobody wants riot or mob justice by preference. It differs from deliberative justice. Deliberative justice stabilizes society, whereas riot threatens social disorder, can harm the very communities already feeling victimized, and can destabilize a society into civil war, inviting foreign powers to interfere. For these reasons, popular governments traditionally seek remedies to fend off such violence before it happens. What sparks the Roman plebs to "clamour against the senate," Machiavelli asks, or to run "helter-skelter about the streets," to "en masse ... troop out of Rome" in a general strike? This disorder occurs, Machiavelli says, when the Roman Republic denies civil rights. Republics always tend toward income inequality, and the populace is increasingly "oppressed" by the wealthy's insatiable "desire to dominate." The rich are the greatest threat to the viability of a republic. "[S]o great is the ambition of the great that unless in a city they are kept down by various ways and means, that city will soon be brought to ruin." Regular people might riot, but their violence tends to mend things, because they are "more keen on liberty." For Machiavelli, protests and riots in Rome that look "barbaric," actually preserved Roman freedoms because they led to political structures that allowed regular people to hold the rich and powerful accountable. Tribunates allowed any poor citizen to drag before the courts any rich person they suspected of corruption or crimes. Rome survived as long as it did because the upper class were checked by the threat of violence from the lower class.[17]

In this political tradition, then, the *threat* of violence by the people leads to political structures that ensure stability. This tradition has deep roots in the United States as well. Consider the infamous Boston Tea Party. As the US colonies chafed against arbitrary British rule, colonists decided that their protest should mobilize violence against property (tea to be taxed) but draw the line before violence against people (the tax collectors). In the early years of the United States, riot was common enough and goaded policy to prevent its occurrence, not police condemnation to suppress it. Closer to our own time, in 1963, MLK could advocate peaceful political change by threatening the alternative:

> If this [nonviolent] philosophy had not emerged, by now many
> streets of the South would, I am convinced, be flowing with
> blood. And I am further convinced that if our white brothers
> dismiss as "rabble rousers" and "outside agitators" those of

---

17 Niccolò Machiavelli, *The Discourses, vol. 1*, edited by W. Stark (New Haven: Yale University Press, [1531] 1950), 218, 219–220, 298, 220.

us who employ nonviolent direct action, and if they refuse to support our nonviolent efforts, millions of Negroes will, out of frustration and despair, seek solace and security in Black nationalist ideologies—a development that would inevitably lead to a frightening racial nightmare.[18]

The pacifist MLK might be more familiarly known for exposing protesters' bodies, including those of children, to ruthless state violence—dogs and batons—so as to make visible on national television the systemic violence that holds racist political and economic exclusion in place. But King also knows how to employ the threat of violence to mobilize improvements in democratic vitality. The frightening "racial nightmare" is MLK's *threat* of violence. The warning helps his pacifist cause to attain its political and economic aims. As Johnston has it:

[D]emocracy as a nonviolent way of life rests on a background of violence that must not be allowed to move to the foreground. Yet democracy must experience a kind of fear that violence might well erupt and explode in the face of systemic injustice and domination.[19]

John McCormick reads Machiavelli's Rome the same way. The mass citywide strikes, the riots—this threat of violence led to political structures that kept the rich in check.[20]

Joker nevertheless reminds us of the dangers and limits of violence as a solution. Most movements that license violence to achieve political goals, whether those goals be economic or social justice or

---

18   Martin Luther King, Jr., "Letter from Birmingham Jail," africa.upenn.edu, April 16, 1963, np.

19   Johnston, *American Dionysia*, 182.

20   John P. McCormick, *Machiavellian Democracy* (Cambridge: Cambridge University Press, 2011), 31–35.

the preservation of one-party rule by a coup that disrupts the peaceful transfer of power, operate from a sense of righteousness. But as we see in Chapter Nine, those ideals might easily be fashioned from conspiratorial lies that feel truthful but are false, or might be rooted in a just desire for power sharing and dignity that warps into an entitlement to supremacy and a willingness to use violence to defend it.

In the US, there is a crisis of resignation and despair, catalyzed by the complete capture of income and productivity gains by the wealthy over the last decades. Wolin writes that pessimism and despair ought to be understood as "suppressed revolutionary impulses." What's more, he argues that revolution might even be "politically and morally justified by democratic standards." Nevertheless, he finds it "neither possible nor prudent—if by revolution we mean launching a campaign of violent insurrection or civil war. Revolutions of that nature are plainly pathological under contemporary conditions of interdependency."[21] The protests in Gotham against inequality are morally justified by democratic standards. But the movie also cautions that Arthur's violence, which transforms political protests into violent riot and assassination, is also "pathological," as if aware that we'd be naive to think that American resignation and despair that expresses itself in tumult would advocate democratic renewal.

One reason to see violence as pathology is that the United States lacks a clear class politics, if we can put it this way, such as those that exist elsewhere, that even existed in Rome. Scholars have long known this: the United States has a non-class politics. Neither Democrats nor Republicans seek to mobilize the workers who vote for them against capital.[22] Instead, Republicans have capitalized on suppressed revolution-

---

21   Sheldon S. Wolin, "What Revolutionary Action Means Today," in *Fugitive Democracy and Other Essays*, edited by Nicholas Xenos (Princeton: Princeton University Press, 2016), 375.

22   Dylan Riley and Robert Brenner, "Seven Theses on American Politics," *New Left Review* 138 (2022), 9.

ary impulses by riling up ethnonationalism that claims to increase the value of the labor power of the white working class by keeping down non-whites and keeping out immigrants; just as mainstream Democrats generally appeal to a different faction of the working class, to those who seek to preserve their status through credentials such as degrees, or those who aim for more equitable racial representation in positions of power and tiers of wealth, without threatening overall structural inequality. The lack of class awareness means that the "revolutionary impulses" of the working-class can be channeled into a failed anti-democratic coup that wants to "hang Mike Pence," but achieves only prison terms.

Conversely, it means that when a Democratic president seeks to undo our massive wealth inequality—by giving the Fed the economic space to reverse policies that benefited those with assets, space provided by massive fiscal policies—the class politics at play are hidden, and popular disapproval of Joe Biden high. The fiscal policies that Biden enacted to benefit the working class range from one-year child credits that cut childhood poverty in half to long term investments in infrastructure and clean energy. Those latter bills brim with corporate incentives, it's true, but the incentives are linked to required high wages, childcare, and union support. Even these economic programs designed to reduce inequality and the threat of tumult cannot be presented, discussed, or recognized in those terms. As a result, delivering economic justice fails to defuse violent revolutionary impulses, and leaves the polity just as factionalized as before.

Further reading

Slavoj Žižek, *Violence* (London: Picador, 2008).

John P. McCormick, *Machiavellian Democracy* (Cambridge: Cambridge University Press, 2011).

Sheldon S. Wolin, *Fugitive Democracy and Other Essays*, edited by Nicholas Xenos (Princeton: Princeton University Press, 2016).

Chapter Eleven

Send in the Clowns!

Solutions

Fleck goes into Gotham to confront his father at Wayne Hall and gets caught up in the clown protests. Modern Times is on the big screen and there is big clown energy on the streets. Police line the avenue, some on horseback, guarding the red carpet. People are chanting and holding up placards: "We are <u>all</u> clowns," "Clown for Mayor!", "Kill the Rich." Fleck pushes through the crowd, sensing the energy. He scoots past a cop, smiling, ra-ra-ing, mimicking what he sees. Gotham is on the brink. Fleck seems thrilled by the spectacle of it all. He turns to take it all in, gasping with joy. Up front, things kick off as a protester lashes out and some cops jump the barricade. Sensing his opportunity, Fleck ducks under the cordon rope and slips into Wayne Hall. The crowd jeers outside as, comfortably ensconced in Wayne Hall, the rich settle in for a night with Charlie Chaplin. Fleck disguises himself as an usher and goes to find his father. (1:02:18–1:03:10)

Arthur Fleck's mistake in *Joker* is to ignore politics while investing in revenge. He personalizes things. When he learns of the protests that are planned at Wayne Hall, Fleck determines to go find his father. He arrives on a carnival scene of collective indignation. The *demos* has arisen, incensed by Wayne's dismissal of its grievances. As Fleck moves through the crowd, he seems transported by the spectacle of organized dissent. He senses what it might mean to join a movement, to build solidarity, to speak truth to power. He might even enjoy himself, if his sudden burst of joy is anything to go by. But Fleck turns away from politics. Instead, he uses the crowd for cover, ducking under the ropes to find his Daddy. The clowns on the street are just a distraction, so much background noise. Their indignation preoccupies the police such that Fleck can pursue his own agenda. In *Joker*'s allegory, Fleck is failing to connect with the power of the people and has determined to go it alone. He seeks personal satisfaction not political solidarity. He instrumentalizes the *demos* to pursue a grudge.

What's a clown supposed to do? The point of *Send in the Clowns!* is that Fleck may not know what to do, since he embodies the depoliticizing effects of neoliberalism on the *demos*. Fleck says he doesn't "believe in anything" (1:35:40). He doesn't feel like "the kind of clown that could start a movement" (1:42:52). Power feels like the prerogative of other people: the system. Politics happens *to* Fleck, or without him. The reasons for this disconnection are many: the prioritizing of economic rights over political inclusion under neoliberalism, the preoccupation of precarious workers with their daily survival, the time tax of welfare bureaucracy, the penalization of poverty, the narcotic effect of the mainstream media. All of these converge to make dignified participation in politics impractical, if not impossible, for the many. To this diagnosis, we might add the many ways capital has been legally coded to shield assets and redistribute costs to the voiceless, the toxic ideals of bro-culture capitalism and its glorification of violent competition, the systemic invalidation of the precariat by state institutions that enforce the law, and the debilitating impact of neoliberal feminism on working mothers. Together, these help to explain the anti-democratic impetus of neoliberalism when pursued as public philosophy.

Sheldon Wolin predicted as much in 1981. He saw very clearly how Reagan's administration had substituted economics for politics as the main responsibility of government. Political freedom was redefined as economic freedom (from regulation and accountability). And downturns in the business cycle would be solved, no longer with fiscal policy, but through monetary policy determined outside the realm of political (i.e., democratic) meddling. If you wanted to know how the people were doing, you needed to ask how the economy was doing. It was a tactical substitution "intended to reverse, change, and even destroy a fair number of established rights, institutions, and powers." And it would do so in the name of freedom. The people were free to sink or swim. They were free to choose. Rugged individualism—Reagan's cowboy capitalism—trumped social inclusion as America's new public philosophy. Wolin also saw how this retreat from welfare would result in increased state power despite all talk of a turn to small government. State security agencies would be lavished with funds while state bureaucracies would be disciplined. The prerogatives of business— global as well as national—would be enforced against the people. *Clowns!* bears out the sobering extent to which Wolin was right on both counts.[1]

Neoliberalism promises freedom for the people but prioritizes economic liberty alone. In doing so, it becomes increasingly resentful of democracy and opens to authoritarianism. This is the founding paradox of neoliberal governance. *Joker* opens on the prospect of the National Guard being brought in and "cleaning up" the city. By the film's end, city blocks are in flames. The clowns' protests, grounded in legitimate rights, degenerate into riot, providing further pretext for a crackdown. A state of emergency seems inevitable. We have suggested that the popular rage in *Joker* expresses the masses' frustrations with the structural humiliations of precarity in a false meritocracy: "you get what you fuckin' deserve." And violence against property has a long tradition—from ancient Roman tumults to Boston Tea Parties—for provoking the state into recognizing and mitigating the systemic violence of unchecked plutocracy. We might ask what alternatives might there be to riot? And what should the clowns

---

1   Sheldon S. Wolin, "The New Public Philosophy," in *Fugitive Democracy and Other Essays*, edited by Nicholas Xenos (Princeton: Princeton University Press, 2016), 395, 397.

demand that would roll back the neoliberal reversion? Is it even possible to put the people first anymore? And if it *is* possible, how? How might we discipline finance capital, reinvigorate democracy, and prioritize the needs of society over those of the economy?

There are no easy answers to such questions. We need practical solutions to the problems we have identified in these pages. No single measure will suffice to prevent a final fracturing of the *demos*. And even as we propose solutions, we are acutely aware that the scope of inequality and depoliticizing extends deeply into international spaces, in ways that contravene national solutions. *Send in the Clowns!* says that everyone must participate in multiple ways, and on multiple fronts, to shift the needle back toward social democracy. Thomas Piketty is right. The solution to popular rage is more democracy and more equality.[2] And that means more engagement on the part of the clowns. We need to reclaim our politicalness. A main lesson of the neoliberal turn is that free markets cannot do the work of politics. Only mass political engagement can steer us to social justice and meaningful equality. The solutions proposed here are offered in the spirit of experiment. We identify certain contradictions that burden our system and think of ways to fix them, politically and economically. Some of the measures will entail big picture adjustments in our public and political philosophy. Other measures will be more targeted and specific. None is guaranteed to work by itself. Together, they might focus the *demos* on aims we can collectively achieve.

Dignify the Social Contract

We need a new public philosophy. Neoliberalism advocates that economic liberties are foundational whereas political liberties and democracy come

---

2   Thomas Piketty, "The Fall of the US Idol," in *Time for Socialism: Dispatches from a World on Fire, 2016–2021* (New Haven: Yale University Press, 2021), 333.

second.[3] That priority must be reversed. Political liberty and democracy must be held as intrinsic, with economic liberties relegated to a supporting role. The reasons, we've seen, are clear. When we prioritize economic liberalism, democracy gives way to oligarchy, then to authoritarianism. Laissez-faire economics demands state intervention at home and abroad, prison and police expansion, and the hollowing-out of political rights. Even capitalists admit that economic rationality leads to political irresponsibility: that financial models overvalue the short term, discounting existential threats such as climate change until suddenly upon us, and too late. More profoundly, economic liberalism is unable to value societal resources that fall outside the logics of profitability and so trashes them: pride in meaningful work, belonging in community, self-worth in politicalness, friendship, happy children, nature. By prioritizing political democracy, we champion the human dignity found in the formation of political power and, from this basis, see a foundation to protect society.

Democracy First

Such a philosophical reorientation makes demands of us all. First among them is that we advocate policies that actually expand people's chances to share in forming political power. Some remain wary of the people. They point to the enormous turnout to elect Donald Trump. We note how many more voted to oust him after seeing the mistake. These reversals indicate renewed vigor in the democratic process, not its failing. What follows is that voting must be made easier and participation broader. We should not have to choose between voting and missing work. The citizens of Washington DC deserve Senate representation, just as in a presidential election, the blue voters in Alabama and the red voters in California

---

3   Noberto Bobbio, *Liberalism and Democracy*, translated by Martin Ryle and Kate Soper (London: Verso, [1988] 2005), 81.

deserve to have their votes matter. No citizen should have their voting rights revoked, whether or not they have committed a crime. The dignity of civic participation is a mode of rehabilitation that must be open to everyone. Such changes call for abolishing the electoral college, or, more plausibly, for circumventing it through state agreement.[4] They call for passing the *Freedom to Vote Act*, which expands access to the ballot, removes dark money from elections, and bans partisan gerrymandering.[5] The architects of the US Constitution were scared of the *demos*.[6] It is time to trust the people with their democracy.

Let the Clowns Decide

Citizens need more ways to share in the formation of political power than elections. We must consider new mechanisms that provide "systematic possibilities for ordinary people to contest the doings of government."[7] In one sense, this has us join Eitan Hersh, who reminds us that the point of politics is not newsfeed hobbyism and outrage adrenaline. The point is to form power and effect change. He is right to say that local political spaces—more grounded in practicality, more gratifying in immediacy, and more generous to civic friendships and alliances—are ideal places to begin.[8] In another sense, our celebration of people power has

---

4   Kristin Eberhard, *Becoming a Democracy: How We Can Fix the Electoral College, Gerrymandering, and Our Elections* (Seattle: Sightline Institute, 2020), np.

5   Brennan Center for Justice, "What the Freedom to Vote Act Would Do," brennancenter.org, July 13, 2023, np.

6   Sheldon S. Wolin, "Norm and Form: Constitutionalizing Democracy," in *Fugitive Democracy and Other Essays*, edited by Nicholas Xenos (Princeton: Princeton University Press, 2016), 79.

7   Philip Pettit, *Republicanism: A Theory of Freedom and Government* (Oxford: Oxford University Press, 1999), 277.

8   Eitan Hersh, *Politics Is for Power: How to Move Beyond Political Hobbyism, Take Action, and Make Real Change* (New York: Scribner, 2020).

us join Jeremy Waldron in advocating legislation made in meaningful consultation with the people.[9]

The overwhelming threat of oligarchy, however, calls on us all to consider more radical experiments in empowering the people at the national level. In *Machiavellian Democracy*, for example, John McCormick suggests we revamp a model used by ancient republics to prevent oligarchy from destroying the republic by provoking the masses into rage politics and civil war: the people's tribune. Fifty-one citizens, randomly selected and paid to serve a one-year term, are empowered to veto one piece of congressional legislation, one executive order, and one Supreme Court ruling in a term.[10] A non-binding version of this idea is employed successfully in Ireland. In 2013, a first assembly deliberated on the voting age and the presidential term.[11] Ninety-nine citizens, randomly selected, were invited to assembly, provided with expert testimony, Q&A sessions, and time to debate. They then proposed solutions. Subsequent assemblies have deliberated over the decriminalization of drugs and abortion, policies for biodiversity loss, and climate change.[12] In each case, assembly reports have been more radical than anything the government itself was willing to propose.[13] Imagine a body of citizens with a year to evaluate the Supreme Court's *Citizens United*, the 2010 ruling that granted corporations rights of individuals and sluiced corporate cash into politics. Or imagine they address the Supreme Court ruling of 1980 that allowed

---

9   Jeremy Waldron, *The Dignity of Legislation* (Cambridge: Cambridge University Press, 1999).

10 John P. McCormick, *Machiavellian Democracy* (Cambridge: Cambridge University Press, 2011), 178–185.

11 Citizens' Assembly, "Convention on the Constitution," citizensassembly. ie, nd, np.

12 Citizens' Assembly, "Previous Assemblies," citizensassembly.ie, nd, np.

13 James Bridle, "The Conspiracy of the Algorithm," *Jacobin* 49 (Spring 2023): 73–78.

corporations to patent parts of DNA, transforming life forms into monopoly capital. Most Americans are fed up with the concentrated power of the wealthy. Let's find ways to reject the false binary that asks whether markets or government are the solution. The people can be a solution.

Dismantle Oligarchy

Neoliberalism produces astonishing income inequality. It suppresses and undermines democracy's ability to regulate capital, prompting calls to overthrow democracy under the banner of reclaiming citizen power. It villainizes government oversight of private contracts, but, in a crisis, blackmails the citizens for bailouts. It expects state power to enforce property rights, but evades taxes when it is time to foot the bill. It stirs up anti-government sentiment, but relies on state currency to convert assets and store wealth. It begrudges fiscal policy solutions when they help the poor and middle class—sadofiscalism—only to leave economic stimulus to the Fed, whose tools are to lower borrowing rates or gush trillions into the economy, inevitably inflating assets for those who have them: the rich become supremely richer. From early 2020 to 2024, the net worth of the top .01 percent in the US—that's 131,238 families—increased by $7.4 *trillion* dollars to $19.8 trillion, up $56 million more per family.[14] Expanding the child credit in 2021, on the other hand, cut child poverty by 46 percent—a provision that costs just $100 billion, but which Congress let expire. These obscene paradoxes are produced by oligarchy. And their political face is a disempowered citizenry that becomes susceptible to demagogic superheroes who promise they alone can clean up government or punish villains, superheroes who nevertheless preserve venal capital structures and punch down for their scapegoats. Here are some solutions:

---

14   FRED, "Net Worth Held by the Top 0.1% (99.9th to 100th Wealth Percentiles)," fred.stlouisfed.org, Q4 2023, np.

Make the rich pay their way

The federal debt has ballooned over decades of neoliberal misgovernance—trillions borrowed to invade and privatize Iraq, with more trillions in tax cuts for the wealthy; decades of slashed capital gains tax rates, so that hedge fund billionaires, employing carried interest loopholes, pay lower tax rates than nurses. That trickle-down economics is a lie is now generally recognized. The need for emergency tax measures is not. Piketty reminds us that it was "exceptional levies"—income taxes of up to 70 percent—that restored stability after the Great Depression and provided the foundations for the postwar, New Deal consensus.[15] Make tax rates on the wealthy great again! In 2013, Piketty called for a "progressive global tax on capital."[16] More recently, he advocates for wealth taxes of 90 percent on assets over one billion dollars.[17] This sounds extreme, until you remember that monetary stimulus artificially enriched the wealthy in the first place. Transaction taxes, what's more, would go some way to pay for inevitable bailouts. If capitalism cannot pay for the risks to which it exposes the people, those practices should be banned: speculative contracts, derivatives, short sales, and the like. Restoring stability with higher rates allowed the United States to avoid the threat of fascism in the early twentieth century. Tax justice is social justice. It is time to tax wealth.

Recode capital

Taxing wealth is a worthy and necessary fight. The 15 percent minimum corporation tax implemented globally in 2024, for example, marks an

---

15 Thomas Piketty, "What to Do with Covid Debt?" in *Time for Socialism*, 321.

16 Thomas Piketty, *Capital in the Twenty-First Century*, translated by Arthur Goldhammer (Cambridge, MA: Belknap of Harvard University Press, 2014), 572.

17 Thomas Piketty, *Capital and Ideology* (Cambridge, MA: Belknap of Harvard University Press, 2020).

important first step toward increased corporate citizenship.[18] But tax alone will not bring capital under democratic control. We agree with Katharina Pistor that capital's legal privileges need to be rolled back. International corporations operate beyond legal accountability to the jurisdictions where they operate.[19] Like Wayne Enterprises, they fly above the law and under the radar. We can all make it harder for capital to "go on a legal shopping spree" by evading democratic law through tax shelters and shell companies; states must roll back conflict-in-law rules, which allow corporations to shirk their responsibilities in a global game of legal hide-and-seek.[20] Class action—the ability of citizens and consumers to take on corporations at their own legal game—needs to be strengthened, and arbitration for cases involving public interest denied.

In addition, laws can be recoded to expand rights and entitlements for societal values other than capital. Admittedly, the forces are mismatched: deep-pocketed corporations face off against not-for-profits—groups such as Common Cause, Public Citizen, and Public Advocates—while individual suits can only claw back monopoly patents for public use, for instance, one at a time. Pistor is right that courts should rescind the benefit of doubt traditionally given to enterprises who argue for exemptions because their profits benefit everyone; *the onus should be on them to prove it*. Corporate law protects shareholders' expectations of future profit, but workers are told to expect a future of insecure and flexible labor. Why? If corporations deemed persons can devour resources for profit, nature can also be deemed a person and claim the right to self-defense.[21] Ecuador led

---

18   Richard Rubin, Jennifer Williams, and Paul Hannon, "A New Global Tax Is About to Raise Billions. The U.S. Is Missing Out," *Wall Street Journal*, February 1, 2024, np.

19   Katharina Pistor, *The Code of Capital: How the Law Creates Wealth and Inequality* (Princeton: Princeton University Press, 2019), 221.

20   Pistor, *Code of Capital*, 225.

21   On corporations as persons, see Pistor, *Code of Capital*, 47–76.

the way in 2008, establishing rights for nature in its constitution. Bolivia followed suit. In 2023, sixteen youths took on the state of Montana arguing their right to a "clean and healthful climate" and won.[22] Extending rights is one way to defend the commons. In *Joker*, the clowns take to the streets. Pistor says they must also take to the courts. If capitalism persistently attacks society, thwarts democracy, and trashes nature, more radical options must be sought. Limited liability for corporations could be abolished, for example.[23] Law can be a major force in the fight for social justice and against environmental destruction.

Politicize monetary policy and socialize investment
The US central bank, or Fed, claims to be politically neutral, with a double mandate to keep inflation and unemployment low, through the mechanism of adjusting (short term) borrowing rates. But since the Great Recession of 2008, as the Fed slashed interest rates, the economy has remained tepid, even when real interest rates have been kept near, or below, zero.[24] In the absence of robust fiscal stimulus, the Fed resorted to extraordinary measures, called "quantitative easing." This entails spending trillions of dollars buying long-term mortgages and corporate bonds, in order to lower long-term borrowing rates. While these policies temporarily stabilize the economy, they increase systemic risks as easing unwinds and they dramatically inflate asset prices, cultivating ever-widening wealth inequality that undermines democracy. Far from being politically neutral, then, monetary solutions deployed in isolation solidify upper-class wealth and come up short for the overall economy.

The obvious conclusion is to have fiscal policy play a larger role in economic stabilization going forward and, when deciding between

---

22 Lesley Clark, "Kids Sued Montana Over Climate Change and Won," *Scientific American*, August 15, 2023, np.

23 Pistor, *Code of Capital*, 53–54.

24 Nic Johnson, "Times of Interest," *New Left Review* 143 (2023): 109–142.

monetary or fiscal remedies, to have the class (i.e., distributional) effects of these choices made clear for the citizenry. Neoliberals have preferred monetary solutions over fiscal policy (with the exceptions of military spending and tax cuts for corporations and the wealthy). Yet, over the last fifteen years, growing dissatisfaction with a rigged economy, the limits of monetary stimulus, and the anomaly of the COVID pandemic have combined to make fiscal policy acceptable again. Biden's *Infrastructure, Investment, and Jobs Act*, *Inflation Reduction Act* (a climate bill), and *Chips Act* are all fiscal policies that stimulate domestic industrial and corporate investment. Even if structured as corporate stimulus, they at least have attached dignified labor requirements. Other emergency fiscal stimuli have helped regular people as well. Where fiscal policies play a wider role, new political spaces open; we must insist investment be directed toward social justice and democratic stability—greening the global economy, providing affordable housing, expanding healthcare and childcare, preserving dignity for people and nature—and away from the lure of fiscal militarism. Winning that political fight requires guarding against melodrama.

Call Out Neoliberal Melodrama

In literature and film, melodrama has been central to the democratic imagination because it condenses social conflict into individual allegories and moves us by feelings, even as it can reprimand our naivete.[25] Before democratic revolutions, villainous aristocrats sexually assault hapless servants; once a revolution disciplines aristocratic privilege, Disney says Belle can marry the Beast. Now, as we live through the reassertion

---

25   Thomas Elsaesser, "Tales of Sound and Fury: Observations on the Family Melodrama," in Marcia Landy, ed., *Imitations of Life: A Reader on Film and Television Melodrama* (Detroit: Wayne State University Press, 1991), 68–91.

of class hierarchy, *Batman* glamorizes reaction, whereas *Joker* lashes out with pre-revolutionary vigor.

We recognize these meanings, not to incite guilt about whether the movies we enjoy match our politics, but because *melodrama also shapes political policy*. Under capitalism, poverty is slammed as a moral failing and the poor ridiculed as "undeserving," so that we can cut welfare payments and unleash a powerful incentive to work.[26] Crime designates poor people as savage, so we can lock them up.[27] Foreign regimes are categorized as evil, so we can mobilize "superpower" for war.[28] We even find melodrama in neoliberal philosophy. Social policies that mitigate capitalism's inevitable damage—whether through recessions and automation or insecure wages and environmental degradation—are tarred as "collectivism" and lumped together with National Socialism, as "abhorred tyranny."[29] In movie melodrama, an individual allegorizes a class position; in real-life neoliberal melodrama, individuals become perverted allegories. They are made to bear the full brunt of social costs and internalize the obligation to face them alone. Melodrama is politically effective: it isolates blame for structural problems into the shame of victims themselves. It provides psychic relief for those who profit from damage, by reassuring them that societal consequences were unintended and neglect counts as moral good: financial success is virtue, military adventurism is righteousness, over-punishment is justice, denying society is responsibility.

---

26   Michael B. Katz, *The Undeserving Poor: From the War on Poverty to the War on Welfare* (New York: Pantheon, 1990).

27   Loïc Wacquant, *Punishing the Poor: The Neoliberal Government of Social Insecurity* (Durham: Duke University Press, 2009).

28   Sheldon S. Wolin, *Democracy Incorporated: Managed Democracy and the Specter of Inverted Totalitarianism* (Princeton: Princeton University Press, 2008), 82–94.

29   Milton Friedman, "Introduction," in Friedrich A. Hayek, *The Road to Serfdom*, fiftieth anniversary edition (Chicago: University of Chicago Press, [1944] 1994), x. Hayek, *Road to Serfdom*, 6.

But such narratives exact their own revenge. When money is scarce, but still designates the value of all things, people feel slighted. When leaders drum up "felt legitimacy" to justify war, [30] with stories of evil that turn out to be lies, they provide a model for conspiracy at home: fully one-third of US citizens tell pollsters that 9/11 was an inside government job. The majority of people on welfare are mothers with children under five.[31] When we demonize them, insisting they must work if they want benefits, yet fail to ask how a $7.25 minimum wage will allow them to afford childcare, our moralizing justifies neglect. When we incarcerate their brothers and fathers in for-profit prisons, at rates double the police state of Russia and eightfold the countries in Europe, we punish whole communities.[32]

We may not *intend* for white working men to die off ever younger each year from deaths of despair: drug poisoning, alcohol, and suicide.[33] We may eschew racism, even as we build a racist system that gives a young Black man a one-in-three chance of doing hard time across his life.[34] And we might well disavow misogyny and child neglect, notwithstanding that domestic violence affects not just survivors, but is the leading cause of "homelessness for children in the United States."[35] In all these cases, liberal law, which relies on a standard of *intentional* harm, might

---

30   Elisabeth R. Anker, *Orgies of Feeling: Melodrama and the Politics of Freedom* (Durham: Duke University Press, 2014), 27. BBC News, "The Evolution of a Conspiracy Theory," news.bbc.co.uk, July 4, 2008, np.

31   Joel F. Handler, "On Welfare Reform's Hollow Victory," *Daedalus* 135.3 (2006): 114–117.

32   National Research Council of the National Academies, *The Growth of Incarceration in the United States: Exploring Causes and Consequences* (Washington, DC: The National Academies Press, 2014), 36.

33   National Academies of Sciences, Engineering, and Medicine, *High and Rising Mortality Rates Among Working-Age Adults* (Washington, DC: The National Academies Press, 2021), 101–104.

34   Wacquant, *Punishing the Poor*, 37.

35   "Five Facts About Domestic and Sexual Violence and Homelessness," americanbar.org, nd, np.

protect us from suit.[36] But we should not be surprised that when a strongman runs for office, selling nostalgia for the time before oligarchy with policies that keep oligarchy in place, he taps into melodrama's currents—that the system is rigged, goodness is a fiction, liberalism is a conspiracy, Mexicans are "rapists"[37]—and people moth to his flame.

Solutions to neoliberal melodrama are difficult, but we should not despair. They are difficult because melodrama chimes with a media culture whose forms and profit structure arouse emotion for their effect and bind politics to entertainment;[38] difficult because melodrama cultivates compliance for US interventionism among citizens who dislike war; difficult because the sadism in villainizing others thrives on the humiliation of thwarted entitlement. And not all entitlements can or should be restored, whether masculinity resentful when denied access to a woman's body, or whiteness assured that humiliation only happens to others. Our solutions call for a dignity pact.

Dignify the Social

We dignify the social when we reduce structural humiliations for everyone; when we acknowledge that policies borne from melodrama overlook very real social costs. Even where such structural racism and structural misogyny are initially unintentional, they clearly become intentional when we resist reforms to rectify them. Poor mothers are smothered when we require them to work yet fail to account for the labor of raising their children. Mother nature is smothered when we contract

---

36   Charles R. Lawrence III, "The Id, the Ego, and Equal Protection: Reckoning with Unconscious Racism," *Stanford Law Review* 39.2 (1987): 317–388.

37   Jake Miller, "Donald Trump Defends Calling Mexican Immigrants 'Rapists'," cbsnews.com, July 2, 2015, np.

38   Neil Postman, *Amusing Ourselves to Death: Public Discourse in the Age of Show Business* (Harmondsworth: Penguin, 1985).

to extract yet fail to account for replenishment. Karl Polanyi is right: labor and land *are* fictitious commodities. Left to the mercies of a self-regulating market, biological life will be exhausted and destroyed. The aim must be to embed institutions that safeguard the health of society and nature. Childcare should be publicly provisioned, much like elementary schooling. In addition to recoding capital, federally protected lands and national monuments could be further expanded, here and abroad, especially if achieved in cooperation with indigenous populations. Using the 1906 *Antiquities Act*, President Obama quadrupled the size of the Papahānaumokuākea National Marine Monument; 582,578 square miles of land and sea by Hawaii placed beyond the grasp of commodification: an ecological nursery. Profit logics are unceasingly rapacious, and legal logics tirelessly offload costs to those without voice. New life must be put beyond their bounds.

Dignify Rehabilitation

Instead of investing in social safety nets, neoliberalism invested in cages. Public housing budgets dropped in inverse proportion to outlays that expanded jails and prisons. In the US, nearly two million people are incarcerated at any one time, with millions more on parole.[39] Mandatory sentencing laws, and ill-founded three-strike theories, force judges to mete out punishments they themselves consider unjust.[40] Incarceration culture also requires judges to ignore society's wider interests: the damage to children who lose a parent to prison, the cost to communities that lose so many men—social injuries predictably indexed to class and race. The results of this experiment are in: prison fails to reform. Prison

39   Wendy Sawyer and Peter Wagner, "Mass Incarceration: The Whole Pie 2023," prisonpolicy.org, March 14, 2023, np.

40   Danielle Sered, *Until We Reckon: Violence, Mass Incarceration, and a Road to Repair* (New York: The New Press, 2019), 27.

actually harms society, producing crime and recidivism not repentance.[41] Being tough on criminals is not the same as being tough on crime. The latter must involve strategies for prevention and rehabilitation. We know that lowering incarceration rates correlates to less crime, not the reverse. We know community-based drug-use programs yield better results in reducing recidivism than incarceration, and that peer-to-peer connections interrupt violence as it is happening.[42] But the incentives are skewed: incarcerated workers produce more than $2 billion a year in goods and commodities and over $9 billion a year in services for the maintenance of the prisons where they are warehoused.[43] Imprisonment is ostensibly cheaper than public housing, social programs, and education. Incarceration satisfies capitalist and media melodrama that blames individuals alone for crime, even if it costs society $182 billion a year as well as untold social devastation.[44]

We join Danielle Sered who proposes that we invert the logic of penalization altogether and imagine incarceration as a last resort. Instead, she has us ask: "who are we incapable of holding in our communities and what would it take to hold them?" She suggests we abolish minimum sentencing laws and apply changes retroactively; limit the power of prosecutors, especially in plea bargaining, which is "rife with racial disparities"; and expand community-based, restorative justice approaches that are proven to work.[45] Groups such as Common Justice provide models for what success looks like, and states could build such models into their own procedures. The enormous sums spent on housing millions of people in prison could be shifted back to public housing schemes.

---

41 Sered, *Until We Reckon*, 33.

42 Sered, *Until We Reckon*, 70, 79.

43 ACLU and University of Chicago Law School Global Human Rights Clinic, *Captive Labor: Exploitation of Incarcerated Workers* (2022), 6.

44 Sawyer and Wagner, "Mass Incarceration," np.

45 Sered, *Until We Reckon*, 40, 69–71.

Dignify Labor

Breathtaking incarceration rates owe to policies that punish poverty. One immediate solution is to pay workers more. As the top 1 percent have seen their wages grow 138 percent since 1979, the bottom 90 percent saw gains of just 15 percent.[46] In Chapter Two, we saw that the minimum wage, indexed to inflation and gains in worker productivity, should be $19.43 today, not $7.25. Wage stagnation exacerbates wealth inequality and worker resentment. "Work hard and you will be rewarded" is the meritocratic ideal. When meritocracy is false—a cover story for structural humiliation—it lays the groundwork for a politics of rage. We need fair opportunity, not false meritocracy.[47]

Insecure work is not simply about money—making cents—just as the loss of a coherent work ethic is not a character flaw. Work should also make sense: be supported by organizing as a political force and societal good. In 2023, for example, American autoworkers and UPS workers, through the power of union solidarity, won big, while Amazon and Starbucks resorted to dirty tricks to prevent unionization among their workers.[48] Both outcomes signal the potential of union solidarity as a force for liberation. Yet unions must learn from their rout under neoliberalism. Union density in the private sector has plummeted to 6 percent, down from 30 percent in the 1960s.[49] We agree with Jared

46   Lawrence Mishel, Elise Gould, and Josh Bivens, "Wage Stagnation in Nine Charts," epi.org, January 6, 2015, np.

47   Michael J. Sandel, *The Tyranny of Merit: What's Become of the Common Good?* (New York: Farrar, Straus and Giroux, 2020).

48   Camila Domonoske, "The UAW Won Big in the Auto Strike—But What Does It Mean for the Rest of Us?" npr.org, November 12, 2023, np. Ali Asad Zulfiqar, "UK Union Blasts Amazon for 'Dirty Tricks' After Drive Fails," bnnbloomberg.ca, June 8, 2023, np.

49   Jared Abbott, "Why We Need Union Halls in Every Town," jacobin.com, January 29, 2024, np.

Abbott who suggests that if "union revival" is to succeed, unions must master "place-based community organizing" as well as "long-distance solidarities."[50] They must foster conversations and education about wealth and income inequality, and remain open to winning what Italian Marxist, Antonio Gramsci, called the "war of position."[51] By embedding themselves in communities, making union halls spaces for celebration and local politics, unions would not simply demonstrate how solidarity improves work conditions, but model how a work ethic at its root means fashioning a social identity that participates in the formation of political power.

Send in the Clowns!

A dignity pact, in short, means broadening who can share in the formation of power. Successful policy, once achieved, makes future policy change easier.[52] When more people share in power, new power formations become possible. Angela Davis calls on us all to "resist the depiction of history as the work of heroic individuals" so that everyone can "recognize their potential agency as a part of an ever-expanding community of struggle."[53] The protesters in *Joker* are right. We are *all* clowns. And instead of waiting for our blockbusters, we need to participate in political power and reinvigorate the *demos*. We need to send in the clowns.

---

50   Abbott, "Why We Need," np.

51   Antonio Gramsci, *Selections from The Prison Notebooks*, edited and translated by Quintin Hoare and Geoffrey Nowell Smith (New York: International Publishers, [1929–1935] 1971), 238.

52   Theda Skocpol quoted in Michael B. Katz, "Was Government the Solution or the Problem? The Role of the State in the History of American Social Policy," *Theory and Society* 39.3/4 (2010): 495.

53   Angela Y. Davis, *Freedom is a Constant Struggle: Ferguson, Palestine, and the Foundations of a Movement* (Chicago: Haymarket Press, 2016), 2.

Further reading

Steve Duncombe and Steve Lambert, *The Art of Activism: Your All-Purpose Guide to Making the Impossible Possible* (New York: OR Books, 2021).

Vanessa Machado de Oliveira, *Hospicing Modernity: Facing Humanity's Wrongs and the Implications for Social Activism* (Berkeley: North Atlantic Books, 2021).

Glossary

Agitation – personal discomfort and/or political activity. The idea being to turn the former into the latter

Allegory – narrative device in which individuals embody abstract concepts or problems (happiness, justice) in plots that ask to be read on two levels: literal and figurative

Cannibal Capitalism – Nancy Fraser's term for the innate tendency of capitalism to devour the bases of its own viability

Carnival – political festivities that interrogate power dynamics by temporarily subverting them

Coding of Capital – Katharina Pistor's term for how the law transforms assets into capital by endowing them with properties of convertibility, durability, and priority

Comedy – narrative genre in which the social order is first challenged then restored in a happy ending

Commodity – resource that is traded—bought or sold—in a market economy

Commodity (Fictitious) – Karl Polanyi's term for the fiction that land and labor can be treated like commodities without destroying them or society

Compliance – psychological predicament wherein children become beholden to the fantasies and desires of their parents. Submission to power

Consumerism – buying stuff but also buying into stuff (e.g. gentrification), most often without realizing what you are buying into

Conspiracism – political genre in which power is ascribed to alien forces, malevolent individuals, or corrupt elites, e.g. Fleck's view of "the system"

Contradictions – structural anomalies in systems or arguments that make them vulnerable to critique or collapse, e.g. my freedom to do what I want is limited, in principle, by another's freedom from interference. Therefore, the positive moment (freedom to) and the negative moment (freedom from) of the concept exist in contradiction

Corporation – a business entity that is treated like a person for legal purposes. Economically, it can enter into contracts, own assets, and incur debt, as well as sue and be sued. Legally, it can shield assets, shift losses, and immortalize wealth

Democracy (Liberal) – mode of government defined by free elections, in which citizens possess equal rights, e.g. to association and free speech; freedom is imagined negatively with minimal government; and citizens are inhibited from regulating the economy. The pre-eminent roles of government are to secure borders, protect property, and promote free markets

Democracy (Social) – mode of government defined by free elections, in which citizens possess equal rights, freedom is imagined positively with government decisions in citizens' hands, and citizens have the freedom to regulate the economy. The pre-eminent roles of government are to secure borders, promote economic equalization, and nurture society

Demos – the people as proper vehicle of power in a democracy

Depoliticization – under neoliberalism, the detrimental effect of consumerism, atomization, insecure labor, media melodrama, and legal double-standards on people's willingness and ability to be political

Durability – the ability to preserve capital over time by dint of legal coding

Flexploitation – intensified worker exploitation under the guise of flexible (i.e., insecure) work arrangements

Free Market – *see* Market (Free)

Great Replacement Theory – race theory that reframes social democratic gains achieved by the disenfranchised as an assault on the privileges of white heteropatriarchy. Often presented as a conspiracy of Western elites who aim to replace majority "white" populations with "non-white" immigrants

Grip-Reading – slow-reading popular culture to unfold social critique in everyday language

Incel – involuntary celibate: a person who wants sex but cannot seem to get any. A condition that becomes toxic if the person also believes they have a right to sex

Individualism – the collective fiction of selfhood as solitary. The prioritization of self over society

Inflation – the rising cost of goods in a market society

Intimacy Delusion – understanding reality based on personal feelings rather than evidence, reason, or collective deliberation

Invisible Hand – Adam Smith's fiction of how the pursuit of individual self-interest inadvertently promotes the common good, one consensual transaction at a time

Keynesian – economic approach derived from the theories of John Maynard Keynes, who argued for stimulus, not austerity, to create consumer demand in a downturn

Late Capitalism – the epoch of capitalism inaugurated after 1940, characterized by the inexorable rise of finance capitalism, corporate oligopoly, and integration of global markets

Legislation – laws enacted by deliberative process rather than court rulings

Liberalism (Classical) – a political philosophy of minimal government that advocates state security for property and person, grounded in individual political rights and free markets

Liberalism (Embedded) – the determination to embed liberal rights and privileges in legislation, policy, and social institutions to protect them from political interference, e.g. the postwar consensus

Liberalism (New, or Neoliberalism) – economic policy defined by privatization of public goods, deregulation of markets, and dismantling of the welfare state

Market (Free) – an economic system in which prices are determined by supply and demand and unrestricted competition between privately owned businesses

Market (Protectionist) – a market system defined by sectional or national interests. Demand and supply are controlled to meet political goals

Melodrama – a genre in which individuals represent moralized versions of wider social and political struggles, and moral binarisms are conveyed and challenged through techniques of style (e.g. music, lighting, camera angle)

Melodrama (Neoliberal) – a genre of political discourse in which social conflicts are recast as stories of individual merit and failure, e.g. poverty as a choice, while social dynamics are reduced to moral binarisms, e.g. free markets good, government planning evil. Also employed to expand state power, e.g. the state as an innocent victim fighting foreign evil through domestic surveillance and international war

Meritocracy – a hypothetical society which distributes reward based on individual talent or industry

Meritocracy (False) – the myth that industrious and/or talented individuals get what they deserve in a free market society. In truth, numerous advantages pervert meritocracy, e.g. inheritance, law, norms of conduct

Monetary and Fiscal Policy – monetary policy controls the circulation of money as a means to manipulate the economy, whereas fiscal policy uses taxation and spending to the same end

Neoliberalism – *see* Liberalism (New)

Penal Pornography – the use of crime as a political spectacle to incite support for repressive policing

Politicalness – political literacy and engagement

Possessive Individualism – the idea that individuals are defined primarily by what they own

Postwar Consensus – the broad agreement after World War II that, as the economy made strides in productivity and income, workers would also profit through gains in wages and state benefits

Precarity – a state of economic vulnerability defined by poverty, insecure labor, and/or unmanageable debt. Living from paycheck to paycheck, or on subsidies

Precarity (Structural) – the historical predicament of the working classes, who have only the fictitious commodity of their labor to sell

Stagflation – a combination of economic stagnation and inflation

Sadomonetarism – punitive use of monetary policy to discipline the poor and reward the rich

Sadofiscalism – punitive use of fiscal policy to discipline the poor and reward the rich

Social Contract – the liberal fiction that society is governed by a contract that we all sign. We agree to give up some natural rights to achieve security enough to pursue our own happiness

Social Welfare – the provision of a social safety net to citizens, e.g. healthcare or unemployment benefits

Social Warfare – the withdrawal of social welfare under neoliberalism. Rationalized as incentivizing the undeserving poor to work

Toxic Masculinity – the psychological blend of presumption and privilege that defines masculinity as pre-eminent in patriarchal societies

Two-Body Problem – the dual exploitation of women, as mothers and workers, in capitalism

Tragedy – narrative genre in which personal flaws produce disastrous results for self and society

Trust – a legal fiction that allows an owner (called the settlor) to transfer an asset into a legal shell to protect it from creditors

Utilitarianism – Nineteenth-century political philosophy, which rejects social contract theory for a policy-based approach. The aim is the greatest happiness of the greatest number

Wage Labor – a main innovation of capitalism, whereby workers exchange their labor for pay

Work Ethic – traditional view of labor, whereby work includes self-recognition, social identity, and awareness of labor as a political force. This ethic is lost under neoliberalism

Bibliography

Abbott, Jared. "Why We Need Union Halls in Every Town." jacobin.com (January 29, 2024), np.

Accurso, Anthony. "$12.5 Million to Settle Class Action Suit Over Strip Searches of NYC Jail Visitors." *Prison Legal News* (October 2018).

ACLU and University of Chicago Law School Global Human Rights Clinic. *Captive Labor: Exploitation of Incarcerated Workers* (2022).

ACLU. "NYPD Officer Pleads Guilty in Torture Case." aclu.org (May 26, 1999), np.

Alexander, Michelle. *The New Jim Crow: Mass Incarceration in the Age of Colorblindness,* tenth anniversary edition. New York: The New Press, [2010] 2020.

Allen, Robert C. "Engels' Pause: Technical Change, Capital Accumulation, and Inequality in the British Industrial Revolution." *Explorations in Economic History* 46.4 (2009): 418–435.

Allon, Gad, Kimon Drakopoulos, and Vahideh Manshadi. "Information Inundation on Platforms and Implications." *Operations Research* 69.6 (2021): 1784–1804.

Anderson, David C. *Crime and the Politics of Hysteria: How the Willie Horton Story Changed American Justice.* New York: Random House, 1995.

Anker, Elisabeth R. *Orgies of Feeling: Melodrama and the Politics of Freedom.* Durham: Duke University Press, 2014.

Aragão, Carolina. "Gender Pay Gap in U.S. Hasn't Changed Much in Two Decades." pewresearch.org (March 1, 2023), np.

Atwood, Margaret. "Writing the Male Character." In *Second Words: Selected Critical Prose, 1960–1982,* 412–430. Toronto: House of Anansi, [1982] 2000.

Bakhtin, Mikhail. *Rabelais and His World,* translated by Helene Iswolski. Bloomington: Indiana University Press, [1965] 2009.

Batman. Directed by Tim Burton. Warner Bros, 1989.

Baudrillard, Jean. *For a Critique of the Political Economy of the Sign*. London: Verso, 2019.

BBC News. "The Evolution of a Conspiracy Theory." news.bbc.co.uk (July 4, 2008), np.

Ben-Ghiat, Ruth. *Strongmen: Mussolini to the Present*. New York: W. W. Norton, 2020.

Bentham, Jeremy. *Principles of the Civil Code*, in *The Works of Jeremy Bentham, vol. 1*, edited by John Bowring, 538–659. Illinois: Liberty Fund, [1802] 2011.

Best, Michael H. and William E. Connolly, *The Politicized Economy*, second edition. Lexington: DC Heath, 1982.

Blyth, Mark. *Great Transformations: Economic Ideas and Institutional Change in the Twentieth Century*. Cambridge: Cambridge University Press, 2002.

Bobbio, Norberto. *Liberalism and Democracy*, translated by Martin Ryle and Kate Soper. London: Verso, [1988] 2005.

Boltanski, Luc. *Mysteries and Conspiracies: Detective Stories, Spy Novels and the Making of Modern Societies*. Cambridge: Polity Press, 2014.

Bourdieu, Pierre. "Job Insecurity Is Everywhere Now." In *Acts of Resistance: The Tyranny of the Market*, translated by Richard Nice, 81–87. New York: The New Press, [1997] 1998.

Brennan Center for Justice. "What the Freedom to Vote Act Would Do." brennancenter.org (July 13, 2023), np.

Bridle, James. "The Conspiracy of the Algorithm." *Jacobin* 49 (Spring 2023): 73–78.

Brock, David, Ari Rabin-Havt, and Media Matters for America. *The Fox Effect: How Roger Ailes Turned a Network into a Propaganda Machine*. Milwaukee: Anchor Books, 2012.

Brown, Wendy. *In the Ruins of Neoliberalism: The Rise of Antidemocratic Politics in the West*. Columbia University Press: New York, 2019.

Caplan, Paula. "Mother Blaming." In Molly Ladd-Taylor and Lauri Umansky, eds. *"Bad" Mothers: The Politics of Blame in Twentieth-Century America*, 127–144. New York: New York University Press, 1998.

Cardi B and Megan Thee Stallion. "WAP." Track 2 on *WAP*, Atlantic Records, 2020.

Cavanaugh, Patrick. "Elon Musk Claims to Be Doctor Strange, but Marvel Director Lets Him Know Otherwise." comicbook.com, June 29, 2018, np.

Chung, Gabrielle. "Sheryl Sandberg Opens Up About Family Leave, Says Women Can't 'Lean In' Without 'Right Corporate Policies'." people.com (December 10, 2020), np.

Citizens' Assembly. "Convention on the Constitution." citizensassembly.ie (nd), np.

Citizens' Assembly. "Previous Assemblies." citizensassembly.ie (nd), np.

Clark, Lesley. "Kids Sued Montana Over Climate Change and Won." *Scientific American* (August 15, 2023), np.

Coday, Dennis. "Pope's Quotes: An Economy That Kills." ncronline.org (November 26, 2013), np.

Cohen, Michael Mark. *The Conspiracy of Capital: Law, Violence, and American Popular Radicalism in the Age of Monopoly*. Amherst: University of Massachusetts Press, 2019.

Crenshaw, Kimberlé. "Mapping the Margins: Intersectionality, Identity Politics, and Violence Against Women of Color." *Stanford Law Review* 43.6 (1991): 1241–1299.

Dale, Iain, ed. *Margaret Thatcher: In Her Own Words*. Hull: Biteback, 2010.

Davies, William. "The New Neoliberalism." *New Left Review* 101 (2016): 121–134.

Davis, Angela Y. *Are Prisons Obsolete?* New York: Seven Stories Press, 2003.

Davis, Angela Y. *Freedom Is a Constant Struggle: Ferguson, Palestine, and the Foundations of a Movement*. Chicago: Haymarket Press, 2016.

Davis, Mike. *Old Gods, New Enigmas: Marx's Lost Theory*. London: Verso, 2018.

Dewey, John. *Democracy and Education: An Introduction to the Philosophy of Education*. New York: The Free Press, [1916] 1944.

Domonoske, Camila. "The UAW Won Big in the Auto-Strike—But What Does It Mean for the Rest of Us?" npr.org (November 12, 2023), np.

Duncombe, Steve and Steve Lambert. *The Art of Activism: Your Guide to Making the Impossible Possible*. New York: OR Books, 2021.

Eberhard, Kristin. *Becoming a Democracy: How We Can Fix the Electoral College, Gerrymandering, and Our Elections*. Seattle: Sightline Institute, 2020.

Economic Policy Institute. "The Productivity-Pay Gap." epi.org (October 2022), np.

Elsaesser, Thomas. "Tales of Sound and Fury: Observations on the Family Melodrama." In *Imitations of Life: A Reader on Film and Television Melodrama*, edited by Marcia Landy, 68–91. Detroit: Wayne State University Press, 1991.

Encyclopaedia Britannica. "Factory Act, United Kingdom [1833]." britannica.com (nd), np.

Eyal, Nir. *Hooked: How to Build Habit-Forming Products* (New York: Portfolio, 2014).

Fairlie, Simon. "A Short History of Enclosure in Britain." *The Land* 7 (2009): 16–31.

Federal Reserve Bank of Chicago. "The Federal Reserve's Dual Mandate." chicagofed.org (October 20, 2022), np.

Feemster, Ron. "Naked City?" salon.com (June 1, 1999), np.

Findlaw Staff. "Paid Parental Leave in the U.S. vs Other Developed Countries." findlaw.com (January 31, 2023), np.

Fisher, Mark. *Capitalist Realism: Is There No Alternative?* London: Zero Books, 2014.

"Five Facts About Domestic and Sexual Violence and Homelessness." americanbar.org, (nd), np.

Fraser, Nancy. *Cannibal Capitalism: How Our System Is Devouring Democracy, Care, and the Planet—and What We Can Do About It*. London: Verso, 2022.

Fraser, Nancy. *The Old Is Dying and the New Cannot Be Born: From Progressive Neoliberalism to Trump and Beyond*. London: Verso, 2019.

FRED. "Net Worth Held by the Top 0.1% (99.9th to 100th Wealth Percentiles)." fred.stlouisfed.org (Q4 2023), np.

Freud, Sigmund. "Family Romances." In *On Sexuality: The Penguin Freud Library, vol. 7*, 221–225. Harmondsworth: Pelican, 1977.

Friedman, Milton. *Capitalism and Freedom*, fortieth anniversary edition. Chicago: University of Chicago Press, [1962] 2002.

Friedman, Milton. "Introduction." In *The Road to Serfdom*, fiftieth anniversary edition, 1–12. Chicago: Chicago University Press, [1944] 1994.

Friedman, Milton. "Negative Income Tax II." In *There's No Such Thing as a Free Lunch: Essays on Public Policy*, 200–201. La Salle: Open Court, 1975.

Friedman, Milton. "Nobel Lecture: Inflation and Unemployment." *Journal of Political Economy* 85.3 (1977), 451–472.

Friedman, Milton. "*Playboy* Interview." In *There's No Such Thing as A Free Lunch: Essays on Public Policy*, 1–38. La Salle: Open Court, 1975.

Friedman, Milton. "Steady as You Go Revisited." In *There's No Such Thing as a Free Lunch: Essays on Public Policy*, 49–51. La Salle: Open Court, 1975.

Friedman, Milton. *Why Government Is the Problem*. Stanford: Hoover Institution on War, Revolution and Peace, 1993.

Friedman, Milton and Rose Friedman. *Free to Choose: A Personal Statement*. New York: Harcourt Brace Jovanovich: 1980.

Friedman, Myra. "My Neighbor Bernie Goetz." *New York Magazine* (February 18, 1985), 35–41.

Garvey, Stephen P. "Racism, Unreasonable Belief, and Bernhard Goetz." *Cornell Law Faculty Working Papers* (2007), scholarship.law.cornell.edu, 1–58.

Gentili, Dario. *The Age of Precarity: Endless Crisis as an Art of Government*. London: Verso, 2021.

Gilmore, Ruth W. *Abolition Geography: Essays Towards Liberation*. London: Verso, 2022.

Gorz, André. *Critique of Economic Reason*, translated by Gillian Handyside and Chris Turner. London: Verso, 1989.

Gramsci, Antonio. *Selections from the Prison Notebooks*, edited and translated by Quintin Hoare and Geoffrey Nowell Smith. New York: International Publishers, [1929–1935] 1971.

Guth, Madeline, Rachel Garfield, and Robin Rudowitz. "The Effects of Medicaid Expansion Under the ACA: Studies from January 2014 to January 2020." kff.org (March 17, 2020), np.

Handler, Joel F. "On Welfare Reform's Hollow Victory." *Daedalus* 135.3 (2006): 114–117.

Handler, Joel F. *The Poverty of Welfare Reform*. New Haven: Yale University Press, 1995.

Harvey, David. *A Brief History of Neoliberalism*. Oxford: Oxford University Press, 2005.

Hayek, Friedrich A. *Law, Legislation and Liberty: A New Statement of the Liberal Principles of Justice and Political Economy*. London: Routledge, [1973] 2013.

Hayek, Friedrich A. *The Road to Serfdom*, fiftieth anniversary edition. Chicago: Chicago University Press, [1944] 1994.

Hersh, Eitan. *Politics Is for Power: How to Move Beyond Political Hobbyism, Take Action, and Make Real Change*. New York: Scribner, 2020.

Hester, Helen and Nick Srnicek. *After Work: A History of the Home and the Fight for Free Time*. New York: Verso, 2023.

Hobbes, Thomas. *Leviathan*, edited by Richard Tuck. Cambridge: Cambridge University Press, [1651] 1996.

Hochschild, Arlie with Annie Machung. *The Second Shift: Working Parents and the Revolution at Home*. New York: Viking, 1989.

Honig, Bonnie. *Democracy and the Foreigner*. Princeton: Princeton University Press, 2001.

hooks, bell. *The Will to Change: Men, Masculinity, and Love*. New York: Washington Square Press, 2004.

Investopedia. "How the 2008 Housing Crash Affected the American Dream." investopedia.com (September 28, 2021), np.

Jameson, Fredric. "Cognitive Mapping." In *Marxism and the Interpretation of Culture*, edited by Cary Nelson and Lawrence Grossberg, 347–360. Champaign: University of Illinois Press, 1988.

Johnson, Kirk. "Goetz Account of Shooting 4 Given on Tape." *New York Times* (April 30, 1987), Section B, 1.

Johnson, Nic. "Times of Interest." *New Left Review* 143 (2023): 109–142.

Johnston, Steven. *American Dionysia: Violence, Tragedy, and Democratic Politics*. Cambridge: Cambridge University Press, 2015.

Joker. Directed by Todd Phillips. Warner Bros and DC Films. 2019.

"Joker (2019)." the-numbers.com, (nd), np.

Kane, Bob and Bill Finger. *Batman #1*. New York: Marvel, 1940.

Katz, Michael B. *The Price of Citizenship: Redefining the American Welfare State*, updated edition. Philadelphia: University of Pennsylvania Press, [2001] 2008.

Katz, Michael B. *The Undeserving Poor: From the War on Poverty to the War on Welfare*. New York: Pantheon, 1990.

Katz, Michael B. "Was Government the Solution or the Problem? The Role of the State in the History of American Social Policy." *Theory and Society* 39.3/4 (2010): 487–502.

Kentikelenis, Alexandros and Thomas Stubbs. *A Thousand Cuts: Social Protection in the Age of Austerity*. Oxford: Oxford University Press, 2023.

Keynes, John M. *The General Theory of Employment, Interest and Money*. New York: Harcourt, Brace and Co., 1936.

King, Jr., Martin Luther. *"All Labor Has Dignity."* Edited and introduced by Michael K. Honey. Boston: Beacon Press, 2011.

King, Jr., Martin Luther. "Letter from Birmingham Jail." africa.upenn.edu, April 16, 1963, np.

Klein, Naomi. *The Shock Doctrine: The Rise of Disaster Capitalism*. London: Picador, 2007.

Klippenstein, Ken. "US Military Training Document Says Socialists Represent 'Terrorist' Ideology." theintercept.com (June 22, 2021), np.

Kroll, Andy. "Big Law Firms Promised to Punish Republicans Who Voted to Overthrow Democracy. Now They're Donating to Their Campaigns." rollingstone.com (December 9, 2021), np.

Kundnani, Arun. "The Neoliberal Idea." In *What Is Antiracism? And Why it Means Anticapitalism*, 155–182. London: Verso, 2023.

Langley, Travis. *Batman and Psychology: A Dark and Stormy Knight*. New York: Wiley, 2012.

Laplanche, Jean. "Interview: The Other Within." *Radical Philosophy* 102 (2000): 31–41.

Lawrence III, Charles R. "The Id, the Ego, and Equal Protection: Reckoning with Unconscious Racism." *Stanford Law Review* 39.2 (1987): 317–388.

Limburg, Joanne. "Am I Disabled?" aeon.co (December 10, 2020), np.

Locke, John. *An Essay Concerning Human Understanding*, edited by Roger Woolhouse. Harmondsworth: Penguin, [1689] 1997.

Locke, John. *Two Treatises of Government*, edited by Peter Laslett. Cambridge: Cambridge University Press, [1689] 1988.

Lorde, Audre. *Sister Outsider: Essays and Speeches*. London: Ten Speed, [1984] 2007.

Lowrey, Annie. "The Time Tax." theatlantic.com (July 27, 2021), np.

Lui, Brendan. "US Waste Exporting Explained." rePurpose.global, (April 16, 2019), np.

Luo, Tian, Amar Mann, and Richard J. Holden. "The Expanding Role of Temporary Help Services from 1990 to 2008." *Monthly Labor Review* (August 2010): 3–16.

Machiavelli, Niccolò. *The Discourses, vol. 1*, edited by W. Stark. New Haven: Yale University Press, [1531] 1950.

Machado De Oliveira, Vanessa. *Hospicing Modernity: Facing Humanity's Wrongs and the Implications for Social Activism*. Berkeley: North Atlantic Books, 2021.

Malthus, Thomas R. *An Essay on the Principle of Population*. Edited and introduced by Geoffrey Gilbert. Oxford: Oxford University Press [1798] 2008.

Mamdani, Mahmood. *Good Muslim, Bad Muslim: America, the Cold War, and the Roots of Terror*. New York: Doubleday, 2004.

Martin, Janos. "Today in New York History: The Great Garbage Strike of 1968." untappedcities.com (February 11, 2015).

Marx, Karl. *Capital: A Critique of Political Economy, vol. 1*. Harmondsworth: Penguin, [1867] 1990.

Marx, Karl. *Economic and Philosophical Manuscripts of 1844*. Buffalo: Prometheus, [1844] 1988.

Matthews, Dylan and Dara Lind. "Vox Sentences: 'When You're a Star, They'll Let You Do It. You Can Do Anything'." vox.com (October 8, 2016), np.

McCormick, John P. *Machiavellian Democracy.* Cambridge: Cambridge University Press, 2011.

McFeely, Shane and Ryan Pendell. "What Workplace Leaders Can Learn from the Real Gig Economy." gallup.com (August 16, 2018), np.

McManus, Matt. "Was John Stuart Mill a Socialist?" jacobin.com, (May 30, 2021), np.

Menke, Christoph. *Critique of Rights.* Translated by Christopher Turner. Cambridge: Polity Press, 2020.

Mill, John Stuart. *On Liberty,* in *On Liberty, Utilitarianism and Other Essays,* Edited and introduced by Mark Philp and Frederick Rosen, 5–112. Oxford: Oxford University Press, 2015.

Mill, John Stuart. *Socialism.* Chicago: Belford, Clarke, and Co., 1879.

Mill, John Stuart. *The Subjection of Women.* In *On Liberty, Utilitarianism and Other Essays.* Edited and introduced by Mark Philp and Frederick Rosen, 409–505. Oxford: Oxford University Press, 2015.

Mill, John Stuart. *Utilitarianism.* In *On Liberty, Utilitarianism and Other Essays.* Edited and introduced by Mark Philp and Frederick Rosen, 538–659. Oxford: Oxford University Press, 2015.

Miller, Jake. "Donald Trump Defends Calling Mexican Immigrants 'Rapists'." cbsnews.com (July 2, 2015), np.

Mills, Charles W. *The Racial Contract,* twenty-fifth anniversary edition. Ithaca: Cornell University Press, [1997] 2022.

Mintz, Frank P. *The Liberty Lobby and the American Right: Race, Conspiracy, and Culture.* Westport: Greenwood, 1999.

Mishel, Lawrence, Elise Gould, and Josh Bivens. "Wage Stagnation in Nine Charts." epi.org, January 6, 2015, np.

Modern Times. Directed by Charlie Chaplin. United Pictures, 1936.

Morgenson, Gretchen and Joshua Rosner. *These Are the Plunderers: How Private Equity Runs—and Wrecks—America.* New York: Simon and Schuster, 2023.

Mouffe, Chantal. *The Democratic Paradox.* New York: Verso, 2000.

National Academies of Sciences, Engineering, and Medicine. *High and Rising Mortality Rates Among Working-Age Adults*. Washington, DC: The National Academies Press, 2021.

National Conference of State Legislature, "Brief: Felon Voting Rights." ncsl.org (June 6, 2024), np.

National Research Council of the National Academies. *The Growth of Incarceration in the United States: Exploring Causes and Consequences*. Washington, DC: The National Academies Press, 2014.

Olmsted, Kathryn S. *Real Enemies: Conspiracy Theories and American Democracy, World War I to 9/11*. Oxford: Oxford University Press, [2009] 2011.

Pateman, Carole. *The Sexual Contract*. Stanford: Stanford University Press, 1988.

Peaslee, Robert Moses and Robert G. Weiner, eds. *The Joker: A Serious Study of the Prince of Crime*. Jackson: University of Mississippi Press, 2015.

Pettit, Philip. *Republicanism: A Theory of Freedom and Government*. Oxford: Oxford University Press, 1999.

Phillips, Adam. "Just Rage." In *The Beast in the Nursery: On Curiosity and Other Appetites*, 121–140. New York: Vintage, 1998.

Phillips, Todd and Scott Silver. *Joker: The Official Script Book*. New York: Insight, 2022.

Piketty, Thomas. *Capital and Ideology*. Cambridge: Belknap of Harvard University Press, 2020.

Piketty, Thomas. *Capital in the Twenty-First Century*, translated by Arthur Goldhammer. Cambridge, MA: Belknap of Harvard University Press, 2014.

Piketty, Thomas. "The Fall of the US Idol." In *Time for Socialism: Dispatches from a World on Fire, 2016–2021*, 329–333. New Haven: Yale University Press, 2021.

Piketty, Thomas. "What to Do with Covid Debt." In *Time for Socialism: Dispatches from a World on Fire, 2016–2021*, 317–320. New Haven: Yale University Press, 2021.

Pistor, Katharina. *The Code of Capital: How the Law Creates Wealth and Inequality*. Princeton: Princeton University Press, 2019.

Polanyi, Karl. *The Great Transformation: The Political and Economic Origins of Our Time*. Boston: Beacon Press, [1944] 2001.

Pope Francis. "Apostolic Exhortation Evangelii Gaudium of the Holy Father Francis to the Bishops, Clergy, Consecrated Persons and the Lay Faithful on the Proclamation of the Gospel in Today's World." vatican.va (November 24, 2013), 1–288.

Postman, Neil. *Amusing Ourselves to Death: Public Discourse in the Age of Show Business*. Harmondsworth: Penguin, 1985.

Rancière, Jacques. "The Fools and the Wise." versobooks.com (January 21, 2021), np.

Reagan, Ronald. "First Inaugural Address." Speech at the US Capitol. January 20, 1981. reaganlibrary.gov, np.

Reagan, Ronald. "State of the Union Address." Speech at the Joint Session of Congress. January 26, 1982. reaganlibrary.gov, np.

Reagan, Ronald. "State of the Union Address." Speech at the Joint Session of Congress. February 4, 1986. reaganlibrary.gov, np.

Riley, Dylan and Robert Brenner, "Seven Theses on American Politics." *New Left Review* 138 (2022): 5–27.

Rose, Jacqueline. *Mothers: An Essay on Love and Cruelty*. New York: Farrar, Straus and Giroux, 2018.

Rosenof, Theodore. "Freedom, Planning, and Totalitarianism: The Reception of F. A. Hayek's *Road to Serfdom*." *Canadian Review of American Studies* 5.2 (1974): 149–165.

Rothberg, Erika, ed. *The Joker: 80 Years of the Clown Prince of Crime!* Burbank: DC Comics, 2020.

Rousseau, Jean-Jacques. *On the Social Contract*, translated by G.D.H. Cole. Mineola: Dover Thrift Editions, [1762] 2003.

Rubin, Richard, Jennifer Williams, and Paul Hannon. "A New Global Tax Is About to Raise Billions. The U.S. Is Missing Out." *Wall Street Journal* (February 1, 2024), np.

Rule, John. *The Laboring Classes in Early Industrial England, 1750–1850*. London: Longman, 1986.

Ryan, Frances. *Crippled: Austerity and the Demonization of Disabled People.* London: Verso, 2019.

Sandberg, Sheryl and Nell Scovell. *Lean In: Women, Work, and the Will to Lead.* New York: Alfred A. Knopf Inc., 2013.

Sandberg, Sheryl. "Why We Have Too Few Women Leaders." ted.com (December 2010), np.

Sandel, Michael J. *The Tyranny of Merit: What's Become of the Common Good?* New York: Farrar, Straus and Giroux, 2020.

Sawyer, Wendy and Peter Wagner. "Mass Incarceration: The Whole Pie 2023." prisonpolicy.org (March 14, 2023), np.

Schmitt, Carl. *The Concept of the Political,* expanded edition. Chicago: University of Chicago Press, [1932] 2007.

Sered, Danielle. *Until We Reckon: Violence, Mass Incarceration, and a Road to Repair.* New York: The New Press, 2019.

Shmerling, Robert H. "Why Life Expectancy in the US Is Falling." health.harvard.edu (October 20, 2020), np.

Smith, Adam. *The Theory of Moral Sentiments.* New Delhi: Gyan Books, [1759] 2017.

Smith, Adam. *The Wealth of Nations,* introduction by Alan B. Krueger. New York: Bantam, [1776] 2003.

Smith, Neil. "Giuliani Time: The Revanchist 1990s." *Social Text* 57 (1998): 1–20.

Solnit, Rebecca. "A Rape a Minute, A Thousand Corpses a Year." *Guernica* (January 25, 2013), np.

Solnit, Rebecca. "The Problem With Sex Is Capitalism." In *Whose Story is This? Old Conflicts, New Chapters,* 91–96. Chicago: Haymarket Press, 2019.

Spiderman 2. Directed by Sam Raimi. Columbia Pictures and Marvel Enterprises, 2004.

Srinivasan, Amia. *The Right to Sex.* London: Bloomsbury, 2021.

Strike. Directed by Sergei Eisenstein. 1st Goskino Factory, 1925.

Stuckler, David and Sanjay Basu. *The Body Economic: Why Austerity Kills.* New York: HarperCollins, 2014.

Sugrue, Thomas J. *The Origins of the Urban Crisis: Race and Inequality in Postwar Detroit*. Princeton: Princeton University Press, 2014.

The Dark Knight. Directed by Christopher Nolan. Warner Bros, 2008.

The Dark Knight Rises. Directed by Christopher Nolan. Warner Bros, 2012.

The King of Comedy. Directed by Martin Scorsese. 20th Century Fox, 1982.

The Man Who Laughs. Directed by Paul Leni. Universal Studios, 1928.

Thompson, E. P. "Custom, Law and Common Right." In *Customs in Common: Studies in Traditional Popular Culture*, 97–184. New York: The New Press, 1993.

Townsend, Joseph. *A Dissertation on the Poor Laws*. London: Poultry Press, 1786.

Uggen, Christopher, et al. "Locked Out 2020: Estimates of People Denied Voting Rights Due to a Felony Conviction." sentencingproject.org (updated October 30, 2020), 1–20.

US Bureau of Labor Statistics. "Contingent and Alternative Employment Arrangement Summary." bls.gov (June 7, 2018), np.

Wacquant, Loïc. *Punishing the Poor: The Neoliberal Government of Social Insecurity*. Durham. Duke University Press, 2009.

Wacquant, Loïc. "Race as Civic Felony." *International Social Science Journal* 57.183 (2005): 127–142.

Wacquant, Loïc. "Three Steps to a Historical Anthropology of Actually Existing Neoliberalism." *Social Anthropology/Anthropologie Sociale* 20.1 (2012): 66–79.

Waldron, Jeremy. *The Dignity of Legislation*. Cambridge: Cambridge University Press, 1999.

Wallace, Daniel. *The Joker: A Visual History of the Clown Prince of Crime*. New York: Universe, 2011.

Winnicott, Donald W. "Ego Distortion in Terms of True and False Self." In *The Maturational Processes and the Facilitating Environment: Studies in the Theory of Emotional Development*, 140–152. London: Karnac, 2006.

Winnicott, Donald W. "Primary Maternal Preoccupation." In *Through Paediatrics to Psycho-Analysis: Collected Papers*, 300–305. London: Routledge, [1975] 1992.

Winnicott, Donald W. *The Child, the Family, and the Outside World*. London: Pelican, 1964.

Wolin, Sheldon S. "Democracy and the Welfare State." In *The Presence of the Past: Essays on the State and Constitution*, 151–179. Princeton: Princeton University Press, 1989.

Wolin, Sheldon S. *Democracy Incorporated: Managed Democracy and the Specter of Inverted Totalitarianism*. Princeton: Princeton University Press, 2008.

Wolin, Sheldon S. "Norm and Form: Constitutionalizing Democracy." In *Fugitive Democracy and Other Essays*, edited by Nicholas Xenos, 77–99. Princeton: Princeton University Press, 2016.

Wolin, Sheldon S. "The New Public Philosophy." In *Fugitive Democracy and Other Essays*, edited by Nicholas Xenos, 394–404. Princeton: Princeton University Press, 2016.

Wolin, Sheldon S. "What Revolutionary Action Means Today." In *Fugitive Democracy and Other Essays*, edited by Nicholas Xenos, 368–378. Princeton: Princeton University Press, 2016.

Yang, Maya. "'Incels' Are a Rising Threat in the US." *Guardian* (March 16, 2022), np.

"You Have to Think in a Cold-Blooded Way." *New York Times* (April 30, 1987), Section B, 6.

Žižek, Slavoj. *Violence*. London: Picador, 2008.

Zuboff, Shoshana. *The Age of Surveillance Capitalism: The Fight for a Human Future at the New Frontier of Power*. London: Profile Books, 2019.

Zulfiqar, Ali Asad. "UK Union Blasts Amazon for 'Dirty Tricks' After Drive Fails." bnnbloomberg.ca (June 8, 2023), np.

Index

Printed in the USA
CPSIA information can be obtained
at www.ICGtesting.com
JSHW021927041224
74686JS00005B/1